Wole Soyinka

The Interpreters

WITH NOTES BY

ELDRED JONES
Professor of English
University of Sierra Leone

HEINEMANN

IN ASSOCIATION WITH
ANDRÉ DEUTSCH

Heinemann Educational Books Ltd
22 Bedford Square, London WC1B 3HH
P.M.B. 5205 Ibadan · P.O. Box 45314 Nairobi
EDINBURGH MELBOURNE AUCKLAND KINGSTON
HONG KONG SINGAPORE KUALA LUMPUR NEW DELHI
Heinemann Educational Books Inc.
70 Court Street, Portsmouth, New Hampshire 03801, USA

ISBN 0 435 90076 5

First published by André Deutsch 1965
First published in African Writers Series 1970
Reprinted 1972, 1974, 1976, 1978, 1981, 1985

Notes will be found on page 253
and a glossary of dialect words will be found on page 259

Printed and bound in Great Britain by
Richard Clay (The Chaucer Press) Ltd, Bungay, Suffolk

PART ONE

1

'Metal on concrete jars my drink lobes'. This was Sagoe, grumbling as he stuck fingers in his ears against the mad screech of iron tables. Then his neck was nearly snapped as Dehinwa leapt up and Sagoe's head dangled in the void where her lap had been. Bandele's arms never ceased to surprise. At half-span they embraced table and chairs, pushed them deep into the main wall as dancers dodged long chameleon tongues of the cloudburst and the wind leapt at them, visibly male-volent. In a moment only the band was left.

The 'plop' continued some time before its meaning came clear to Egbo and he looked up at the leaking roof in disgust, then threw his beer into the rain muttering.

'I don't need his pity. Someone tell God not to weep in my beer.'

Sagoe continued to rub his neck. 'You are a born hang-woman, leaping up like that. It could snap a gorilla's neck.'

'I had to think of my hair.'

'Her hair! My neck to her hair. Why don't you use wigs like all fashionable women?'

'I don't like wigs.'

'If you go around wearing your own hair people will think you are bald.'

Separate only by the thigh-high bamboo wall giving the so-called 'party privacy'—try our Club Cambana Cubicles etc etc —Egbo watched the rising pool in which his polluted beer dissolved in froth. A last straggle of white clung stubbornly to the bamboo, rising with the water; the rest thinned fast under direct whipping off the roof.

'Well, I made a choice. I can't complain.'

Bandele looked up at him.

'Oh I was only having a chat with me and this talkative puddle.'

Two paddles clove the still water of the creek, and the canoe trailed behind it a silent groove, between gnarled tears of mangrove; it was dead air, and they came to a spot where an old rusted cannon showed above the water. It built a faded photo of the past with rotting canoe hulks along the bank, but the link was spurious. The paddlers slowed down and held the boat against the cannon. Egbo put his hand in the water and dropped his eyes down the brackish stillness, down the dark depths to its bed of mud. He looked reposed, wholly withdrawn.

'Perhaps you've guessed. My parents drowned at this spot.'

The canoe began to move off.

'Your Chinese Sages would say that is a lie, of course. How can I say my parents died at this spot when it isn't the same water here today as was here last year, or even yesterday. Or a moment ago when I spoke. Anyway, my grandfather is no philosopher. He buoyed the cannon there to mark the spot, and so, my parents died at that spot.'

They inclined their heads away from him not knowing what to say. From the receding cannon a quizzical crab emerged, seemed to stretch its claws in the sun and slipped over the edge, making a soft hole in the water. Mudskippers the colour of the water lined the canoe hulks, tenants of once-proud war-canoes. The mangrove arches spread seemingly endless and Kola broke the silence saying, 'Mangrove depresses me.'

'Me too,' said Egbo. 'I suppose I can never wholly escape water, but I do not love things of death. I remember when I was in Oshogbo I loved Oshun grove and would lie there for hours listening at the edge of the water. It has a quality of this part of the creeks, peaceful and comforting. I would lie there, convinced that my parents would rise from the water and speak to me. That they had turned into waterman and wife I had no doubt, so I expected they would appear wherever the conditions were right. And Oshun had the same everhung greyness, so night after night I went and called to them and placed my ear against the water, on the line of water against the bank.' He laughed, 'I only got beaten for my pains. My guardians thought I had become an Oshun follower. What use, I ask you, would I have for Oshun?' He trailed his hand in the water as he went, pulling up lettuce and plaiting the long whitened rootstrands.

'That was only a phase of course, but I truly yearned for the dark. I loved life to be still, mysterious. I took my books down there to read, during the holidays. But later, I began to go further, down towards the old suspension bridge where the water ran freely, over rocks and white sand. And there was sunshine. There was depth also in that turbulence, at least I felt down into darkness from an unfettered sky. It was so different from the grove where depth swamped me; at the bridge it was elusive, you had to pierce it, arrowed like a bird.'

He felt a sudden qualm with frustration and some embarrassment, wishing now more than ever to emerge plain, unambiguous.

'I am trying to explain why memories do not hold me. I have made no pilgrimage to this place since my parents died. Occasionally my aunt brought me here of course just to tell the old man I was still alive. The last time, I was fourteen, and I wish it were still the last time.'

Bandele was frowning and Egbo noticed. 'Why do you frown?'

Bandele merely shook his head.

'You don't agree? Sekoni, what do you say? If the dead are not strong enough to be ever-present in our being, should they not be as they are, dead?'

'T-t-to make such d-d-distinctions disrupts the d-d-dome of c-c-continuity, which is wwwhat life is.'

'But are we then,' Egbo continued, 'to continue making advances to the dead? Why should the dead on their part fear to speak to light?'

'Ththat is why wwe must acc-c-cept the universal d-d-dome, b b because ththere is no d-d-d-direction. The b-b-bridge is the d-d-dome of rreligion and b-b-bridges d-d-don't jjjust g-g-go from hhhere to ththere; a bridge also faces backwards.'

'There should be more Alhajis like you, Sheikh,' Egbo said. 'You all violate the silence but yours insists on a purpose.'

Lethargy had crept on him and it spread imperceptibly; each voice grew a projected echo far cast as the dusk wailing of the muezzin catechist. And the suddenness of the creektown, distant still in a heavy noon haze violating the peace by rounding on them without warning robbed them for some moments more of any desire to speak. Slowly, as if any sudden action might ruffle the archine balances, Kola drew out the crayons and placed a hand on the nearer paddler. The canoe slowed and paused.

'It is,' Egbo murmured, 'as I remember it. An interlude from reality.'

Mud-dark stilts, and above them, whites and greys on smooth walls, and over these a hundred nests of thatch roofing. Dry-docked canoes in bright contrasts beneath plank flooring, relics of the days when fishes over whom hunting rights were fought fed on the disputants. Now they awaited the annual race and re-enactment of the war of the long canoes. Osa drowsed in hard shadows and sun vapours, in vivid whites reflecting momentary blindness, motionless, until a shallow bark emerged from a hidden inlet and drew up among the row of idle boats. From it stepped a barrel figure, half naked, a soft sheen over his paunch as if oil from his last meal was seeping gently through. Even from that distance they saw no softening corpulence; the boatman grounded his craft easily, heaved a sack over his shoulder and receded into shadows.

The paddlers had begun to move but Egbo stopped them again.

'Wait.'

The unknown man had broken the crust of time; Egbo saw dwarfs sitting at the foot of a warlord whose deadly laugh bred terror in a huddled group to whom he granted audience. Into the centre of this scene he was thrust by his aunt, impervious ever to her father's dignity and shouting almost in his ear, 'I've brought your son'. And Egbo could remember the sudden transformation of the ancient strong man, his laughter of menace changed to true delight and a sudden incomprehensible strength which lifted him clean above the dwarfs and onto his knees. Egbo felt again the contact of a terrifying virility, of two hands which felt him all over the face and the head, the head especially, of fingers which pressed beneath the hair and into the skull as if it would feel into the bumps and crevices of his brain. And tested his muscles and his chest, and the sound of a tornado which was again his grandfather's contented laughter. That was their last meeting. And now something, something, a vision of the warlord retiring from audience, for although he walked firmly enough, even out-striding the two dwarfs his eternal companions, yet Egbo had had the feeling they were his guides, that he rested his hands lightly on their heads to obtain an initial direction. Sifting them carefully, he began to re-read his memories. . . .

'In such a setting,' it was Kola talking, hardly taking his attention off the sketch book '. . . controlling every motion of the place in a rigid grasp, to all purposes a god among men . . . that is how I anticipate your old man. And a wholly white head of hair.'

'Blind too by now, I imagine?' Egbo made it a question turning to the paddlers. They hemmed and stuttered, uneasy. Vaguely Egbo sensed a code of taboos, and with it returned a feeling of remoteness. 'But I am his son,' he protested. 'You are not talking to a stranger.'

But still the paddlers kept silence. Egbo persisted, 'I was a child when I saw him last and his sight had begun to fail. Can he see at all now?'

The elder of the paddlers took refuge in a proverb; 'When asked why they wore leather shields over their thoughts, the counsellors replied, "the king says he's blind".'

The spectre of generations rose now above him and Egbo found he would always shrink, although incessantly drawn to the pattern of the dead. And this, waiting near the end of the journey, hesitating on the brink, wincing as he admitted it— was it not exhumation of a better forgotten past? Belatedly thinking, who am I to meddle? Who? Except—and this counted for much—that he knew and despised the age which sought to mutilate his beginnings.

And there was the personal threat to his grandfather but then, he did not doubt that the old man understood the political risks and would accept reversals. And Egbo wished, if that could be all! If the fight were only political, nothing more. But Egbo had felt a virile essence, a redeeming grace in the old man and in that existence. And this was being destroyed he knew, and by cozening half-men who came bloated on empty wind. There is also my pride of race Egbo said, I am after all, an Egbo.

Well, he could stay. Osa Descendants Union sent their spokesmen to plague him daily, all bitten by the bug of an 'enlightened ruler', and gradually Egbo had begun to wonder and to set the warlord of the creeks against dull grey file cabinet faces of the Foreign Office. And a slow anger built in him, panic and retraction from the elaborate pit. What did they demand of him? How dared they suggest obligations? And this stranger whose halting breath he could hear in their every plea—and stranger he was, separated by a generation no less tenuous—a father whose dug-out moved among the settlements spreading a Word which in spite of ritual acceptance altered little, a father whose careless death left a bigger doubt than the conversions in a life-long evangelism. And his mother was the princess Egbo whose burden it was he now carried; hers was the line of inheritance and she had gone down at the same spot and there was nothing but the rusted cannon left of her. . . . Mentally he surrendered the effort of unravelling blood skeins and was left only with their tyrannous energies.

The paddle dipped from time to time straining the canoe against the tide to maintain an even length from the shore. Sekoni's head slid down on his chest, succumbing to a general somnolence. But the rest of them gradually turned, unsure, suspicious of their coming intrusion and the motives.

'Are we meeting this progenitor of yours or not?'

'I really don't know,' Egbo answered.

For it had become different at this point, waiting to go on shore and grapple with his failure to insulate, different from the distant disillusionment, his fears for the dignity of his roots, and the fate of a burnt out fire-eater. He acknowledged it finally, this was a place of death. And admitted too that he was drawn to it, drawn to it as a dream of isolation, smelling its archaic menace and the violent undertows, unable to deny its dark vitality.

'What do you mean, you don't know? Don't tell me you've brought us all this way only to say you don't know.'

'Over there is a blind old man and a people, waiting on some mythical omniscience of my generation. But what on earth can such an existence hold out for me?'

Bandele said, 'As many wives as you can handle, for one.'

'Oh yes, that. I admit that's a strong point.'

'And power too?' Kola said.

'That kind of power would only be a hobby. And there is plenty of it as these tempters from home always impress on me. Oh there is power, all right. Either way. Ally with the new gods or hold them to ransom. Osa controls a lot of these vital smuggling routes and to hell with your helicopters and speedboats. The government only gets what the old man wants to sacrifice. It's a small place, but it's the richest of these creek-towns. And the neighbouring areas know where their secret bread is buttered. They've gone with Osa from the days of tributes.'

'But they all crack, don't they? Sooner or later they crack.'

'I don't want to see it happen.'

'Who will stop it? Your tired grandfather?'

'No. But we could.'

'But do we want to? Or try?'

'No. Too busy, although I've never discovered doing what. And that is what I constantly ask—doing what? Beyond propping up the herald-men of the future, slaves in their hearts and blubber-men in fact doing what? Don't you ever feel that your whole life might be sheer creek-surface bearing the burdens of fools, a mere passage, a mere reflecting medium or occasional sheer mass controlled by ferments beyond you?'

Bandele shrugged. 'I don't work in the Civil Service.'

'But you acquiesce in the system. You exist in it. Lending pith to hollow reeds.'

'Is that why power attracts you?' Bandele asked.

'I merely want to be released from the creek-surface.'

'From apostasy.' Kola said.

'What's that?'

'What? Oh you mean apostate? An apostate, that's a face I cannot draw, even badly. You know, an absolute neutrality.'

One paddler felt in the water for movement. Anxiously he said, 'The tide, it changes direction by late afternoon.'

'Changes how? Away from the shore?'

The man nodded.

Affecting innocence Kola asked, 'How many wives has the old man?'

For a moment Egbo was deceived, then he laughed. 'I've admitted that's a powerful consideration. I've thought of that. Long and seriously. Just think, not only to be able to fill my house with women but to have it regarded as befitting and manly. I don't know how many he has but I won't be skimpy, I tell you.'

'You don't need to.'

'Oh I've dreamt of me and a household like that dozens of times. And the future prospects for the country's traditions. By example to convert the world.'

'You are the first genuine throw-back of this generation.'

'On the contrary. Polygamy is an entirely modern concept. Oh I don't deny the practice is old, but whoever thought it was polygamy then?'

'Okay, okay, do we get ashore or not?'

As if he hadn't heard, 'I have, I sometimes suspect, strained objectivity to its negative limits. What choice, I ask myself, is there between the ugly mudskippers on this creek and the raucous toads of our sewage-ridden ports? What difference?'

'None.'

'That is the answer I dread to find if I yield to temptation and reclaim my place here. None. Sometimes I even go so far that I say, "What is my grandfather but a glorified bandit?" Only that doesn't help either. Sooner a glorified bandit than a loud-mouthed slave.'

The canoeman pointed at the water. The currents had become discernible, sluggish veins beneath a sleepy coil of python. It strokes you, the creekmen would say, strokes you with voluptuous mermaid arms to the deepest caves, infinitely coy and maternal. 'Not yet,' Egbo said, 'not another Egbo so soon, you nymphomaniac depths.' But there remained the question of a choice still and he had made none, none at least that he was directly conscious of.

'All right, let's go.'

'Which way, man? You haven't said.'

Perhaps he had hoped they would simply move and take the burden of a choice from him, but it was like Bandele to insist although motiveless. So, leaving it at that Egbo simply said,

'With the tide.'

Kola grinned. 'Like apostates?'

A shade of anger over his face, resentment at his failure to bury the abortive quest finally, especially the promise it still held for him like a salvation. He looked around the club seeking an object to frizzle and be warmed in turn by energies he had aroused. There was only Lasunwon the politician-lawyer. He dogged their company always, an eternal garbage can for such sporadic splurges, and uncomplaining. Silently he watched him choke slowly on his college tie which had assumed a will of its own and pressed its knot on the gulping Adam's apple. The beer reversed direction and Lasunwon's nostrils were twin nozzles of a fireman's nose. When Egbo opened his eyes he was astonished to see Lasunwon beaming across the floor to an acquaintance.

The party between them and the rain scrambled up and fled as a sudden uplift swamped them, spraying Sagoe's table in hard mists. Bandele reached a long thin leg and tripped the deserted table on its edge, so it made a shield. Sagoe shivered suddenly and Dehinwa's tone turned anxious.

'You are shivering,' testing Sagoe's head for fever.

'It's only the damp,' he said, 'I am not shivering but I can't get used to the damp.'

'Liar. It's the cold you caught yesterday.' She turned to the others. 'He went out again on Apapa road. And you know why he does it? To crow over stalled cars.'

'That's not true. I go prospecting for oil from the pot-holes.'

'Very funny.'

'You look for seepage in the middle of the road, that is all there is to it.'

'Riding a bicycle in that weather. That is why they all call you a communist. You know you are top of the preventive detention list.'

'At least wait for the bill to be passed.'

Dehinwa, still angrily protective, turned to Bandele, 'He came home with his head blocked and his nose streaming. Serve you right.'

Sagoe grimaced and covered up his ears in the shawl, and for some moments there was silence.

The trumpet stabbed the night in one last defiant note, and the saxophone slunk out of light, a wounded serpent diminishing in obscene hisses. Kola had exhausted the paper napkins forced from waiters, now Sekoni joined him in searching for any forgotten space among the jumbled doodles. He pointed to a modest corner but Kola shook his head. 'Couldn't draw a bean there.' He began to wave the napkins, hoping to attract a waiter. Sekoni took the ball-pen from him and drew an object in the rejected space, shaped like an onion.

Kola gave up. The waiters were huddled near the bar. They all had the vacant stare of boredom, and two were wholly mesmerised by cascades from the roof. He looked briefly at Sekoni's onion and turned to Egbo.

'What did you begin to say?'

Somewhere in blind air, a loud rending, the agony of pitch-soaked beams torn against the grain, and they all waited for the crash of zinc. It was very near and they strained over the low roofs of the courtyard towards the sound. But Sekoni's were the cat's eyes. 'Th-there, it is over th-th-there.' And immediately the crash came, a damp thud of bricks, and later the higher-pitched collapse of rusted sheets.

'One tooth,' Egbo announced. 'The sky-line has lost a tooth from its long rotted gums.' Sekoni stammered worse than ever. 'Th-th-they will b-b-be homeless to . . . n-night. P-p-p-perhaps we should stop there and see if wwwe can h-h-h-help.'

Sagoe had begun to snore gently. Normally Egbo would thrill to a storm, his face unnaturally animated. Tonight, he merely glowered, muttering imprecations at the sky, 'Didn't beg you to join in celebrating my depression'. Using his left palm for surface, Kola resumed his sketches. Bandele fitted himself, wall-gecko, into a corner.

Like a secret weapon, something called a stronga-head; for him it was always a term for the stubborn child, and Egbo felt resentful at his helplessness. They said it too when he was rescued—they, the world of grown-ups, of strangers, of wise humanity—they pronounced it as they saved him from the water, fully conscious; this one they said, has a strong head. But not the two, the preacher his father and a king's daughter, whose bodies were recovered only hours afterwards. From then it was from parent to parent, for his aunt who really took charge of him was a restless spirit and her face even now remained for him undefined. The school-teacher, his first guardian, wore out canes on him. And his aunt returned suddenly from Dahomey, took one look at the weals and broke an inkwell on the teacher's head. Then to Oshogbo to a trading partner. But the merchant's wife only took the weals to cross them with new ones. For one thing, he would refuse to mind the shops. 'My aunt is your trading partner,' Egbo would ask, 'so how does that make me your shop-keeper?'

But there was worse. 'When you greet your elders,' the merchant said, 'you prostrate yourself.' 'You mean, lie flat on my belly?' 'On your belly, you son of the devil.' And Egbo would correct him gently, 'My father was a reverend pastor and he never taught me to prostrate.' Seizing his *koboko* the man tore at Egbo's skin crying, 'You are a small child. You will learn the hard way or the path of whips!' Years later he went to a boarding school and only returned to the merchant's home for holidays. But his guardian was awaiting him, his flabby paunch overflowing downwards, huge rolls of soft *amala* over a leather rim. And Egbo set down his box, braced himself and greeted him standing. Out from under the chair flew the whip, only there were intellectual arguments to be used now. 'If I only kneel to God why should I prostrate to you?' And the merchant paused on the blow trembling. Suppose God overheard the argument and took Egbo's side? That was a long cheat in time for divine vengeance. For days he moved meekly, spoke only in whispers, waiting for God to forget the precocious thought and his own existence. But nothing happened for a week, then three, and gradually he regained his boldness. Only, Egbo's point remained, and could he presume to dismiss it as mere child's talk? It was not difficult to find new excuses, Egbo was discovered at midnight lying at the water's edge in the grove of Oshun, one ear against the ground. 'What were you doing there?' they asked. He said he was praying. So they beat him for paganistic leanings. 'All well-trained children pray in church,' the woman screamed, 'not in some evil grove of heathens.'

They waited for the rain to release them, dozing off in fits.

Sagoe stirred, drew Dehinwa's head to him and whispered, 'Honestly now, do I look as blank as the others?' But he was very loud and Bandele overheard. 'Vacuous,' he assured him, and Egbo added, 'as a politician in press conference.' Dehinwa said, 'These two are still very much alive,' meaning Kola whose palm was now a mess of ink lines and Sekoni who was fighting the cobbles over heaven knew what topic. The cobbles were in fact his own myth, his one aberration of humour in a life of

17

painful sincerity. . . . 'D-d-during my ch-ch-childhood, I wwwas fond of swallowing c-c-c-cobbles. Now when I hic . . . cup they rrrush to my throat, and I c-c-can't speak.' The 'hic-cups' were most violent when Sekoni was excited and his excite-ment as he spun this case-history was only equalled by that of the listeners. For this was, from Sekoni, wildly humorous. It was dumbfounding, and the effort left him a child in forced feeding, his head rebellious to the stress of entry. In his case, ideas. Bizarre, unintelligible, commonplace, inspired, even things he had himself said or done and taken daily for granted —when the novelty reached him he stood assaulted.

For minutes Sagoe screwed his eyes and opened them out again weaving back and forth in sudden striking-snake motions, indifferent to Dehinwa's plaintive 'For heaven's sake, keep still!' Some event powered his neck and he lunged finally at Egbo's face and remained there a mere foot away. Egbo watched him indulgently, then encouraged him with his drunk imbecile grin.

'Have you found what you want?'

Sagoe shook his head and sighed, 'What a waste.'

Only Dehinwa would persist in searching for sense in a drunk Sagoe. 'What,' she demanded, 'is a waste?'

With difficulty, they made out Sagoe's complaint. 'Do you see Egbo's face in ultramarine? This club has atmosphere.'

Light from the blue bulb in the aquarium had spilled on Egbo. There were fluttering spots on Lasunwon's face also, and they seemed to act as meat-tenderising rays. His muscles were slacked about the mouth and cheeks and resisted all Kola's efforts to reset them. Dehinwa continued to insist, 'But what is a waste?'

'The atmosphere, girl, the atmosphere. We should be love pairs. Even scheming lechers and their gulls would do but what do we have? Five drunken sots.' Dehinwa's retort was lost half-way as Sagoe mummified her in her shawl. From the shadow of a pillar, Bandele emerged from a cat-nap, unwrapped his eyes and inspected the scene.

'It hasn't stopped then.'

'The rain, no.'

Sekoni chuckled suddenly, his usual brief retracted ration. Kola stopped and looked up, but did not press for explanation. Nothing particularly funny seemed to be happening and he went back to his work. No doubt, some forgotten incident. Sekoni would not laugh at the actual moment of an event. Often he would react with alarm, with worry, and if the others were strangers to him they would wonder if they had not been guilty of some callousness. But invariably, prompted by some accident or whatever reviewing device Sekoni had built in him, he would recollect the scene and laugh, a short illicit laughter.

The fish began a little amphibious game thrashing wildly and darting suddenly behind a rock to stare at some unseen pursuer. Lasunwon watched, turned maudlin. Wagging a finger of admonition at the aquarium he said, 'We human beings are rather like that, living in a perpetual trap, closed in by avenues on which escape is so clearly written.' The fish, outraged, paused in mid-motion, assaulted through the mouth; Sekoni fought the cobbles valiantly but lost, shook his head in pitying disapproval. Egbo simply took Lasunwon by his college tie, jerked his head forward with a 'God punish you.'

Sagoe sat up at last and looked for the waiter. 'I need a brandy to shake the ague.'

'No more no more. You are already drunk.'

'As the only woman in the party, you should efface yourself. Never be heard, never, never, in male company.'

'You see, you are drunk.'

'No I am low. Damn it, I *am* low. And that wretched band was really to blame. They depressed me the moment they began to play. And then this transition from high-life to rain *maraccas* has gone on far too long. Rain rhythm is too complex and I am too slow to take it in. You too, tootsie.'

'You are talking too much.'

'You should not be talking at all I told you. Anyway, I refuse to go down like these others. Just look at them. And if the Sheikh weren't too preoccupied with his cobbles he'd be talking too.'

'Now you are up, bring your shoulder here.' Dehinwa leant and was soon dozing. Sagoe looked round in alarm, wondering if he had been left alone to cope with Sekoni. Alone with the Sheikh's intensity! As if by accident he kicked Egbo underneath the table, but the legs only retracted. Cautiously he tried to peep beneath Bandele's lids only to find the eyes surveying him with their familiar mildness. 'Don't worry, I am not asleep.'

Sagoe leant across the table and lowered his voice. 'He depresses me and I am sad enough as it is.'

'What's wrong with *you*?'

Sagoe smiled. 'You won't believe it, but it's our dead chairman. Sir Derinola. I never thought I could shed a tear for him.'

'The ex-Judge?'

'Ay. The lawyers nicknamed him the Morgue. He was all right until he let the politicians buy him over. It's funny but I despised him when he was alive!'

'I thought you were trying to get away from morbid thoughts.'

'That's true, Sheikh set me off.' He lowered his voice. 'It's this earnestness of his really, and one never quite knows what to do . . . like a cripple coming out of a car and you don't know how to help him. Place your hands under his elbows or leave him alone and merely open the door? Or bring out his crutches and hold them out. You know what I mean, why does he have to be so bloody pig-headed! I can't get used to it.'

'You don't have to. Just be indifferent.'

'That's easy said. Well for you, maybe, but not me. Sometimes when I interrupt him and sense him still struggling in the background, I feel I have somehow strangled him, you know what I mean, strangled him but not quite finished him altogether. How Kola copes . . .'

'Kola keeps him from getting bruised.'

Kola could hear him of course. For the first time he thought of himself in that role and decided it was not quite true. 'But tell me,' Sagoe continued, 'what is it between him and the Dome?'

Bandele hurriedly glanced round. Sekoni wasn't listening, but just the same he said, 'Later, later. Kola will explain it better.'

Few people achieved the right indifference to Sekoni, and his fantasies needed so much time to unburden.

A new band took the stand, but they had not come to duel the rain. The small *apala* group had slowly begun to function as the string trio, quartet, or the lone violinist of the restaurants of Europe, serenaders of the promising purse. This was an

20

itinerant group, unfed; their livelihood would depend on alms. Normally their haunts were the streets, the markets and even private offices where they could practise a mild blackmail. They had a great nose for the occasion and were prepared for the naming-day before the child was born. They grew bolder, took in the urban needs, taught style to the new *oyinbos*, and became as indispensable to the cocktail party as the olive on a stick. First their tunes, then their instruments—the talking-drum especially—invaded the night-clubs. And later they re-formed, and once again intact, exploited intervals and other silences wrought by circumstance. As this group now did. Just the one box-guitar, three drums which seemed permanent outgrowths of the armpits, voices modulated as the muted slur by the drums' controlling strings. And they gauged the mood, like true professionals, speaking to each other, not to their audience, who would, if they chose, not *know* this language. But fashion had changed. Denial was now old-fashioned and after the garish, exhibitionist, bluff of the high-life band, this renewed a cause for feeling, hinted meanings of which they were, a phase before, half-ashamed.

Not that anyone would dance. The manager stormed out suddenly, waving his arms about and shouting 'Who let those people in?' But that was only to test the reaction of his wealthier patrons. They waved at him to shut up and chuckling he went back behind the bar. Contentment lay in taking something for nothing.

'Couriers of the after-wash,' Egbo said. He had woken up fully, beginning to be excited. Kola looked up.

'What was that you said?'

The waiters seemed to be alive again and Kola secured more napkins.

Sagoe was moaning. 'I must lie down flat on my belly. I know you won't believe this, but that drum timbre makes my belly run.'

Dehinwa, wearily: 'Oh Sagoe . . .'

'But it is true. It is something about the vibration. I'm not lying I tell you. The music is okay only my stomach won't take it.'

'There is too much the matter with you. I just don't know how you ever survived childhood.'

'Shut up, you two,' snapped Egbo.

21

Thrown back to some far distant past, plucking the faintest memories, the men sang to supplement the wash of rain, not now on a beleaguered air but a grey lassitude; and one by one their listeners stirred, disquietened but submissive. All at once Egbo lost it, and the others, for Sekoni had again begun to fight his cobbles. His distress was apparent although he had not yet succeeded in getting out a word. Glaring, Egbo waited for him to erupt.

'Nnnnihilist!' At last, forced out like the sudden follow-out of air from a tyre valve. 'T-t-to be afraid of gog-g-goodness. In an intelligent man, a fffear of b-b-beauty or g-g-good is c . . . cowardice.'

'Can't we even listen to these wanderers before you bicker?'

Egbo took the offending drawing from Kola and examined it, Kola merely saying 'I was bored with her', as if this was enough to explain why he had planted a goitre on the woman's neck and encased her feet in Wellington boot canoes or perhaps it was a platypus. Only then did Egbo see the original herself, alone on the dance floor. None of them, except obviously, Kola and Sekoni, had seen her take possession of the emptied floor. She had no partner, being wholly self-sufficient. She was immense. She would stand out anywhere, dominating. She filled the floor with her body, dismissing her surroundings with a natural air of superfluity. And she moved slowly, intensely, wrapped in the song and the rhythm of the rain. And she brought a change again in the band, who now began to play to her to drape her in the lyric and the mood.

They watched her slowly lose herself, her head thrown back the better to hold private communion with palm fronds, with banana rafters or with whatever leaves faked tropical freshness on the artifact of the floor's centrepiece. The lead drummer moved on her, drawing, as it were, her skin on the crook of the drum. Rain ribbons in club greens and orange ringed her, falling off the edges of the open 'state umbrella', and her reflections were distorted on the four sides of the mirror stem. The wind shifted lightly from time to time and drove some water on her and she danced on; but the drummer retreated, rubbing the drum skin quickly, chafing it to restore its texture, though his voice never left her side.

A long arm reached from the dark corner, long and thin, deceptively frail, Bandele's. It slipped the drawing from

Lasunwon who was going to throw it on the wet floor. 'I wish you had let him,' Egbo said.

'It belongs in the puddle,' said Lasunwon.

'You more than the drawing. And that is where you would have landed.'

'Oh, let the lawyer express an opinion,' said Sagoe.

'I don't mind that at all,' Egbo replied. 'But he was going too far. He was going to express a feeling.'

Bandele laughed. 'Leave Lasunwon alone,' Sagoe adding, 'You leave him alone. The man can't help what he is.'

Bandele passed the drawing to Egbo who said, 'Just the same, Sheikh is right. You are a goddamn cynic. And now let's listen to this group.'

'But what is wrong?'

'Ignoring the goitre and your irrelevant houseboats on the feet . . .'

'Why irrelevant? Look at the floor. How do you suppose she dances in that pool?'

Egbo threw the drawing back in disgust. 'They should do something to your head.' The song, a cry and a legend of the past, brought back his own commitments and he tensed.

And then he turned to the dancer leaning back against the wall and losing himself immediately in her own self-immersion. But first Kola's sketch would intrude, a transparency stuck on his retina, and he would curse him silently and wave away the outrage. 'It was much too busy anyway. The woman dances in one piece, not merely buttock by buttock.'

And she was still by herself, her feet in water, her shimmering velvet wrapper with designs of a past fashion rage— Owolebi—trailed irreverently, soggy, by a corner. So Egbo called her Owolebi, murmuring the name again and again, Owolebi, Owolebi. Till Dehinwa overheard and cried, 'That's it. I was trying to remember what that design was called.' But Egbo no longer heard. Seeking to see through the dancer's eyelids which closed slowly until she saw nothing of the leaking armpits of the umbrella centrepiece, and the water ran through her indulgent as hidden hills, sacred. She should have, Egbo decided, *iyun* around her ankles, antimony rings on her breasts and light tooth marks, a full circle of flat valleys sunk in antimony. And on nights like this, to the clang of iron bells and the summons of shaved drums, even old women opened their wrinkled thighs to heaven. The dancer turned her head and her brows arched a rainbow and her hills and runnels were bared clearly to his sight.

'Like a river swollen on fresh yam hillocks.'

And Egbo shut his eyes shutting out the division in the stream, moist banks on which his shoulders itched to rest.

'That isn't all rain-water on her you know.' Kola continued to defend himself. 'Sweat. Most of it is sweat. She is hard worked inside the muscles or do you think it is all automation in that bulk?'

Bandele squinted again at the original.

'That light,' Kola persisted, 'is deceptive, and I admit that the face is peaceful, still, but . . .'

'Still!' Egbo bellowed. 'Still! O Still that passeth all understanding. Transcendental stillness of the distanced godhead! The maid of Sango after possession is still. A bed after impassioned loving is still. Still! From the deep vast centre of love—still?'

'D-d-do what you lllike,' Sekoni said. 'She is a b-b-beautiful woman.'

'Is that all you can say?' Egbo began. 'Before you, the exultation of the Black Immanent, and all you say is . . .' Kola thrust under his nose an amended portrait of the woman.

Egbo studied it solemnly for a while. Very gravely he said, 'Sometimes, you godless dauber, I would gladly kill you.'

And Kola threw up his pen. 'Now what do you find objectionable in that?'

'What is wrong! Where are the dark closing hills and the cloud crevices? Well, where are they? Instead of which you have merely drawn twin orange slices.' It was true. And even on that paper they heaved independent of the body.

'Look man, take a pen and draw your own.'

'I can't draw,' Egbo said, turning most dejected. 'No, I can't draw and that is why you deserve to be drowned.'

Lasunwon said, 'I don't see what the oranges are doing there, but at least it has improved now.'

'The QC approves,' said Sagoe.

'You needn't be so ready to sneer,' Lasunwon was beginning to get ruffled. 'What do you know about it anyway?'

'Enough to see that Egbo is dying to go to bed with the original?'

'With that?' And Lasunwon's guffaw turned several heads in their direction. 'Go to bed with that?'

Egbo demanded, 'Why not?'

'She is revoltingly fat that's all. Why, I can almost hear her buttocks squelch, like these oranges in Kola's drawing.'

'You are just crude. Bush.' Egbo fastened his eyes on the subtle independence of the buttocks. Sagoe was looking too. 'They make me think of two satellites bouncing gently in space, just touching each other.' Egbo glared at him, so he tried to appease him.

'You know, a white woman that size would be wholly amorphous. Quite revolting. But black woman eh. . . .'

'That,' said Lasunwon, 'is just another of your baseless generalities.'

'Not so baseless. I have seen both colours on their home ground and I know what I am talking about. That woman for instance. She is ample but she isn't surplus. She uses every ounce of her flesh and she is feminine.'

'But can you see yourself going to bed with her?'

'Try me.' Dehinwa gave him a violent clout.

And Egbo, his eyes all the time on the dancer: 'I would put my head between her breasts and smother my ears in them. And let even God Almighty shout "Egbo" and I'll reply, "Call back later, can't hear a word you're saying".'

Sekoni, instantly horrified, began to struggle. 'N-no, really you must not. A woman . . . she is the body of religion. T-t-to bring her in c-c-conflict . . .'

Nervously Sagoe interposed, 'Don't be so serious, Sheikh. Can't a man have his joke?'

From side to side Sekoni shook his head with increasing violence and Bandele said quietly, 'Now you've gone and made it worse.' They waited a few more seconds for it and Sekoni erupted at last with 'P-p-p-profanity!'

Egbo, without withdrawing his gaze from the woman, 'I don't know why you think I'm joking.' He looked again at her breasts, seeing them as huge moments and longing to seal himself in time. 'As the rain isolates,' he murmured, 'beating out the world and surrendering you to a lover. What,' and he turned to Sekoni, 'do you find wrong in snuffing out the world with the fruits of God's own cornucopia?'

Sekoni was struggling with his reply, but his eye fell on

the paper and he saw for the first time the changes Kola had made. He drew it to him almost desperately and excitement nearly stifled him. 'B . . . but this is . . . I didn't know you had ch-ch-changed it. Mmmmore honest . . .'

Kola stared at him open-mouthed. 'There is really no predicting you, Sheikh.'

Lasunwon, with equal surprise: 'So you approve the orange business?'

'Or . . . range, pumpkin . . . sssame thing . . . all d-d-domes of moisture . . . feminine.'

Sagoe laughed. 'That is no feminine thing he has done to the buffers. Sheer Kola nastiness—ask him.'

'N-n-no. Oh no, Kkkola is right. After all, lllife, lllove, th-they are p-p-paths to the Universal D-d-dome. And d-d-domes of moisture . . . optimistic ap . . . proach, view of hhhumanity. Wh-what Kola hhhas d-dd-done wwwith our friend's c-c-creative symbols. Re . . . member, a woman is the D-d-dome of love, sh-she is the D-d-dome of Religion. . . .'

Sekoni, qualified engineer, had looked over the railings every day of his sea voyage home. And the sea sprays built him bridges and hospitals, and the large trailing furrow became a deafening waterfall defying human will until he gathered it between his fingers, made the water run in the lower channels of his palm, directing it against the primeval giants on the forest banks. And he closed his palms again, cradling the surge of power. Once he sat on a tall water spout high above the tallest trees and beyond low clouds. Across his sight in endless mammoth rolls, columns of rock, petrifications of divine droppings from eternity. If the mountain won't come, if the mountain won't come, then let us to the mountains now, in the name of Mohammed! So he opened his palm to the gurgle of power from the charging prisoner, shafts of power nudged the monolith along the fissures, little gasps of organic ecstasy and paths were opened, and the brooding matriarchs surrendered all their strength, lay in neat geometric patterns at his feet. Sekoni shuffled them like cards and they reshaped to magic formulae in sweeping harbours. Atomised, they paved the land end to end. Into earth delved one channel, breaking earth a thousand miles away with iron-plate catalogues of energies below the surface; over them Sekoni ran a knowing selective eye and ticked them carefully. And the logic of nature's growth was bettered by the cabalistic equations of the sprouting derrick, chaos of snakes and other forest threads by parallels of railtracks, road extravagances and a nervous electronic core. Sekoni rushed down the gangway, sought the hand of kindred spirits for the flare of static electricity, but it slipped with grease and pointed to his desk. . . .

'In here. Let me know if there is anything else you need. That is a bell for the messenger.'

Air-conditioned too, Sekoni had no cause for complaint.

'Letters for signature sir . . .'

'If you'd just look over these applications for leave and put up a roster . . .'

'Bicycle advance . . . bicycle advance . . . let me see now, that should be File C/S 429. I'll check among the B.U.s in the S.M.E.K.'s office. In the meantime will you also take charge of . . .'

'Can I have your contribution sir? For morning tea, or do you prefer to take coffee yourself sir?'

'Please join a preliminary Committee of Five to sort out the applications for the post of a Third Class Clerk. . . .'

'Don't forget the meeting of the Board. You are one of our ex-officio members. . . .'

The fluid rose slowly at that meeting, bursting outside the minutes and agenda of the Board and they all stared, unbelieving.

'You realise, Mr Sekoni, that you are out of order.'

'I realise, Mmmmister Ch-chairman, that I c-c-cannot conttinue to be ssigning vouchers and llletters and b-b-bicycle allowances . . .'

Pandemonium, except for the practised chairman, calm and full of instant calculations. 'Just wait outside a moment, please, Mr Sekoni.'

'Is he mad?'

'*Omo tani?*'

'Why do we employ these too-knows?'

'No, no, no,' and the chairman soothed them. 'He obviously needs a transfer. He's one of the keen ones.'

And to Ijioha Sekoni went, 'where you may work with your hands until your back blisters' and Sekoni built a small experimental power station. And the chairman chuckled and said,

'I knew he was our man. Get me the expat. expert.' Hot from his last lucrative 'evaluation', came the expatriate expert. Expatriate, therefore impartial.

'Constitute yourself into a one-man commission of enquiry and probe the construction of our power station at Ijioha which was built without estimates approved expenditure.'

'Is it unsafe for operation?' and he winked, a truly expert expat. expert's wink.

'That's the safest idea. You put it in technical language.'

And the expatriate expert came to Ijioha, saw, and condemned.

And the chairman read the report and said, 'that expert never fails me,' salivating on the epithets, a wasteful expenditure, highly dangerous conditions, unsuitable materials, unsafe for operation.

'Bring me the Write-off file,' chortled the chairman.

And the project was written off while parliament at question time resounded to 'the escapade of the mad engineer'.

'Interdict him shall we? Bring me Form S2/7 Interdiction of Senior Civil Servants and Confidential File Sekoni Chief Engineer in charge Ijioha.'

And the chairman—for his subsidiary company registered in the name of his two-month-old niece had been sole contractor for Project Ijioha—cleaned out a few thousands in immediate compensation and filed claims for a few thousands more. 'I always say it, the Write-Offs pay better than fulfilled contracts.' And to Sekoni, 'the expert says that was junk, Engineer, junk.'

And Sekoni, bewildered, repeating 'J-j-j-junk? J-j-j-junk . . . ?'

And the papers resounded to 'the escapade of the mad engineer'.

Sekoni, obscuring himself in the streets of Ibadan, plodding among the easels in Kola's art classes, moving around without a sense of intrusion, without comment, waiting for a decision to be taken on his fate by the next meeting of the governing board. Hearing often the whirr of motors that he had built, the assemblage of a million parts that he had scavenged touring the various stations under his command more like a junk-cart than as a Senior Civil Engineer in charge, prodding crumpled heaps of motor cars and lorries, tractors, railway yards, scrounging and—oh yes—that obliging contractor's agent ready to supply the sky on a government requisition estimate or no estimate—Sekoni remembered him with fondness.

'J-j-j-junk?' The Chairman had called it junk. And the plant had never even been tested! Bigger towns still worked their refrigerators by kerosene, but Sekoni's plant would bathe Ijioha maidens in neon glow—the Village Head had chuckled at that, and Sekoni, carried forward on the excitement, began plans for a waterworks, to be constructed as soon as the power station was finished. Incredulous on his observation perch, the Head had promised him three wives, to include his own daughter.

And this the chairman had called it 'J-j-j junk!' When the furnace had never even been lit!

At Ijioha the weeds were reaching high among the baked brick huts of the power plant. A stalk of elephant grass had bent into the furnace inspection vent, like an ear being tickled, and for one moment, Sekoni thought he heard a rasp of laughter from the walls. A dirty head looked out from hiding, then another. The children saw they were discovered and ran off. The silence descended round him, of a grass snake coiled beside a plastered ledge, of buckets rusting on conveyor cables. Following them he came to the tipping device which knocked the coal into a chute and led straight into the furnace. He had been rather proud of that. He walked towards the control chamber. There were new bolts on the door beside the lock, and on the wall someone had splashed in whitewash— DANGEROUS. KEEP OFF in two languages. He looked round for a heavy object, found a large stone and stooped to pick it.

'Oh, so it was you, Engineer.'

Sekoni spun round, came face to face with the village Head.

'Did I scare you? Some children came and told me of a stranger prowling round the place. So I thought I would come up and see.'

Stranger! It was only two months. Sekoni knew those children, and they must have remembered him. The Head appeared to sense what he was thinking. 'It must have been your beard. You didn't have that when you were here.'

His hand moved involuntarily to his chin, scraping the beard with the back of his hand. He had forgotten about that, no, it was more accurate to say he had never really been conscious of it. And he began to think of it like a new problem, some cause for a decision, amazed that he had never really noticed it sprout.

The Head looked at him with some apprehension, and seemed to feel his way around the engineer. Something he could not quite decide, and it urged him to be wary.

'You didn't even come back to say good-bye to us.'

'I . . . I . . . have cccome back.'

'Oh yes, oh yes. There are many people who still talk of you.'

'I-er . . . I came to t-t-test the plant.'

At first the Head did not believe he heard right. He looked at him in doubt, pointed towards the plant. Sekoni nodded, as if in confidence.

The Head put it in words. 'You want to get this thing going?'

More eagerly, Sekoni nodded. 'Th-they say it c-c-can't work, b-b-but th-that is all rrrubbish.'

The Chief's hostility was now unmistakable. 'They don't say it won't work. It will not only work, it will blow up. It will blow up and blow up the village with it.'

Sekoni became incoherent, a throbbing vein out on his forehead and his neck-muscles working with self-destructive strength. 'D-d-don't believe it. D-d-d-don't bbbelieve it. If ththey only allowed me to tttest . . .'

'If you want to test it, my friend, just uproot your funny thing and carry it with you. Go and test it in the bush, or in your home town. Electricity is government thing, we all know that. The white men know about it, and one came here and told us. They know what they are talking about.'

'Lllies. Lllies. The-they c-c-called it jjunk. Jjjunk! And ththat man even came here without my p-p-plans.'

'Look, take my advice, just go back before more people see you.'

Sekoni could not believe it. 'We only nnneed firewood. If you g-g-get the ch-children to ffetch firewood, I will use that in ssstead of c-c-coal.'

'My friend, just go home.'

'One llload from every ch-ch-child, th-then you will see it work. If yyyou find me the wood, you will s-s-see lllight g-g-glowing from th-that post.'

'Thank you very much. We've used oil-lamps until now.

When government is ready, they will build us a proper one.'

'Only one t-t-test, one test. You have to sssee for your . . . self.'

'Come now, before people begin to gather . . .' And as he placed a hand on Sekoni's arm, Sekoni broke suddenly loose and seized the boulder. The Head screamed for help and fled, not even looking round to see Sekoni who had begun to batter the door. It flew away from the lock and the bolts and the reinforcement of six-inch nails. When the chief returned with help, they found Sekoni oiling the machines and inspecting the meters. He turned round, seeing the chief and asked, 'Have you brought the firewood?'

Surprisingly, he had allowed the police to lead him off without resistance. There was another Commission of Enquiry, but by then Sekoni lay in a mental hospital.

2

They left the club towards morning. Egbo started them up, following out the lone dancer when the singers left, and the spell shattered about her.

'You have a rendezvous in space?' Sagoe said.

'Get lost.'

'In space, certainly, what do you say, my little Secretary?'

'Egbo at least is sensible. Time we all went home.'

Bandele rose, 'When do you set off for Ibadan?' Sagoe asked him.

'Soon as I get up. I'm setting off before those two.'

'I doubt that. Sheikh wants to get back early. But if you are ready before me, he can ride back with you.'

'Anyway, if I don't see you before you go, just leave the houseboy in charge.'

'You won't be back. Good-night, Dehinwa. Don't let him drive.'

'Don't you worry. I don't intend to commit suicide.'

'What do you mean . . .' With half his weight on her, Dehinwa steered Sagoe through the puddles and into the little car.

'Please,' said Sagoe. 'Drive to the beach. I need some salt wind to clear my head.'

'It is all very well for you, you are a newspaper man. But don't forget I have to be in the office at eight this morning.'

'Career girl, career girl, don't get mixed up with a career girl.'

They drove in silence some distance, then Dehinwa turned to him, and her tone, even through his beery obfuscation, Sagoe recognised as very dangerous. 'Just what did you mean that time, what you told Bandele?'

He knew quite well but he asked, 'What?'

'You said in case you didn't see him and the others before they left.'

'Well?'

'Well what? They are staying with you aren't they?'

'I gave them my flat.'

'You know what I am talking about.'

'My dear young lady, I don't know what you are talking about.'

'Biodun, let's not go through this again. You can't stay in my place.'

'Why do you get so suspicious? I only asked you to drive me to the beach.'

She took the next corner vindictively, and Sagoe lurched against the door and it flew open. 'That's right,' he said. 'Kill me. Kill me on mere suspicion.'

Sagoe slept off before they arrived on the beach. And he fell out helpless when Dehinwa opened the door for him, hoping he would get out and walk. That woke him, murmuring, 'Sand. Is it now raining sand?'

Suddenly chilled by the desolation, Dehinwa looked round, hearing stealth and robbers in every movement of the wind. 'Where are we, Dehin?'

'The beach.'

'The beach!'

'At this hour?'

'You wanted to come?'

'I did? Suppose my friend Sir Derin rises from the sea, where will I run?'

'The man is dead. Can't you leave him alone?'

'Meaning I suppose, respect the dead?'

'Let's go, Biodun.'

'Ho ho, the woman is afraid of ghosts.'

'Biodun, come on.'

'Not to mention prowlers. Have you thought of our getting attacked? All those prowlers? Even in the best condition I am not Egbo you know. Or even Bandele with his gorilla limbs.'

'You should have thought of that.'

'I should have thought of that.' And lifting his voice high up to the winds he shouted, 'Did you hear this mermaid? She says I should have thought of that.'

Dehinwa got up, looked apprehensively round. 'Let's go.'

'Now I have got her scared, though why, I cannot think. You are lucky. What after all will they have but your treasure. But me, I may lose my life. At least I will lose an ear like that politician who came here to frolic.'

'She was in league with them.'

'Some frolic, enh. You can never tell with frolics. How do I know you are not also in league with them? After all, have you ever given that which I desire? You hold me off with hoping—why?'

She took him by the shoulders and tried to drag him up. 'Moreover, you have chosen to bring me here when I can neither defend myself nor assert my manhood. I mean, at five in the morning, alone on the beach, and you will still return to your bed unbroken . . .'

She got him in at last and slipped the safety catch on the lock. She drove off madly, terrified until they saw the lights of the first bridge approach them. Sagoe fell against the steering wheel and she had to extricate his fingers from the spokes.

'You know something? That *apala* band, they were demoralising.'

'What was wrong with them?'

'Demoralising that's all. At three-thirty in the morning and with that gloomy rain, it was no time for them to come vibrating a man's stomach was it?'

Dehinwa took his hand off the wheel.

33

'Well was it? You are a sensible girl so you tell me, was it fair?'

'No Sagoe, it wasn't.'

'You see, that was why I drank so much.' Upon which he promptly fell asleep. He woke later to a succession of bumps as Dehinwa turned into a side-street and hit one pot-hole after another.

'Careful, careful. What are you doing?'

'I didn't make the road.'

'You are jarring my drink lobes.'

'You are shivering again. Wind up the glass.'

'I should have stuck to beer. Those whiskies burnt out all my negritude.' Another jolt smacked his head on the roof. 'Are you sure we are on the road?'

'It's nearly over, cheer up.'

Throwing up his arms suddenly, he shouted, 'To thine tent, O damsel.'

Dehinwa stopped the car. 'We are home.'

Sagoe slunk down into the seat. 'Which home?'

'Yours.'

'I am not coming out.'

'Biodun, be reasonable. You cannot stay at my flat.'

'My house is full. Three full-grown men in it. Where do you expect us to sleep?'

'Why didn't one of them stay with Lasunwon?'

'With his wife and two children? And anyway who wants to be saddled with that bush wife of his? And Egbo was out. You saw that woman yourself. She would need a double bed and a half.'

'No, Biodun, you really must come down.'

'If it is *that* you are worrying about, I promise I'll behave. In any case, I am in no condition.'

Sagoe had begun shivering again. Anxiously Dehinwa looked at him and felt his brow. 'Biodun, you're ill!'

'No, no . . . it's just the damp, you know . . .'

She drove home furiously while he kept mumbling, 'You should watch my drink lobes. You keep jarring them.'

He did not wake even to the different surface of gravel, and Dehinwa had to shake him awake. 'The garage is some distance. You come down here and go straight up to my flat. I'll park the car and come up directly.'

34

Sagoe got out, swayed and leant against the car. Dehinwa opened the door quickly and ran to him. 'I'd better help you up.'

'No no. I can walk.'

'Are you sure?'

'Of course. Seriously, though, something has happened to my drink lobes. You know where the drink lobes are, don't you?'

Hastily she said yes, dreading the explanation which she already knew and he hadn't the strength to give. 'Everyone is born with them, but you have to find them you see. You get to know them when you become professional. Then it gives a delicate trill and you know you're there. The first time, it is like confirmation . . . a truly religious moment . . .'

She had urged him gently towards the stairs. 'Don't keep supporting me like a crock. I can walk, I tell you.'

'Okay, I'll be right back.' She ran to the car and drove off.

Sagoe climbed the stairs slowly, taking short rests to fight his dizziness. With difficulty he opened the door, only to be met by signs of occupation as light from the landing fell on a figure in an armchair. For a moment he stood still, and then he hurriedly slammed the door murmuring, 'Beg pardon, wrong door.' Flying down the stairs with false energy, he nearly collided with Dehinwa. 'What's the matter?'

'Opened the wrong door.'

'You really are trying. Surely you should know my door by now . . .' and then she stopped, wondering, 'But you say you opened it.'

Handing her the key he said, 'See for yourself. Black shape in a chair and I thought I saw a few more in the background. I stood a few seconds and then something urged me to run. I ran.'

'You *are* in a bad way.' They had now reached the landing. 'You are sure it was this door?'

'Open it. They looked like monstrous bats . . . witches even.

'Stop trembling.'

'Couldn't quite decide what they were, but the one I saw looked clear enough. Looked like a woman.'

Dehinwa stood with the key in her hand, thoughtful. 'A woman? You are sure it was a woman?'

'One moment it looked like a woman, the next like a winged

35

rodent. Especially those others in the dark. The place was like a cave.'

Muttering, 'It would be my mother. She and some relations, I am certain. And God, I am so tired.'

As she opened the door a figure rose from the gloom, a black shawl slipped down and an enormous head-tie bristled. Sagoe fell backwards, hitting his head against the balustrade. All went dark but for a few moments he heard voices from Gehenna . . .

'So Dehinwa, this is what you people do in Lagos . . . is this a decent time for a young girl to be out?'

'Ah Mamma . . . and auntie too . . . I am so sorry. Have you been waiting long?'

'What is the matter with that man?'

Because Sagoe was screaming, 'Don't let them near, don't let them near me!'

And blissfully, before they even touched him, he went limp and fully lost consciousness.

'Drunk, I bet,' and she was familiar with that edge of distaste in her mother. 'Drunk, but you bring him home. You think you can trust yourself with that kind of man?'

At other times, Dehinwa would be knocked up in the night. How had they got in anyway? The houseboy of course; they knew where the servants' quarters were. Once her mother had travelled down to see her, arriving late in the night. Then Dehinwa's mind still ran to reasons. To reasonable reasons, disasters, emergencies. That time her mind flew to a grandfather who had been in hospital for some time. It was nothing of the sort. Not that time, not this, not any other time.

'Why mother, what is the matter?'

The mother settled herself and asked if she had tea in the house, but first she turned the lock on the bedroom where Sagoe lay unconscious or asleep. She never came alone, perhaps she sensed a change, some time of decisions when an aunt's moral support would count for much. Inevitably it was an indigent aunt or cousin who could be hustled down to Lagos at the moment's notice, one who sat and sighed and chorused 'For your own good; listen my child, what your mother says is for your own good. We had no one to tell us these things, so count yourself lucky.'

The tea was made and the aunt asked for bread with sardines.

'I had no time to eat, you see. Would I stop to eat where my own children were concerned? Not likely. And what touches your mother touches me. I regard you as my own children. Oh, perhaps some stew then, if you have no sardines . . .'

The aunt, sucking steaming tea as through a straw began, 'Your mother's *aladura* had a vision concerning you.' Tension in the mother more that the heat raised huge drops of sweat on her face. The aunt scooped hot peppers with the bread, began to sweat in sympathy. 'Your mother was very worried. She chartered a taxi and called on me to accompany her. As you see, we are here. This is what brought us.'

'What was this vision?' Dehinwa wanted to know.

'He saw you brought to bed. You gave me a grandson.'

Dehinwa could not help smiling. 'Did he see the father?'

Tension now, and the strain of gossip. The aunt took refuge in the cant, deferential, even obsequious to her companion. 'Just listen to what your mother will tell you. I know what she has suffered for all you children. You must listen to her now, for your own good.'

'Well, won't you tell me? Who was supposed to be the father?'

The mother braced herself for battle. This was the whole point now, the entire point of the midnight visit. 'He didn't say. But people have been telling me that you are going with a Northerner.'

The aunt interjected, 'It has made us all very unhappy.'

'Are men so short in town? Enh? Tell me Dehinwa, are good-looking, decent men so hard to find that you must go with a *Gambari*? Don't you know what your name is that you even let yourself be seen with a *Gambari*?'

'But mamma, you shouldn't listen to that kind of talk. Next time tell them to mind their business.'

The aunt left her mouth open in mid-swallow. 'What did the child say? Tell people to mind their own business when it is their love for your mother that prompts them to speak?'

'Who I move with is my own business.'

'Oh no, it isn't your own business, and you don't go with who you like, not if you are my own daughter. I should think I have a say in the matter. I haven't worked and slaved to send you to England and pulled strings to get you a really

37

good post nearly in the Senior Service only to have you give me a Hausa grandson.'

'Mamma . . .'

'Well what did your father do? He didn't lift a finger to help you. He sent all his sons to England, but when it came to you, you remember what he said, don't you? But how could you? Sisi, better tell her what her father said. It was no secret, he repeated it all over town.'

The auntie nodded. 'He said he wasn't sending any girl to England only to go and get herself pregnant within three months.'

'His very words. I had only my petty trade, but from it I saved enough to send you on my own.'

Dehinwa bristled gradually. They had come to familiar grounds and now she was bored. 'All right, mamma, all right. I am saving as fast as I can. I'll pay you back what you spent on me before I ever get married.'

Tears now, tears for ingratitude, for toil and sacrifice unappreciated. Contrition, allowances, resuscitation of love and a little ground given. 'It isn't that I am even thinking of marriage or anything like that.' Always a mistake. 'Don't you see it is all in your own interest. We have no more use for the world. God has spared us this long only to look after you.'

The tone becomes lighter, everyone is crying and blissfully unhappy. As once, months before, at such a moment Dehinwa playfully said, 'But really, mother, you mustn't make any more of these midnight journeys. Suppose I had a man with me?'

And the tears froze on the instant, and a slow disbelief replaced the brief contentment. 'What was that you said?' Anxious not to spoil things, ready to sacrifice for the sake of peace, 'Come, mamma, I was only joking.'

'I heard you. I heard what you said and you were not joking. Suppose you had a man with you? Enh, is that the sort of life you want to cut out for yourself? God protect me, what sort of a daughter have I born? If I found a man in your house at any awkward hour I will let him know that my family bears the name of Komolola. A man in this house at night? I will cry *ibosi* on him and humiliate him in public. . . .'

But tonight there was tact. By mutual consent Sagoe did not exist, locked away like soiled linen from decent sight. Only, the mother could not quite forget and the aunt was slowly weighing up the risks—did the mother wait for her to open up that door? She was the whipping dog, but at such times her function was nearly insupportable. Was this a truce or was the battle to begin? She wiped the bread-crumbs from the plate, avoiding the mother's eyes. And Dehinwa, steeling herself for the final act that must pronounce the break, was slowly being worn down from the midnight visitations of aunts and mothers bearing love, and transparent intentions, and manufactured anxieties, and, quite simply, blood cruelty . . .

3

Monica Faseyi was always in disgrace. And so at the entrance to the embassy reception her husband stopped and inspected her thoroughly. Satisfied, he nodded and quickly checked the line of his own bow-tie. He smiled then and kissed her formally on the forehead.

'You might as well put on your gloves now.'

'What gloves? I didn't bring any.'

Faseyi thought she was teasing, and out of character though it was, Monica was certain that her husband was teasing.

'Come on now, put on the gloves.'

'You stop teasing, now. Who do you see wearing gloves in Nigeria?'

Faseyi was no longer joking. He had snatched the handbag from her and found that there were no gloves inside. 'Do you mean you didn't bring them?'

'Bring what, Ayo?'

'The gloves, of course. What else?'

'But I haven't any gloves. I gave the ones I had away soon after I came.'

'I am not talking about two years ago. I mean the gloves you've bought for tonight.'

'I didn't buy any. Ayo, what's all this?'

'What's all this? I should ask you what's all this! Didn't I give you an invitation over a week ago?'

'Yes you did, but . . .'

'Darling, I gave you a cheque for fifteen pounds to get yourself all you needed.'

'I thought you wanted me to have a new dress.'

'For heaven's sake, what about the gloves?'

'But you didn't say anything about gloves.'

'Was it necessary to say anything? It was right there on the card. In black and white.' He took the card from his pocket, dragged it from the envelope and thrust it under her eyes. 'Read it, there it is. Read it.'

Monica read the last line on the card. 'But Ayo, it only says those who are to be presented. We are not, are we?'

Ayo held his head. 'We *are* to be presented.'

'You didn't tell me. How was I to know?'

'How were you to know! It took me two weeks to wangle the presentation, and now you ask me how were you to know. What would be the whole point of coming if we were not to be presented?'

'I am sorry,' said Monica, 'it never occurred to me . . .'

'Nothing ever occurs to you!'

Bandele and Kola continued to hug the shadows where they had gone for fresh air, unwilling eavesdroppers, but it was too late to move.

'Do you know them?'

'Ayo Faseyi, Teaching Hospital.'

The emphasis shifted somewhat, Faseyi saying, 'But at least you could have used some initiative. Even if there was no question of being presented, you knew Their Excellencies would be here.'

'I am sorry.'

'Darling, if the Queen was attending a garden party, would you go dressed without your gloves?'

'I've said I am sorry, Ayo. I really am. Perhaps I had better return home.'

'But would you? Answer my question. Would you attend the same party with the Queen without gloves.'

'I really don't know, Ayo. I never moved in such circles.'

'Darling, I am surprised at you. These are simple require-

40

ments of society which any intelligent person would know.' He looked at his watch, thinking rapidly, biting his lips in vexation. And then he hit a solution. 'Of course. Mummy will help out. She is bound to have a pair at home.'

The young girl with the mild voice said, 'No, Ayo. It's much simpler for me just to go back home.'

'What is the use if I cannot be presented with my wife? Let's go back for the gloves.'

'The reception will be over by the time we get back.'

The thought halted Faseyi definitely. 'All right, come on. But you will have to stay behind when we are called.'

'Of course. I am really sorry this happened, Ayo.'

They went in, and Bandele and Kola were released from their long restriction.

'Some domestic scene.'

Bandele sighed. 'I'm going to be told all about it tomorrow.'

'Who by?'

'Faseyi. I know him very well.'

'Oh, is it a regular thing?'

'Once for every social occasion at least, including their own at-homes.'

'It's going to rain.' Kola brushed off a drop on his arm.

'When did it ever stop?'

'What has happened anyway? The season used to be more precise. And four months at the most. Maybe five.'

'Bommmmmmmbs.' Bandele, with his deepest bass.

'Last week I felt suddenly starved for some flare of colours so I woke up early to see in the dawn. And it came, by God it came. A huge suspension of *ewedu*.'

'Come on, let's get in from it.'

Sagoe, locked with the ambassador, full of virtue in the course of duty, had immersed himself in a borrowed dinner jacket, and there was nothing of the journalist in his appearance. Sagoe, desperate. Between him and an 'exclusive statement' lay years of trained caution, and it would not be lulled.

'At that time we were all full of the propaganda, "secret of life discovered by Stalin's doctors". A special plasma extracted from live children, and each injection made Stalin younger by ten years. Stalin could never die—they said.'

'Well,' the ambassador spoke slowly, 'I would agree—in a sense—with that. Stalin, like other dictators, did purchase

41

longevity with human lives. So did Hitler. But it is in the nature of dictators to be rather . . . predatory on human beings.'

'I agree, sir. But still you believe that a dictatorship is often the most sensible government for a nation?'

'It depends on the nation, as I said before.'

'If I may use yours as an example, don't you agree sir, that . . .'

'Ah, will you excuse me a moment, Mr Sagoe. I must welcome the new guests. . . .'

Sagoe charged into Kola and Bandele just outside the door in his headlong rush out. 'What's eating him?'

'He couldn't have got his story. Hey, Sagoe, wait . . .'

'I'll see you back at the house,' he shouted back.

'He must have been pretty well frustrated. He didn't even wait to get drunk.'

The ambassador approached the Faseyis accompanied by a waiter bearing a trayload of champagne. Monica shook her head, and already Faseyi looked displeased. The ambassador was hospitably incredulous. 'But don't you drink at all, Mrs Faseyi?' 'No, only the occasional palm wine when our steward feels kindly towards us.' The ambassador laughed and gestured regretfully. 'I am so sorry, I really wish we had palm wine.'

One of the waiters was passing with more champagne and overheard. Faseyi had wandered off to seek the Master of Presentations; when he returned, Monica had a glass of palm wine in her hand, and a colleague of Faseyi was asking, 'What have you got there, Monica? Mist alba?'

'Where did you get that?' Faseyi shouted.

'One of the stewards brought it. He overheard us talk about palm wine and went to fetch it from his house. Wasn't that sweet of him?'

Faseyi went scrambling towards Bandele. 'You see, she has begun again.'

Bandele wore his mask of infinite patience. 'What has she done now?'

'It was bad enough to refuse the champagne, although mind you I just don't see any necessity for it. After all, how many of these women here touch their drink? They just hold the glass in their hand to be sociable, what is wrong with that?'

Kola murmured, 'Nothing, nothing, I'm sure.'

Faseyi looked at him with love and gratitude. 'But you see, that isn't all. She wasn't satisfied with that. She had to go and ask for palm wine at a cocktail reception. Have you ever heard such a thing? For palm wine!'

Bandele's grave aspect consoled him not at all.

'If she were a bush-girl from some London slum I could understand. But she is educated. She has moved in society. Why does she have to come and disgrace me by drinking palm wine?'

'Oh' Kola looked concerned. 'You mean she even got it?'

Faseyi spun round. 'Look at her if you don't believe me. There she is over there, drinking palm wine if you please. And someone even came along as I saw her, and I bet he is spreading the story all over the place already.'

'Oh, he may not know it was palm wine.'

'He did. He was even sneering. Is that mist alba? that's what he said.'

'You should have said yes,' Kola told him. 'After all it would be more understandable that your wife was taken suddenly ill and had to have some mist alba.'

'Yes . . . I suppose so . . . I suppose so. I should have thought of it. But the trouble is Monica. She would have made some careless slip and given herself away. Look, Bandele, be a friend. If you hear any adverse comments, let me know, will you. Much better if one knew what people are saying in time, then one can do something about it. And also . . .' Faseyi drew closer and whispered, 'about her dress.'

Bandele said, 'What are you talking about?'

'Don't you see she is improperly dressed?'

'I hadn't noticed.'

In Faseyi's eyes a sudden gleam of hope. 'You mean you hadn't? Well that's a relief, perhaps most people won't either.'

'I am afraid you are wrong,' Kola said.

'Oh. So you've noticed.'

Kola improved on it. 'Not me. I don't know much about clothes. But I heard a group over there commenting on her.'

Turning to Bandele, 'You see!'

'I wouldn't pay much attention,' Kola continued. 'You get these spiteful types everywhere, and those ones were'—and a doleful shake of the head—'anyway I don't need to tell you. You know how catty people can be.'

43

'No, no, it's not cattiness. They are quite right. Look, what did they say exactly?'

Bandele interfered and manœuvred Faseyi away and towards his wife. They had hardly come to Monica before Faseyi burst out 'You see how conspicuous you've made us? Look around and see for yourself. Even those in native dress are wearing gloves.'

Bandele withdrew at the first decent opportunity, returning to attack an unrepentant Kola. 'What were all those lies in aid of?'

'The man likes to worry. I only helped him with material.'

Bandele shook his head. 'Don't waste your sympathy on Monica. I know both of them.'

'It is not a question of sympathy.'

'She sounds mild but she isn't. In fact I have still to meet a tougher girl.'

'She looks very young.'

An official, the 'Master of Presentations', moved among the guests with a list, taking the chosen few and leading them to their brief fulfilment, and Faseyi followed him with side-glances. Calculating along the alphabet when his turn approached, he moved away and joined Bandele again. The ruse was obvious to Monica and she lowered her head into the palm wine, pretending not to see.

'Ah there you are, Mr Faseyi. Will you bring your wife and come with me please.'

'Oh my wife is . . . er . . . she is rather shy. I'll have to go by myself.'

'Nonsense, we can't have that sort of thing. Let me talk to her.'

'No, no, no, it's no use believe me. I've done nothing else but try and persuade her all evening. Let's go and get it over with.'

A few moments later, Bandele tugged Kola by the sleeve. 'Look!'

'Your Excellencies, may I present . . . oh . . . that's better, you screwed up your courage at last . . . beg pardon, Your Excellencies, may I now present Mr and Mrs Faseyi, University Teaching Hospital.'

Kola's face was all screwed up in perplexity. 'Just what is the matter with your friend?'

44

'He is supposed to be the best X-ray analyst available in the continent.'

'Is that supposed to be of some relevance?'

Bandele shrugged.

Faseyi stomped out, Monica in his wake, as soon as the presentation was over. Five minutes later he returned by himself, and Monica followed soon afterwards. Outwardly collected, she appeared to be looking for Faseyi. Bandele caught her by the arm. 'Come and join us.'

'Where is Ayo? Have you seen him?'

'He's around somewhere . . . oh there he is with Senator Okot. Shall I fetch him?'

'No no. It doesn't matter.'

'By the way, have you met Kola?'

There was distinct hostility in her voice. 'I am Ayo's wife.'

'Kola lectures on Art. At the Institute.'

'Oh yes of course. My husband was just telling me. He said you overheard some people commenting on my semi-nudity. Is that true?'

Kola felt he should admire her directness. At that moment however he could think of nothing to say.

Her voice changed to genuine concern. 'Have I got him into trouble?'

Bandele laughed. 'You sound worried. Where did you leave your glass? I need another drink myself.' Monica gestured and Bandele strode off.

'How long have you known Bandele?'

'Bandele is a good friend of ours. When Ayo's mother is not around he complains to him.'

'Complains? I don't understand.'

'Oh yes you do. He must have been discussing me just now. How else would you have mentioned what you heard about me?'

Kola remained silent.

'Or are you just a habitual gossip? Oh, most of my husband's friends are. They admit it. In fact Ayo is the only one who gets cross when I say that.'

'I should hope so. A husband has the right to demand some respect for his friends.'

'But they are all gossips. And so much of it is in their

45

imagination isn't it? You don't want to admit it? But surely you know.'

'How long have you been here?'

'Two years. Or don't you consider that long enough to form conclusions?'

'Oh yes. Sometimes even a week can be enough.'

'It was, in this case. I was so horrified when I came, but I soon grew accustomed to it. In fact I enjoy it now, just listening to my husband's colleagues. I had never lived in a university atmosphere, you see, I suppose I expected everything to go above my head. Instead I found it the same as in my old Teacher Training Institute.'

'You think we are just a pack of British schoolmarms then?'

'Oh no, I wasn't trying to be rude.'

Bandele came with the drinks. 'Shall I tell you what I heard about you?' she continued.

'No, I am not really curious.'

'Oh but you are. Everybody wants to know what people are saying about him. You ask Ayo.'

'Well, what did you hear about me?'

'You see. Well, to begin with, you have a friend whom they all think is mad.'

'We were going to talk about me.'

'But that is what I am doing. You are working on an enormous canvas which will contain all your gods and I would like to come and see it.'

'There is nothing to see, I've only started.'

'But you haven't just started. Didn't an angry mother nearly wreck your studio because her daughter was posing for you? Oh I heard all about it.'

'Yes, I'm afraid you are well-informed.'

'So, can I come and see it?'

'Quite frankly, no. It hasn't reached the stage where it means anything.'

'All right. Maybe later.'

'Yes, later.'

'I ought to go and find my husband. Will you excuse me?'

Bandele waited until she had gone. 'What was the matter? You two didn't seem to be very friendly.'

'No, there was nothing.'

46

'In fact, you sounded short-tempered.'

'No. What for?'

'You should know. Anyway, are we going to their house for lunch tomorrow? Faseyi has just asked me.'

'What is that to do with me?'

'He included you. In fact more you than me. You don't know Fash. He has to know what else you heard and it won't wait.'

'Well I heard nothing, so he can forget it.'

'His mother is coming—you'll soon get to know the pattern. After a scene like this he sends for his mother to talk to Monica. Those two get on so well—mother and wife I mean. Anyway I like to indulge in a good meal once in a while, and Mrs Faseyi is a demon of the kitchen.'

'Best of luck then, go and gorge yourself.'

'There is something eating you, Kola.'

'And what should that be? Stop fussing, there is nothing the matter.'

Monica opened the door to them the following afternoon. 'Please feel hungry,' she said, 'My mother-in-law is doing the cooking.'

Faseyi stayed only one moment saying 'Kola hasn't met Mummy has he . . . Mummy, . . .' and disappeared into the kitchen.

'I'll get some beer,' Monica said, and turning to Kola, 'it is always beer in Nigeria isn't it? I never drank at all until I came here and tasted palm wine. Now I don't drink anything else.'

Faseyi returned from the kitchen. 'So sorry, Mummy says she can't leave her cooking now. I've told her you're here, Bandele.'

'That means redoubled effort,' Monica said. 'Bandele is Mother's favourite you know. She can't stand any of Ayo's other friends.'

'Darling, how can you tell such a lie?'

'All right, we'll wait until Mother comes in and then we'll ask her.'

'There will be no more of that nonsense. I don't want you and Mummy discussing my friends any more, I've told you.'

47

From the kitchen came a rich, stentorian voice, 'Moni!'

'I think Mother needs a hand,' and Monica disappeared in the kitchen.

A few moments later, Faseyi, who had never stopped fidgeting, gestured to Bandele and dragged him to the balcony, remembering only at the last moment to say, 'Won't be a minute, Kola, just make yourself at home.'

Through the balcony doors almost at once, 'Did he tell you more about what he heard? Did you find out who they were?' And then Kola deliberately shut his mind off the voice, and heard nothing more.

He was alone a little while. Monica came in once and asked, 'Where are they gone?' and he gestured to the balcony. She said 'Oh,' as if she understood, and was both surprised and saddened by the fact. She stood in the doorway for some time, hesitant, in the end she went in again.

They were a long time talking and Kola soon began to feel the effect of the beer, slowly feeling drowsy. And then he heard the outside door open slightly, a soft furry movement at his back. A warm yellow moth brushed him on the cheek and wedged itself between him and the low table. It peered short-sightedly into the glass in his hand, drank from it, screwed its face at the bitter taste. Then it pressed its face almost against Kola's relaxed fingers from which the nuts had nearly begun to drop. With her back against him, nuzzling his face with short plaited yellow hair stood an albino girl. She was gentle and uncertain, a frail, disturbing twilight child.

Monica had come in. 'Usaye! Oh dear, where are your manners? Come over here.'

Kola blinked, unbelieving.

'Usaye is our cook's daughter,' Monica said.

'Is he albino?'

'No. That is the miracle. Neither he nor his wife. Both of them are as black as you are. Oh, you don't object to black, do you?'

'I object to dark, coloured, pigmented or any of the idiotic euphemisms.'

'I was sure you would. I find one has to be so careful here. Why are most people so touchy? Oh there I go again. I was saying about Usaye, she has four brothers and sisters and three of them, that is three including her, are albinos. And the mother is expecting a sixth. The poor man is really scared to death.'

'She looks too vulnerable.'

'Usaye has the poorest sight of them. She really is short-sighted.'

'I noticed that.'

'I think she comes in here because of me. Colour prejudice you see.'

'She is such a fluffy thing . . . like a day-old chicken. Usaye, come and have some more beer.'

'Oh no, you mustn't.'

'It won't harm her . . . brandy would have been better though. See if the colour rushes to her cheeks.'

Usaye sipped the beer, with the same distaste. And then she began to peer closely into his face, ran her eyes almost an inch away along his clothes. And he became suddenly terrified for her. 'But how on earth does she cross the road?'

'She will have to wear glasses. I've arranged for the optician to test her.'

Usaye attracted and repelled him. 'Like a new-laid egg,' he said, 'when the shell is not full hard . . . or the pulsing soft centre of a baby's head . . . oh ignore me. Sometimes I suffer from fluffy emotions.'

She looked at him then with wonder and he grew uncomfortable. 'You have fluffy emotions, you say?' He tried to brush it aside and she said. 'Come to the window.'

The window looked on the backyard. 'Over there . . . do you see that tree stump? She is so short-sighted she talks to it.'

'Why have you done nothing all this while?'

'Ayo kept promising. The trouble is I haven't a car and anyway I can't drive.'

'It's all right, I'll . . . I'll arrange something.'

'You will come and take her?'

'Yes of course. I'll come myself.'

'Thank you' she said.

'Did I offend you last night?' she asked, a little later.

'Offend me—how?'

'I mean that you were almost unfriendly. Are you one of those who don't believe in mixed marriages? I know that some of Ayo's friends disapprove of me.'

'Isn't that your own business, and your husband's?'

'I am glad you are taking Usaye. Perhaps you think I have taken unfair advantage of you?'

'Of course not, don't be ridiculous.'

'Just the same I think I took unfair advantage, but I can't feel sorry.'

'Nor I, so don't let us talk about it.'

Staring at the wooden stump, Usaye's eyelashes brushing his palms as she gave them detailed examination, Kola did not know when Monica left the room. Suddenly he was returning the action, looking closer at the child and exclaiming softly to himself. For long he had despaired of a suitable face among the neighbouring children for Obaluwaiye's handmaiden, and now Usaye appeared to him a near divine intervention, colour and features achieving his perfect image. He saw Usaye, her skin pure moonstone sitting at the feet of Obaluwaiye, reflecting the phase of the experiments of the divine Scourge, emerging each time, clear, unmarked.

And then there was this other thing, an insidious beginning of a great yearning . . . at such a time surely, not the leavening presence of some tenderness to weaken the laws of his own creation . . . then he heard the doors of the balcony open and Bandele call to him.

He turned abruptly, giving himself no time to think, and fled the house.

4

Even children knew of Simi! Wives knelt and prayed that their men might sin a hundred times with a hundred women, but may their erring feet never lead them to Simi of the slow eyelids. For then men lost hope of salvation, their homes and children became ghosts of a past illusion, learning from Simi a new view of life, and love, immersed in a cannibal's reality.

Simi broke men, and friendships. So innocent was she Simi never fell to the knowledge of age, and each man felt that he betrayed her, never that she had done him wrong, and he protected her from the rage of women in whose eye this innocence could not appear. There were songs of course, the various episodes of Simi's loves, praise-songs and many which spun abuse, not on Simi, not ever on Simi, but on the women who dared profane the goddess of serenity, Simi, Queen Bee, with the skin of light pastel earth, Kano soil from the air. Simi never paid to have her praises sung; the men did. But mostly it was an act of spontaneous homage; the poet saw, and burst forth in song.

In company Simi would sit motionless, calm, unacknowledging, indifferent to a host of admiring men. And yet she noticed them, and when they had gone, bluster emptied, pocket drained, manhood disgraced—for Simi matched them glass for glass and kept her mystery while the men were hollowed out and led out flabby or raucous, sadder but never wiser—then would Simi make her choice, her frozen eyelids betraying nothing.

'Come here! Come here, young Egbo!' The teacher in Geography, the only man in a precipice-lined career who found a spark of good in 'that Egbo!', seized him by his new blazer and dragged him to his classroom. He inspected the blue cloth and the school badge, signs of incipient freedom, for they were bought by the senior class alone, and Egbo had waited until his school-leaving approached. 'Young Egbo,' the teacher said, 'you are something of a miracle. Do you know you came near dismissal six times? Six times in a secondary school career! Young Egbo, you must ask me for a testimonial because that fact must impress any right-thinking man.'

'Yes sir.' Squirming because only this teacher had the power to embarrass him.

'Yes, you have set something of a record. Now listen to this also. I know a sex maniac when I see one. And I see one standing right before me this moment. Keep away from women do you understand? Now get thee gone, thou miserable worm of humanity, get thee from my sight.'

He had a tradition of hyperboles, that teacher, for Egbo was notorious for his fear of women. Until a week before, then the

51

story of a night on the town drifted to the teachers, an escapade which had not merely included Egbo but soon became preserved for his part in it. Drunk on the harmattan euphoria of approaching freedom, six young daredevils, released at last from the tyranny of School Certificate, made a brassy first assault on a night-club. It was some time before his companions realised that Egbo had neither got up to dance nor spoken a word since their arrival. And his gaze had never swerved from the one direction.

'Look at Egbo, enh. Have you never seen a woman before?'

'You can always tell them apart. *Omo alufa*, the greatest womanizers in the business.'

After school-leaving examination, with the last paper flung at the proxy persecutor, there was for them a laxity in time itself; and the period of the year, cold, dry and brittle produced a sensation of airiness; an end of consciousness in space, in time; a general recklessness even in nature, in dust and wisps of charred blades. In the early morning and at night, the air acquired the fore-brush of a sharper sting, and at noon the kestrels would circle the smoke, waiting out the escaping squirrel or rat. But it was that night sting especially which sensitised the skin; walking through the bush-path through tickling waves of *ekan*, the air was a horn of straight palm wine on a ten-day fast, and with a dry throat and cracked lips on the three-mile walk, Egbo knew full drunkenness.

He sat at the table, all awkwardness gone, for he was blind to his own strangeness. Simi, at the immortal period of her life, sat in the midst of a gathering which he was to know quite familiarly, dispensing her favours on none. Her table reeled with laughter, with much emptiness it was true, but Simi seemed untouched by it. She has the eyes of a fish, Egbo murmured, and the boys said, Oh, the creek man has found his Mammy Watta.

Once Simi looked up and saw him. It seemed ludicrous as he looked into the eyes and thought of fresh liver on a butcher's slab, its cold gelatinous depths. For a full moment, Simi let her eyes stay on his and Egbo, confounded and lost, rose slowly, the blood whirling through his head so that he made nothing of the look, could prove nothing by it except that Simi had looked up, and seen him. His hands were clammy, and Egbo stumbled into the street outside, blindly through trays of cola-nut and fried meat while the hawkers laughed and said, Another of them, blind drunk. Remembering the walk back only as an after fever of muted sounds, remote echoes of crickets and furtive rustles in a black night, Egbo reeled with the wanton strike of a snake and welcomed the poison through his veins.

Egbo explained it all in the classroom the following day. 'If I had seen her before the Zoology paper, I would have done the question on the Queen Bee. Just to put the text-books right once for all.'

The teachers always overheard these things. 'Young Egbo, come over here you precocious maniac. . . .'

Later, Egbo would admit to Simi, 'It was my first act of singlemindedness, and my last.' He left school at once, obtained work, and began to save. And his self-denial was such, he thought, that if he should choose to be a seaside holy-man, this training would come useful. He ate just below the starvation line and the library formed his entire pleasure. Eighteen pounds in his pocket, a three-inch crêpe sole for extra height and confidence, a suit of worsted wool, striped, and a tie—the starched white collar had a cutting edge—Egbo stormed Ibadan, where Simi still held court. The choice of a host was of course important and Egbo eventually recalled a student of his age. He seemed ideal, until at the door of his unsuspecting host Egbo hesitated, checked by the card on the door held in place by drawing-pins—E. AYO DEJIADE, secretary S.C.M. KNOCK PLEASE, AND ENTER WITH GOD.

He would have fled at once, but Dejiade opened the door as he stood outside. 'Why, Egbo! What are you doing here?' But Egbo did not even smile. 'What's all this?' rapping the card with his knuckles. 'Don't tell me you are carrying forward the family banner.'

'I wish you would do the same.' Dejiade, son of his dead father's colleague. The Rev Dejiade had fought to take care of his friend's son, at least to put him in care of the parish. But Egbo's aunt was having none of that. Neither you, she said, nor his old devil grandfather will have him. I will arrange his upbringing myself.

Dejiade's student room held the terrors of a sinful life in framed texts round the wall, and Egbo soon saw the futility of his hopes for Dejiade's moral support at the planned encounter. 'That would be immoral support,' said Dejiade. An appeal to his sense of comradeship failed also to budge him. 'I will show true comradeship if I stay in and pray for you.'

'You mustn't neglect your books,' Egbo said. 'Don't concern yourself with me.'

'I always pray before I start swotting,' Dejiade assured him. 'I have a tea-break about eleven. If my prayer is answered, you will see the light and be back in time for tea.'

And Egbo felt genuine terror, seeing Dejiade's prayer answered and he returning home frustrated. As he walked through the campus his fears increased. Dejiade's cause seemed suddenly sensible, just and kindly. Egbo was overwhelmed again by his friend's piety and he began to sweat in fear of the magic of texts. Desperately he pitted his prayers against Dejiade. 'Tonight good Lord, let me be lost to you. Forget my pitiful existence and bless my friend at his books. Make him a shining example Lord, but leave me for his example to shine upon.'

There was piety too, he reasoned, in self-sacrifice, and what was his prayer but this?

He found Simi at the third night-club he tried. Egbo did not immediately see her, but the cluster was unmistakable. The open courtyard was full of Simi, remote and unfluttered, unimpressed as ever. Those who boasted that Simi gave them her love, that she lived for them, could never get the world to accept it, for Simi was cast in the mould of distance, and it made her innocent. As if there never had been contact between her and the world, and these men with whom she slept experienced nothing but desperation, for they must see afterwards that they had never touched her. To recapture the act was, in the dare of Simi's cold liver gaze, a sacrilege. And so men could not tire of her whom they had never possessed, and the illusion maddened them, began a craving they could never end.

She *is* Queen Bee, thought Egbo. Men must dance and play the fool for her. And he stood, not willing yet to commit himself by sitting at a table, and ordering a drink. Egbo stood, bracing himself for the act of submission to the beast that lay in wait to swallow him. As once before he stood on Warri airfield, a scrubby, unkempt field in those early days of civil flight, waiting for the frail Dove to swallow him. Egbo and his aunt, Egbo pondering the foolhardiness of this seasoned flyer who

54

thought more of her cloth trade than the grave danger to which she thought fit to expose his life. Recalling again, mother and father miraculously dead. The Reverend Johnson and his wife the princess Egbo. On his first exercise book, the aunt had scrawled Egbo, and Egbo it was. When he grew older and understood, he found he could not miss a name like Johnson, and Egbo it remained. And to school you must go, said the aunt, to school you must go in Lagos like a civilised being. That pagan grandfather of yours will only teach you how to count wives and reckon the gains of smuggling. And up aloft, once above the smell and the dank of the water-side, fear vanished. He had fought every step of the gangway, kicking, biting, clinging to the rails, and even in the cabin he had tried to open a porthole and the other passengers had laughed. The engine throbbed and the vibrations quietened him a bit, and then his cries sprung out afresh. But the wings of the craft came levelling, suddenly in view, shifting planes, just as he used to do pretending he was flying. Egbo quietened. He looked down and saw the river and the thick sweeping mangroves, and he leapt up and down on the seat. But the sky rose now above him, a vast fan of peacock crest and Egbo turned to his new mother and said, 'Mamma, isn't this where God lives?' Fear vanished wholly, dropped like a dead bird in the vanished creeks below. Egbo was sound asleep the rest of the way.

Egbo had sat down; anxiously he felt in his pockets and was reassured by the thickness of his wad. A small boy came up, a small sharp face with generous cicatrix. He stood there a long time before Egbo realised that he waited on the table. 'Whisky. No, brandy, with lemonade. Er . . . a double shot please. And lemonade.'

The boy left, and Egbo rose. Now, now, even before he took the first sip of spirit, this was the time to move. Now, now, before she raised her eyes and recognising him, filled him with despair that could not be broken.

Astonishing how easy it was. He asked, and Simi rose instantly and came with him. She rose so casually, yielding nothing, meaning nothing, except that she rose and moved as if she had waited to be asked, and that many more would ask, and go. Egbo, apologising that his hands continued clammy, guided her through a graceful fox-trot, for he was a keen member of the dancing class for senior boys, and performed above the average. Thinking, this should suffice me, that I have held her, scared to experiment even by light pressures, thinking only that to ask more would be to ruin the evening. He had worked it out wrong and he was hasty. This should be a slow campaign, building up to the moment when he would not need to ask. Visit her perhaps in her home, when he had been admitted to her honoured circle.

Wondering how he knew it was the thing to say, 'What shall I send to your table? Whisky? Or do you prefer gin?'

'You are very young,' she said. 'Don't start wasting your money.'

Deflated, he returned her to her men, noticing then how the table was filled not with spirits in the glass, but in the bottle. And he had asked to send a pitiful short to her?

The rest of the night was blind, and Egbo kept a long vigil. The men came and left chastened, big business, law, and the doctors were the most confident of all, for at the time this was the prime profession, the sign of maximum intellect, the conquest of the best and the innermost mystique of the white man's talents. But Simi remained the thorn-bush at night, and the glow-worms flew fitfully around and burnt out at her feet.

Hangers-on too, the many she tolerated because they were protection. They ran her errands of tact, invented her whims, took commissions for 'a good word to your sister' and drank from the overflow of eternal hope. Sitting apart, consumed by jealousy and hatred, Egbo swallowed his brandy unthinking and held his breath while the brandy seared his gut and set his chest on fire. Calming down somewhat, he began to consider abandonment at this stage, looking in fact with genuine anticipation to the midnight tea with Dejiade. Dejiade, ah, there lay true comfort.

'Bring me my change quickly': and the boy ran off.

The brandy tinted his vision a dawn harmattan haze; Egbo found his will was towards consummation, even self-destruction in the process, remembering that after all, he was still a virgin, and why not Simi? Why not Simi to initiate him once and thoroughly into his part in the life mysteries. And he said to himself it was not that. It had gone much further, for the truth blighted then his hope of withdrawal and he started up like a madman, nerved by the outstanding simplicity. So this was why he pursued her—he had come to take her away from this, from all this. To make her his wife. Remembering the single-mindedness, past hermit existence, his lack of interest in other women, why, all of that for this one night? For this one night alone? No, he had not come to end it here. Simi must come away, come away and make a home with him.

Standing beside her again, and she must have said No a dozen times. Egbo could not hear. No, I do not want to dance, but Egbo heard nothing. I assure you I am tired, and anyway I do not like this step. Next time, enh? But how could she not want to dance now, when now he had something so important to say and the next moment she might be gone. For he knew about Simi, and her near mystical desertions. One moment, yes, Simi, unmistakable in the centre; the next moment Simi was gone, but with who? And for weeks after Simi would remain in seclusion.

And how could Simi be capable of agonising thwarting and say to him, Not this time, when the next time may be a wait longer than his preparation for this time! Flat of feet, suctioned to her ground, and he knew suddenly that he was trying to pull her from her chair, insistent, 'But I have something to tell you.'

'Can't you say it here?' She was very mild, not patient, simply not impatient.

Egbo, unable to move. . . . Is it not a miracle? Your face is so smooth, the even silt of tidewash but no crab has thought to walk on it, no wanton child has thought to scrawl on the daughter of the rivers when she bathes . . . *ayaba Osa* . . . *omo Yemoja* . . .

'Look young man, go back. You hear the lady does not want to dance.'

A stranger, a man he did not know, who meant nothing to him, stood up to answer for her. I will never be this green again . . . never . . . against all these men, wealthy and important, what did I think . . . ? But to be caught out this way, against all balance, and a hanger-on speaks for her, and a rough hand wet with whisky, on his wrist, removing it, pushing him back. . . .

Egbo heard his own voice across the music, 'Take your hands

off!' Saying, Thank God no one knows me here, but if I should roll him once in a drunk's vomit, just that . . .

'Remove yourself, my friend.' And he pulled again. 'Who do you think you are, shouting here!' And two more guardians rose to meet the threat.

Simi intervened. 'No, no, leave him. Why are you bothering the boy?'

Boy! That was it, really. Boy!

He made the seat somehow. It was shorter than the door, moreover, it would be a wrong time to leave. The wait was no torment for he saw nothing, heard nothing. He did not even see her leave.

Hours and hours later, or perhaps only a few minutes, and a small sharp face, cicatrized, approached him for the seventh time. 'Yes, yes, bring another. Whisky this time.'

'*O ti sah*. Madam *ni npe yin.*'

'Enh?'

'Madam. *Won ni npe yin wa.*'

Egbo looked round wildly, hardly daring to believe. Simi was no longer there. Angrily he gripped the boy by the ear, pinching him on the lobe. 'Are you trying to joke with me?'

The boy twisted in pain, protesting.

'Go on. Which madam? Where? Where?'

'*Nta. Won wa nnu* taxi.'

Egbo sobered with an effort, determined to destroy the hallucination. But the boy remained, and he meant it, that was obvious.

'Change yin sah.' But Egbo was past recalling. . . .

The door of the taxi was open, and Simi sat at the far end. Egbo stood, transfixed.

'Well, won't you get in?'

Egbo fell in, clumsy in every limb.

On this my celebration day, on this my celebration day . . . recalling warnings by the more experienced boys about the state of anxiety, and the possibility of disaster. . . . Limp? God, in this hour of our trial, mock me not with a raw cotton plug. . . .

'You should not try to clash with big men you know. You only get hurt.'

But Egbo could not even look at her. Seeking only a means of escape, longing to be anywhere but here, Dejiade's room

58

took on aspects of happiness of eternal safety. Sooner his spiritual tests than this prospect of humiliation. Could he really have been such a fool? To have come to her, to her with no knowledge but the boasts of other boys and one special lesson in Class IV which now seemed obscene by this, the supreme reality and confrontation.

As the taxi stopped his hand flew towards his pocket, but Simi stopped him, placing her hand on the bulge beneath his pocket and Egbo winced. 'Save it,' she said. In the house she locked the door and turned to him, 'Don't be too anxious. You are not very experienced. In fact, you are not experienced at all.'

. . . if I talk, I shall surely burst. If I speak, this rising boast will surely go down again. And are all women like this, that they know men on sight. That they can tell them inside out . . . ?

She had gone into an inner room, and Egbo looked round, unable to take in anything except the presence of Simi everywhere.

. . . in this hour of my . . .

Simi had entered again and he checked his rising delirium.

. . . God, God, if this is sinful . . . God, may I never lift head another year, but this night, this one night let me worship here, let me never see light again but in the revelation of her woven lights. . . .

'You are not undressed. No, leave it. I'll do it for you.' And at first he felt nothing, for his jaws were clamped in a vice. 'You are young,' she said, and she was kneeling then, so she raised her face to him standing above her. Egbo forgot himself then when he looked at her sensing such sadness that he feared for her and wondered if this was love. But the moment passed, for she had become playful, always in that grave aspect even when she teased, 'Your heart is pounding. You must not be anxious.' And she touched him about and Egbo felt himself lifted, there was no earth beneath his feet.

And he felt in danger now, so that to retrieve himself from a wound he feared he asked, 'Do you never love any man?'

'S-sh.'

A wind rushed through his clenched teeth pile-driving words he could not fathom, stakes to which he clung for self-preservation.

. . . I am that filled bag in a stiff breeze riding high grass on Warri airfield, when it lay fallow . . .

'My dear, what are you saying?'

. . . filled bag in a stiff breeze, high grass on the airfield, when it lay fallow . . .

'What is it, my dear?'

For exquisite though it was, it meant pain, and he who had been ready so long and was ready now found that the fight lay in retaining the moment in hanging by the finger-tips to a sharp-edged precipice while the blood coursed sweetly down his mouth. And his mind flew over his life wondering what this meant within what he ever was or would become.

. . . Good God, in darkness let me be . . .

'Oh my dear, what is it?'

For pleasure must be sinful and excess pleasure is damnation. And Dejiade, Dejiade, he would tell him tomorrow, Dejiade your life is simple, so simple and dead.

. . . through hidden floods a sheath canoe parts tall reeds, not dies, God, not dies a rotting hulk . . .

'But my dear . . .'

. . . And a lone pod strode the baobab on the tapering thigh, leaf-shorn, and high mists swirl him, haze-splitting storms, but the stalk stayed him . . .

'My dear, tell me, what is the matter?'

. . . when it lay flooded when it lay flooded. There were tassels for the man, sweet roots for the child, and above cloud curds waited for the chosen one of God . . .

. . . parting low mists in a dark canoe . . . in darkness let me lie, in darkness cry. . . .

5

It was the maddest morning to pick for riling the girl, but Sagoe had only encountered the wardrobe—he had never been in the bedroom before—and had been senseless through Dehinwa's trial with aunt and mother. Dehinwa finally took them to the bus-stop and was now tearing the room to pieces rushing to be dressed in time for office. The noise woke him and his bloodshot eyes 'made four' with the two handles of her wardrobe.

Finally he asked, 'Did you buy that yourself?'

'What?'

'The wardrobe. Did you buy it yourself?' He was shouting to top the rain which had begun again; the effort split his head but he would not give up.

'I am not kept if that is what you mean.'

'Certainly not by me.'

'You couldn't afford me.'

'That is nothing to brag about.'

'Listen, I have not had any sleep and now I have to go to work, just reserve any insults till I come back.'

'All the women in this goddamn country are so damn eager to be insulted.'

Squeezing into a sheath dress, she wiggled like a trapped fish and Sagoe could not laugh because the effort split his head. Dehinwa felt for the wardrobe handle and pushed out the door, blocking any further view by Sagoe. The wardrobe door swung nearer him and he cringed in distaste.

'You haven't answered my question. Did you pay for that hideous thing?'

'That's right. Just stretch yourself and continue needling me.'

Only then did Sagoe remember the women. The picture returned to him slowly up till the moment when he fell and the world darkened about him. He recovered that moment slowly, with sanity, wondering now into what trouble he had placed Dehinwa and feeling somewhat guilty. Very cautiously he said, 'I suppose those were your people?'

'No. They were blood-sucking witches from my home-town. What on earth did you find to scream about anyway?'

'I . . . don't know . . . they really scared me you know, especially the one with that outer-world superstructure.'

'That was my mother, and now shut up.'

'Oh, I only meant . . .'

'Never mind what you meant.' And she slapped on the powder puff instead of merely dabbing her face. The powder flew up and caught in her hair, settled thickly on the grey dress. 'Now you see what you've made me to do?'

'I didn't make you do anything but if it helps, I'm sorry.'

More gently now he asked, 'Was there much trouble?'

She didn't answer him at all. He leant outwards, trying to touch her, but she moved away. 'Well, tell me at least, did they make trouble?'

She went to the wardrobe and shut the door. It scraped him lightly on his outflung arm. She was astonished by the vehemence of his recoil and she remained there, puzzled now, 'What is wrong with you?'

'There is nothing wrong with me, it's just that goddamn wardrobe.'

'What has the wardrobe done for heaven's sake?'

'What has it done? Good God! You mean you cannot see it?'

'I have to go to work.'

'No, no, wait. Or I swear I'll take it outside and burn it before you come back.'

'Go ahead. It won't burn in this rain.'

'With all that oil dripping from it? But tell me the truth now. You are being forced to live with it aren't you? That was a gift from your aunt or grandma and you daren't throw it away.'

'I bought it.' She was exasperated beyond bearing. 'And if you don't like it keep your dislikes to yourself.'

'The woman is blind . . . but at least you can feel. You open the door, don't you? You must have touched it a hundred times, or are you never revolted by the skin of a lizard?'

'Thank you. I suppose we are back to the old song. You won't let us forget you have been to America and futuristic furnitures.'

'This is not even a question of style. How can you bear to touch the handle?'

'The handle? But that is the best part of it.'

'Then your senses must be frozen, like the disgusting thing. Why on earth would you want to buy a handle of petrified flowers! And look at the varnish, I tell you I'm going to be sick.'

'Yes, you drank a lot last night.'

For vengeance she slammed the door, hard, punishing his hangover. And up on the second floor he felt the revving of the motor engine deep inside his irritated lobes. Only now it wasn't too bad, the horror of the wardrobe had partially paralysed them.

Once, in Seattle, in the morning hours after a swinging binge, Sagoe watched a slow-motion pebble flicked by the motor-car (it was, then, automobile) in front of his. Instinctively he ducked, but the stone clean pierced the windscreen of his car and hit him on the left temple. His head fissured in an instant just as the windscreen would have done, and he waited, agonised, for the whole structure to crumble. But the skull remained intact, it separated and floated round and round his brain waiting to catch the grey pieces when they should disintegrate. It was the waiting Sagoe found inhuman. Like the man in the lower flat, waiting for the other shoe to fall. He fell asleep and woke up in a ditch.

Sagoe stiffened suddenly, waiting for a really bad moment to pass . . . the muddy mid-river spin, once the exclusive routine of a night of Bourbon . . . I end as I began, Sagoe murmured, on the rocks . . . As for this wardrobe, it was thought up by some inspired ghoul.

The obsessing furniture was heart-shaped. Cheap wood overlaid with varnish which looked perpetually running. And the top was clever. The heart completed its normal apex curve ceilingwards but when the doors were opened, they revealed a flat top which stored suitcases and hatboxes. There was a hatbox on it that morning, and he swung his concentration from his sweaty head onto the hatbox. It brought relief. Curiously the hatbox made him think of Sir Someone and his brows were knotted as he tried to remember him.

The effort made him dizzy and he fell back on the pillow, sweat strung as growing beads across his forehead. He wished Dehinwa had not left him alone; she was irritating but she had gentle hands. . . . Aha, Sir Derinola, that was his chairman's name. He turned his head sideways at the hatbox and winked at it. Sir Derinola, of course, that is who you are.

The room tightened further and in utter gloom, Sagoe found his gaze would drop to the repellent skin of the wardrobe.

Salaam, Sir Derinola, salaam. Oh, but you are a lizard, Sir Derin, and your skin is harmattan scabby though you turn on it eternal faucets of rancid oil.

It became obvious that this was the moment to contain the dead knight. Oh, he was dead at last, hat and wig, Sir Derinola was dead. The curtain was flung in and stayed above him like a full sail, buoyed by wet wind. Sagoe did not rise to close the window; the rain was cooling and he caught a few drops on his lips, licking them with some relish. The curtain flapped at the edge, began to tease the hat-box which just kept from falling. And Sagoe remembered news photographs of Sir Derinola in a top-hat, taken when he strolled through St. James's Park to receive his knighthood from the Queen.

'No,' said Sagoe, loudly, 'they couldn't take that away from you, Sir Derin. They'll bury you with the knighthood. But the top-hat now, let's see, the top-hat now, what do we do about the top-hat? Unless of course you use your retired wig.' And Sagoe chuckled to himself, recalling now how Sir Derin was nicknamed The Morgue.

The wind and the weight of Dehinwa's dressing-gown won in the end. The hat-box stayed in place but the wardrobe door pressed outwards, very very slowly, and the good knight himself came out, naked except for a pair of Dehinwa's brassieres over his chest. Sagoe felt suddenly prudish and he outbawled the rain.

'Sir Derin, what do you want? You look indecent!'

The Morgue was solemn. 'Oh you are wrong, You are so wrong, sir. I take it that you do mean that, don't you? In fact it is only a worm.'

'I protest, Sir Derin. Do all board chairmen behave like this? And to think you were even once a judge.'

'Don't remind me. These politicians, you can never trust them. Oh, how they betrayed me.'

'They did?'

'You young men know nothing. But never mind, never mind.

When it falls to you to lead the country . . . oh let's leave that. Any idea how I will be buried? You know my feelings, of course.'

Sagoe was obstinate. 'You'll have to go back. At least put on something. Cover yourself. Or get rid of that worm clinging to your groin.'

'What use would clothes be to me now, young man?'

Sagoe nodded. 'That is true, Sir Derin, you never had much use for clothes.'

'No, I did not and even now I cannot change my principles. The cloth does not make the man. Do you realise the newspapers still quote me on that?'

Sagoe stuck his fingers in his ears. 'Don't go on, Sir Derin. You forget I was there.'

The Morgue nodded, regretfully. 'Of course you were. I see so many of you, how can I remember whom I assault one day to the other? But I hope you bear no rancour. I did my duty according to my lights.'

Sagoe looked him over, humming.

'And anyway, haven't I paid? When the other party came to power they threw me out. Oh I know I resigned, but what else could I do? With all those young men superseding me!' And the Morgue began to laugh, a curious cavernous laugh that somehow was soothing to Sagoe's raw drink lobes. 'But you see, you cannot keep a good man down. I got my knighthood. That is why I keep the brassiere on.'

Sagoe confessed he did not see the connection.

'For the medals young man. The medals. They pin something on you when they give you a knighthood you know. And I do keep the knighthood.'

'Sir Derin, I must rebuke you there. How is the medal separate from the clothes?'

'Come come, young man, don't try to trip me with those legal points. I know my law. My fellow judges acknowledged that. If only those politicians had not led me astray . . .'

'You misunderstand me, good knight. I meant, your philosophy, for instance; did the wig make you a judge?' The Morgue started and the sand grains danced finely in his blind sockets, the eyes of justice.

Sagoe pursued him, gently remorseless, 'So what will a medal make you?'

The Morgue stood silent for a long time, fiddling with brassiere cups below his chin. At that moment he truly fitted the name, earned from his air of mournfulness when, a terror of the Bench, he hooked his glasses down his nose and peered above the prisoner. His voice came mournful as the grave. 'But they have taken everything else, everything . . .'

'You made your choice,' said Sagoe.

And the Morgue was suddenly alert, his pores tingling to a hostile presence. 'Oh-oh, we are observed,' and he dived into the wardrobe.

And then Sagoe watched Dehinwa push open the door.

'To whom were you talking?'

'I was praying.'

'You sounded as if you were talking to someone,' she said.

'Maybe to myself.'

'You are sick.'

'I know it. That wardrobe makes me sick.'

She had begun rummaging in a cupboard, dripping water everywhere. He followed her with his eyes, wondering what was eating her. Suddenly she pulled the bed towards her and bent over him. Scared, truly scared, Sagoe yelled out, 'Don't touch me!'

She bent right over him and peered into space between the bed and wall. Sagoe pulled himself into a knot. 'God, do you have to be so sudden?'

But she only pushed the bed back and its impact with the wall sent him shuddering into the bedclothes.

'Murderer! Murderer!'

And now she stood over him, just looking. 'Hadn't you better see a doctor?'

'There is nothing the matter with me. Just go.'

'Why were you shouting? Did you think I was going to attack you?'

'Did I think? What else have you done but assault me all morning? Just look at my hands, enh, look at them.' And he held them up.

'So they are trembling. What else did you expect from last night's excess?'

'That has nothing to do with it. You slam the bed against the wall, you wait until my head is in the doorway and then you shut the damned door, you walk all over my drink lobes

66

with your wooden clogs . . . why don't you just get a hatchet and sink it in my skull, you damned Jael!'

He sounded hurt and Dehinwa thought, men, they are just like children. They really cannot bear much pain. She sat beside the bed and took his head in her lap, suddenly tender. Sagoe at first submissive, grew ashamed of his weakness. 'Go on,' and he snatched his head away. 'Why the hell did you come back anyway? If you must embrace me at least dry yourself.'

Her reaction amazed him because almost immediately tears came to her eyes. To hide them she began searching the room again, with a ferocity she did not formerly display.

'Is it possible that I might have seen what you were looking for?'

'A file. I brought it home yesterday.'

'An office file?'

'No. A nail file.'

'No need to be so damned sarcastic. Just tell me if its marked confidential.'

'You've seen it?'

'No. I'm clairvoyant.'

'Please, Biodun . . .'

'Under the front seat of the car.'

'But . . .'

'I put it there myself. Looked inside it when I was waiting for you outside the shops. You nearly caught me at it so I shoved it under the seat.'

She looked at him, as if lost in how to kill him. 'I didn't find much in it,' he mocked, 'not enough to make a good scandal story.'

And Sagoe stiffened from head to toe but it didn't save him. She opened the door as far as it would go, gloating. She made him wait and wait and wait. Then, using all her strength, she slammed it hard, juggling his head between the couplings of a shunting train. A woman like that . . . you have to beat them to death . . . and Sagoe, forgetting his weakness leapt up after her, only to crumple at the first step, against the wardrobe. He clutched at it to save himself and his hands came against the petrified slat eyes of his aversion. It sped him back, astonished at such physical betrayal of a body he knew so well. Usually it was only the head that played havoc. In the condition in which he hoped he was, he had climbed once to a third floor window as a student, transversing window ledges until brought down, misunderstood, by the dark revolver muzzle of a New York policeman. 'I am trying to get to my bedroom,' he said, and the man smiled in turn, 'Sure sure, just you come down quiet, nigger.'

Sir Derin emerged once more that morning, after a brief sleep that left Sagoe even worse. Sagoe saw him emerge backwards, and the undulations of the good knight's rear were so comical that he shrieked with laughter and paid instant penalty in his head with the old crackling windscreen sensation.

'Was that your young lady?' asked the Morgue.

Sagoe wanted no more conversation, so he pretended he was asleep.

The knight sounded self-pitying. 'You do not wish to talk to me? You realise you are the only friend I have.'

'I, your friend?'

'Yes. Oh, never mind the past. In fact, by all means, mind the past. You *were* my friend. You tell me the truth at least, and that has lately begun to matter, you see. There was not much time for truth in those days, was there?'

'No, I'm afraid there wasn't.'

'Now I have nothing left except the truth. That is all I get now, watching the rest of you day and night. That is why . . . wait, I will just take this off.' He took off the brassiere. 'Now are you satisfied?'

'What has it to do with me? It was *your* philosophy remember? I happen to like clothes.'

'You were right. Now I am satisfied. Don't let them bury me except as I am now. Not even a shroud.'

'I see what you mean, the shroud does not make the corpse.'

Sir Derin nodded wisely, winking his sockets all the way into the cupboard.

So difficult to think of Sir Derinola as dead. When he first stood before him, applicant before a Board of Interview, the knight had riled him neatly, like a gentleman. Incredible not only that he should have obtained the job but that he should have stuck it up till now. It was not Sir Derinola merely but the whole of *Independent Viewpoint* which stood against his willing presence on those premises. Except of course Mathias, the messenger. Now Mathias was a good augury if ever there was one. And after he took the job, Mathias continued to perform the miracle of pinning him at his desk; he was like a retriever, deftly plonking Sagoe down at the feet of proportion. Or, in strict accuracy, Sagoe took Mathias, imprisoned him and said, Now you rogue, put me down again at the feet of proportion.

To celebrate, for it was Mathias who made him wait for the interview at all, Sagoe sent him out for beer on his first day in office.

'Lock the door, Mathias.' He took the bottles from him and filled his mug. 'Take the other bottle.'

Mathias, embarrassed said, 'Thank you, sir,' and turned to go. 'Where do you think you are going? Sit over there, I'm afraid you will have to drink yours from the bottle, I've only one mug.'

'Oga, make a go drink my own for canteen.'

'What for? I wanted you to drink with me. Or will my presence ruin your drink? I know you are rather sensitive.'

Mathias protested his love for Sagoe's company.

'In that case, don't sit on the edge of the chair. Relax, man, what is the matter with you? I want to talk with you.'

'Oga, sometimes den go want me for other office. Messenger job for newspaper office no get siddon time.'

'As a new man here someone has to show me the ropes. Right?' Mathias nodded. 'Well, I intend to monopolise you this morning for that purpose. Drink, Mathias.'

'Yes sah.' And Mathias dutifully obeyed.

'And please stop answering me Yessah.'

'Yessah. Oh, I sorry, oga.'

'That's all right, but don't forget.'

'Yessah.'

Sagoe winced and Mathias burst out in unselfconscious laughter. 'Ah, you go get patience, o oga, dis one go take time.'

Sagoe took out his bag and from it he drew a bound volume. 'Now Mathias, you are the first good thing that happened to me since I came back. But for you, I would never have taken this job, and if I stay long on it, it will be due entirely to you.'

'How come, oga?'

'That is what I propose to explain to you. You see, you and I are kindred spirits.'

'Spirit? Oga a no sabbe dat one o.'

'Mathias, I can't ask you to call me Biodun, because I believe in some measure of business decorum. But this Oga business is just as bad as Yessah.'

Mathias became a trifle impatient. 'But oga, how we go manage dat one now? Wetin a go call you.'

'Mr Sagoe will do.'

'All right sah.'

'As I was saying, Mathias—oh yes, you wanted to know what kindred spirit is. Well, it means simply that we are, well, let's see, oh yes, it means we see eye to eye.'

'Aha a, I sabbe am.'

'You remember what happened when I came for my interview?'

'Wetin oga?' Sagoe did not immediately answer, and Mathias's eyes suddenly opened wide. 'Abi you mean that business for latrine?'

'Exactly.' Sagoe opened the volume before him. 'And to explain what I mean, I propose to read you part of a very important speech I once made in my philosophising days. I shall read a bit of it to you everyday while I am here, and if you have any questions, you may ask. In fact if we make converts, we will hold discussion groups.'

'Yessah.'

'It was to have been part of my thesis, but unfortunately, my professors did not accept the subject. Found it too esoteric, I suppose. I need to have a friend, Mathias, because, you see, coming here, I have a feeling that I am taking my life in my hands. However, if we read this tract everyday, you know what I mean, make it our bible, it should give us strength and consolation. You are like me, a religious man, I trust?'

Mathias nodded, gravely, and Sagoe waved at his bottle. 'Drink Mathias, it helps. Puts you in a receptive mood.' Mathias dutifully drank, sliding one eye towards the door and wondering. Sagoe's voice recalled him.

'You see Mathias, you are an instinctive Voidante . . .'

'Sah?'

'Voidante . . . eh, never mind. You will understand it all after a few sessions. Don't be in a hurry. You are a natural. It is only a question of grasping the fundamentals of the system. But spiritually, my friend, you are already there . . .'

'Oga, wait small. I done begin confuse.'

70

'There is nothing difficult about it Mathias. You listen and you will understand the philosophy of shit.'

Mathias grinned broadly and Sagoe cleared his throat.

'. . . Of -isms I dirge this day, from homoeopathic Marxism to existentialism. If I am personal, it is because in giving the history of myself, I do neither more nor less than uncover the mystery of my philosophical development, for this is one Ritualism for which I am indebted to no predecessor but the entire world of humanity, this is one vision for which I acknowledge no Cause but the immutable laws of Nature. If I am personal, it is because this must rank as the most inward philosophy in human existence. Functional, spiritual, creative or ritualistic, Voidancy remains the one true philosophy of the true Egoist. For definition, ladies and gentlemen, let this suffice. Voidancy is not a movement of protest, but it protests: it is non-revolutionary, but it revolts. Voidancy—shall we say—is the unknown quantity. Voidancy is the last uncharted mine of creative energies, in its paradox lies the kernel of creative liturgy—in release is birth. I am no Messiah, and yet I cannot help but feel that I was born to fulfil this role, for in the congenital nature of my ailment lay the first imitations of my martyrdom and inevitable apotheosis. I was born, with an emotional stomach. If I was angry, my stomach revolted; if I was hungry it rioted; if I was rebuked, it reacted; and when I was frustrated, it was routed. It ran with anxiety, clammed up with tension, it was suspicious in examinations, and unpredictable in love. My good friends, a prophet has honour . . . I was often suspected of malingering and punishment was swift; and most empathic of the indications of an emotional stomach is the concomitant to a strong sense of injustice. Another influence on the shaping of my Voidant introversion was the aunt of my childhood sweetheart, a sometime visitor to our home. She farted like a beast. And even more illuminating was my own mother with the same affliction. She was a most religious farter. It was her boast, even as she neared the grave that God's voice was a wind which never failed to speak to her any day after evening prayers. And she called the household to witness, and they said—Amen. My conception of the abode of prayer must therefore begin from those days when the cause of my retreat into the lavatory was not so much a physiological necessity as a psychological and religious urge. From this

71

period of my life, I would like to say, began my sense of dedication to the systematic study and objectivisation of digestive behaviourism in a sensitive child. I responded to the well-known posture of a quick finish-and-be-gone. And yet, at other times I experienced a self-communion, a resolution, acceptance, peace attainment, I evolved a spiritual rapprochement with a world of stresses and discord . . .'

Sagoe stopped, looking at Mathias's dropped jaw and clapped shut the pages. 'That is all for today, Mathias. There ended our first lesson.'

Mathias, strangling out a 'Yessah. Tank very much sah', left Sagoe to his thesis, holding his beer bottle with affected ease, masking his eagerness to be gone.

. . . Sagoe, awaiting the arrival of the full complement of the Board of Interview, made his first tour of the premises. The area had been chosen, according to Mathias, for reasons of pure political strategy. Every loud city has its slums, and Isale-Eko symbolised the victory of the modern African capital over European nations in this one aspect of civilisation. A few foreigners seeking off-beat local colour found it always in Isale-Eko; daring its dark maze they admitted that their experience was unique, there was hop-scotch to be played among garbage heaps, and the faint-hearted found their retreat cut off by the slop from housewives' basins. *Independent Viewpoint* owned a large building in the slum; the paper itself was a party organ, its location meant easy patronage of local thugs, and Isale-Eko was rich spawning ground.

Mathias explained, 'Na local brickler come make alteration for inside. De wall done rotten to ground, so den bring them fat woman come lean for the wall. Na private house before before, so dey knack down de wall turn am to office. Na dem own wife dey take body knack de wall for ground.' And he roared away for a full minute.

Sagoe looked through the rear window. The wall dropped sheer onto a canal which led water into the lagoon. This water was stagnant, clogged, and huge turds floated in decomposing rings, bobbing against the wall. He turned to Mathias, 'How do you work in this stench?'

'Ah, na so everybody dey say first time. But make you look me now, I just dey grow fat for the smell.'

Sagoe asked to be shown the canteen. He paid for a coffee

but could not drink it. The two halves of the cup were held together by accumulated filth in a deep crack. And it was difficult to tell what gave the special quality to the smell in the canteen, there was the greasy water in which yesterday's lunch-plates were soaked, or it could be the sweaty girl who served the staff in a stupor, a mere eighteen at the most, and her movements suggested a knee-deep wadding of sanitary towels. And she remained clogged all twenty-eight days of her cycle. Eyelids gelled to—it would appear—her navel, her only extraneous movement was to wipe her forehead with an arm that revealed an armpit in alternate streaks of black and white, powder and grime. Her whitened face further confirmed a daily toilet of powder, never water.

On an impulse Sagoe asked, 'Did you ever answer the telephone?'

'Enh?'

'I asked, are you sometimes the telephone operator?'

'Me myself?'

'Yes, do you sometimes work on the . . . oh never mind.' And Sagoe gave up in despair. For how would he explain to her that the sluggish bilge-water which twice, when he called the paper, lapped the receiver at the other end seemed to evoke the same squelch as her piano-key armpits.

He ran into Mathias at the door. 'Oga, make you no go far o.'

'I'm leaving, Mathias. Can't wait any longer for your board members.'

'Ah oga, no do dat kind ting. Den go come now now. Matter of fac' Chief Winsala done enter. After him na only one remain.'

They both jumped as the hum of machines was harshly supplemented by a sudden H-r-r-r, and a strangulated sound froze Sagoe to the spot. The sound had come from the direction of the receptionist's corner, but there was no longer any receptionist or desk. Instead Sagoe only saw an indoor tent made of ankara cloth and with a design of 'Nigerian Independence 1960.' Astonished, he looked at Mathias to detect the trick, but Mathias was busy chuckling to himself. The sound came again, a ripping sound, and this time Sagoe saw the blade of an office knife hack a straight line down a taut portion of the cloth, a female head pushed through the phony tent, gasping a weak 'Help, he's choking me.' Mathias stood with the

73

tray bearing two coffees in his hand, exclaiming, 'O-ko-ko-ko-o'. And like a masquerade gone to ground, the tent was thrown suddenly back, and an *ikori* cap, the long pouch askew over a high brow, swung nearly seven feet above the ground.

'Where is the bitch?' Chief Winsala demanded, flapping his *agbada* all over the table, 'She was here just now, I had her.' And he felt about in his garments but just failed to seize the entombed receptionist.

Like a demented soul the girl began to fight the folds all over again, her one concern to keep her head in air. There was another Hr-r-r-r-, more ragged and more prolonged as her hands found the original tear and a sleeve of Winsala's Independence Day *agbada* went separate altogether.

'There she is, the slippery bitch. Now come here, my girl.' But there was no holding the receptionist now. As volumes of cloth moved to engulf her again, she ducked under the table, passed clean between his legs, and was seen no more at work that day.

'Who is the giant?'

'Na Chief Winsala wey a mention now now. He and in bottle, den dey like David and Goliat.'

His was a state of deep alcoholic amorousness, but for a man in such an exalted state of tipsiness, Chief Winsala had remarkable balance. He rocked backwards as far down as any *igunuko* could boast at public display, and his weight made the performance all the more impressive. Mathias had moved up to him. 'Chief Chief, at fust a no know say na you.' He was cut short by a heavy blow on the back and the coffee went spilling all over the tray.

'What is the matter with that woman today, enh?' said the Chief when he eventually recovered from his mirth at Mathias's surprise.

'Chief, dat na new receptionist. E no sabbe you yet.'

'New receptionist? No wonder.' And he went into another rocking-chair spasm. Mathias joined, recognising an opportunity.

'Oga, dis coffee done pour finish. How a go tell proof-reader now?'

He knew his man. Chief Winsala dug his hands through deep recesses and brought out a handful of coins. 'You are a bloody rogue Mathias. Go and buy coffee for every man here

—and every woman. Buy the women two coffees in fact, plus sausage rolls. Come on, get away.'

It came to his turn half an hour later and Sagoe thought—how right that Dehinwa sometimes is, we only despise the small criminal. The room into which he was ushered could be a banqueting room. A plush carpet swallowed all shoes below a three-inch soling, contradicting the building itself which had been hurriedly buttressed to pass a second examination by a bribed slums inspector. The boardroom, a different world, contradicted all evidence of other offices. To it belonged the only air-conditioner in the building, and the walls were wood-panelled; hidden behind the panelling was powdering mortar, and there were small curtains to match the wall which screened the cooling machines when they were not in use.

Each seat was a swivelling tilt-back armchair, the table was the best mahogany; a pin scratch on it would have shown up like a bleach mark. A gold-edged pad lay at each place, at scrupulous angles to the table edge. In one corner, an apoplectic radiogram, but no records, only the radio was ever used, and that just for the news. The radio had nine winking lights, all differently coloured, although no one had yet discovered what they proved. This was the pride of the Managing Director. On his visit to Germany on his eleventh round-the-world mission, the grandeur of the thing hit him on the apple and he could only mutter, 'It has class, it has class.' The sales fraulein complimented him on his taste and he paid on the spot with travellers' cheques. 'By the way,' he said, 'do come to my hotel and show me how it works.'

'Aren't we to ship it home for you sir?' 'Of course of course,' said the Director. 'I meant come with the leaflets, and explain it all to me; I don't read German, you see.'

'It is there in English also,' said the girl, 'and in French and Spanish and Arabic.' Dragging his long trail of traditional splendour after him the Director turned to his private secretary and said, 'Aren't these German girls stupid!'

Sagoe paused, seeing the interior through a half-opened door. He returned to the corridor where five other candidates waited, and sent one in his place. Then he went to seek Mathias in the proof-reader's hole.

'Where is the toilet?'

'A-ah, oga, Dey no call you yet?'

'Not yet. Just show me the lavatory.'

And he wondered if he really had to go through with it, recalling a desk of illiterate, unctuous, agravating toads. Who hunted you down from last season's stagnant pools, and constituted you into this obstructive lump and an endowment of the outward sign of matterdom. Matterdom, that was it, and he savoured the word as Mathias led him hastily towards the toilet saying, 'If na only piss you wan' piss, lagoon dey for backyard. Na in we dey take use for common piss.'

'No Mathias, I want a proper sit-down-strike.'

'Siddon wetin? I no sabbe . . . o-oh . . .' and he hunched over to his knees with laughter. 'Oga you too funny. To God I no hear dat one before.'

Mathias was in front, but Sagoe's nose arrived long before them both and the sight of soggy scraps of newspaper stuck in urine only confirmed its probing. Only the toilet of the radio station had, since his return, been so effectively inhibiting. This cistern was caked and unflushed, and its walls matched the radio station's in suspicious smears. The rout was completed and his bowels closed at once. Sagoe turned back.

Mathias, bewildered, 'I think oga say e wan' shit?'

'No no, the ting done disappear.'

'Enh? You mean e go on strike?' And the wit rendered him so helpless that Sagoe feared for his health with such huge intakes of air. 'Let's go', dragging him forcibly. 'Let's go and laugh somewhere else.'

'I dey go oga. But make you siddon small. Sometime 'e fit come back.'

'Siddon where?'

'Siddon where? A-ah, youself oga, wissai person dey siddon for latrine?

'Never mind,' feeling he might lose a friend if he confessed the truth. 'Sometimes my belly dey do dat kin' ting. E no get sense.'

Mathias was not deceived, the outrage at least in Sagoe's voice had betrayed the truth. 'Ah-ha, you no like de place. I sorry oga, na so we dey manage am.'

'You mean you haven't any other lavatory?'

'Unless woman own. Dat one dey for upstair.'

'All right, we'll try it.'

Laughing in the hopeless manner of a man who now considered his companion, finally, an irrepressible wag, Mathias led the way back. 'Matter of fac' he said, 'another one dey, but dat one na for board member and senior service like that. Editor-in-chief get key for dat one. De cleaner dey use am, na foolish man. I done warn am so tey 'e no dey hear. Sometime editor go catch am.'

'So just the three lavatories enh?'

It was indeed. One masculine, one feminine and one for the Neuter Board.

And this helped. In Sagoe's system, a Board which, with true Voidante piety locked a lavatory away for private self-communion could not be wholly soulless. With a new measure of respect for his assessors, Sagoe once again approached the board-room, filled, as with all boards, with Compensation Members.

Lost elections, missed nominations, thug recruitment, financial backing, Ministerial in-lawfulness, Ministerial poncing, general arse-licking, Ministerial concubinage . . . Sagoe occupied the first few minutes fitting each face to each compensation aspect, and found that one face stood out among them. One face did not bear the general vacuity and contempt for merit of the knights of the oval table. It surfaced quietly at the far end of the table and a pair of yellow eyes surveyed him above the silver rims of old-fashioned spectacles. In his own person however, there was something odd. This was his cap. It was a simple *abetiaja,* but worn so that the ears were front and back, not bent above each ear as in normal use. This sage-like oddity possessed a narrow head, tapering backwards like the carved head of an *ibeji,* a true phrenologist collector's piece. Sagoe stared, but he was new in the country and had not heard of the famous cranium of The Morgue, and the ever-growing catalogue of myths which surrounded it. Never without some covering, some said it ended in hole, and others claimed it ended in a triple point and was its own lightning conductor. Others more curious than the rest tried to find his barber and question him. The miracle was that Sir Derin was not an idiot, for this was the average cretin bonce.

'Please sit down.'

Sagoe continued to wonder why Sir Derin chose to wear his

abetiaja front to back and the first question took him by surprise, 'Why do you want this job?'

It came from the man beside Chief Winsala whose mighty paw now cradled a glass of whisky. Sagoe saw the open cabinet, but Chief Winsala was the only one who availed himself of this comfort of the board. He caught the Chief's eyes, and the old rogue winked. Somehow Sagoe knew that Winsala would vote for whichever hand placed the glass of whisky by his side.

Sagoe shivered, wondering if these people knew that an air-conditioner could be adjusted. He turned to face his questioner.

Like two halves of a broad bean, the pachydermous radiogram and the Managing Director. And his attempt to disown his twin brother proved futile, in spite of the delicate china set from which they all, except Chief Winsala, sipped tea. The Director had picked up the set in the tenth economic mission to American China; he donated it to the Board remarking, 'You know, Shanghai Chek has exactly this kind of cup and saucer.'

'Well?' and the Managing Director looked round, obtaining confirmation that the wait was long enough. 'Answer the question. Why do you want this job?'

'I don't know,' Sagoe said.

The reaction was a simple unison of utter disbelief. In their several years of professional boardmanship, not one of them had encountered the like of Sagoe's ignorance.

'Did you say you don't know?' And Sagoe nodded.

It looked as if the interview was over even before it started. This had upset the normal pattern of fly-baiting; procedure had been turned a mockery and resentment mounted round the room. Only Chief Winsala seemed unimpressed.

'Well well,' he said. 'That is what a man can call an honest answer.'

Sir Derin turned such a stern rebuke on his levity that Winsala fled hastily to the friendship of the cabinet. The Managing Director spoke at large, 'Well, if the candidate does not even know why he comes for interview, I think we also cannot know why he is here?'

And now Sir Derin spoke. 'Young man, I hope you do not think you are here to waste our time.'

'No sir.'

'Just let him go, Chairman. How can an interview be conductable with someone who is not taking the matter serious?'

'Wait. Now, young man, you are I presume, an educated person?'

'I hope so sir.'

'I am sure you are even an intelligent man?'

Sagoe was silent. 'No need to be modest, I am sure you consider yourself an intelligent man.'

'That depends in whose company I am sir.'

There was a break in Sir Derin's sureness, but he decided that he would let it pass. 'Now, tell me honestly, as an intelligent man, if you were sitting here and I was sitting where you are now, what would you think if, on being asked why I want a job I say I do not know.'

'I would think, possibly, that you were beginning to feel you had made a mistake.'

The carcass of the Managing Director swelled, spurted greasy globules of the skin in extreme stages of putrefaction and burst in an unintelligible stream through the ruptured throat. 'Do you think we have come here to tolerate your cocky impudence? You small boy, you come here begging for job . . .'

'I have not come to beg.'

'Don't talk when I am talking otherwise just get out. We want the kind of person who is going to respect his superior not conceited boys of your type. Suppose you are not begging who is interested in that? Your betters are begging my friend go and sit down.'

'If you'll excuse me,' and Sagoe rose to go.

'Please go from sight.' And he gave a long hiss. 'These small fries they all think they are popularly in demand, just because they have a degree . . .'

And Sir Derin interrupted him, gravely. 'A degree does not make a graduate.'

It had the pacifying effect of an Oracle. The Director went quiet and the room was hushed and attentive. 'That is the mistake all these boys make. A degree does not make a graduate.'

Chief Winsala grew quite creative in the new atmosphere, feeling at home in the re-establishment of the wisdom of eldero. And he seemed anxious to please, there seemed to be a relationship between the two, like sage and protege. 'The Chairman has said it,' he contributed, 'just as a tree does not

79

make a forest.' The Managing Director nodded in approval but the Chairman cut him short with an indulgent smile and a firm shake of the conical head. 'Not quite the same thing, Chief Winsala. I mean simply that appearances are deceptive. When he came in I felt quite sure that this was the man we wanted.'

'A-ah, you are no judge of character, Mr Chairman.'

And Sir Derin winced as from a treacherous thrust, but the Director was obtusely lost in his moment of world-wisdom and could not see the passage of painful memories across Sir Derin's face. He, not a judge of character? What had he acquired from years at the bench if not this one ability, this wizardry to tell a man apart from his clothes, from his assumed humility or contrition? What was he if not the Oracle Divine who pierced the hearts of men and bared their hidden dreads and passions. For he was unimpeachable. For he was the last word but God. And even that . . . sometimes . . . yes, sometimes, above the common humanity that trembled before him, that in their depths of hopelessness sometimes flared momentarily and aimed slight assaults upon his dignity, when he had struck them down, struck them hard with the look that had no passion, ground them down or broken them in his lofty objectivity, yes, at such times he wondered if God was any more than this. Like this morning's prime cock who went off bristling from his Presence, from Him, the Morgue, from Him! Were these the bygone days . . . and Sir Derin pulled the flap of the *abetiaja* down behind him and found comfort as it tickled him behind the neck, the lawyers knew that gesture . . . when the Morgue pulled down his wig behind him and he moved his neck against its tail in a slow caress, it was the sign of squall. for Sir Derin was confused. This was when he lashed out in anger, raining insults on the brilliance that had overshadowed him.

Sagoe, emerging from the corridor, felt again the promptings of his bowels, attesting once again their Voidante prophecies.

Calling out his name, a man pursued him, but Sagoe only quickened pace. Mathias, ubiquitous Mathias came out from a door just three yards ahead of him, forcing him to stop. 'Ogo, was matter? Na fight?'

His pursuer caught up panting. 'Mr Sagoe. Good God, Mr

Sagoe, are you an athlete? Anyone would think you were running from the devil.' He paused to recover his breath, offered his hand. 'My name is Nwabuzor, I am the Editor-in-chief.' Silently, Sagoe shook hands. 'I am sorry about what happened in there.'

'Oh?' And now he tried to place the face. Nwabuzor forestalled him. 'That's all right, I wasn't in there, but I was listening just the same. I have to, you see. Will you come into my office?'

Sagoe tried to quell the pressure of his bowels but could not immediately succeed. Nwabuzor misunderstood, seeing only his obvious fidgeting. 'Or if you like, we can talk later. In fact I ought to go back right away, hear what they are saying and know whom I can tackle afterwards. You understand don't you? So please leave your address, and phone number if you have any.'

Mathias volunteered, 'I go take am down oga.'

Sagoe said, 'I stay in a hotel—I've only got back from abroad. Hotel Excelsior.'

'Good, good. You mustn't mind what happened there. They get rid of the best people, that board, that is what I'm saddled with. I am supposed to be the editor-in-chief but I am not allowed at the interview. I have to eavesdrop outside the door and try to form my own conclusions. Then the real lobbying starts. That is how I keep going.'

Sagoe murmured 'I see.'

He gave him his hand again. 'I won't keep you then. I shall telephone you tomorrow at the latest and maybe we can meet.'

Sagoe only half-heard, the internal situation had become do or burst. 'To tell you the truth,' he confessed, 'I was rushing to find the nearest hotel. I need to use the toilet very badly.'

'I am sorry . . . oh dear and I've kept talking all the time. But why go all the way to a hotel? Mathias . . .'

'Yessah.'

Sagoe cut in quickly. 'No thank you. I've seen the one up here.'

Nwabuzor grimaced. 'I wasn't going to add insult to injury. Mathias will show you the one we keep under lock and key.'

'Thank you.'

'And I promise to phone tomorrow evening at the latest.

Mathias, you know where the key is kept in my office. Show him to the toilet *you* use.'

'Sah?'

'The one you use, I've caught you several times. Take the key and show this gentleman the place. I must run back to the big shots.'

Mathias's discomfiture was truly pathetic. He heaved the sigh of a man much misunderstood and, led, a slouched figure of resignation to the neuter lavatory. So downcast was he from his exposure that he walked right up to the room, forgetting even the subterfuge and call as instructed at the editor's office. From his pocket he drew a long chain and inserted the key, and only then did he remember, a sheepish grin breaking over his face.

'A-ah, God catch me plenty today. But, make a tell true, no to say a dey go shit for there, a no fit self. Same ting cleaner dey tell me. When 'e siddon, in belly go tight, nuthin' fit commot. How man go fit shit for room wey den make like room an' parlour?' He flung the door and gestured inside with a flourish, 'Abi you no see?'

Sagoe nodded, and Mathias pressed the point. 'You see we trouble? How man go fit shit inside room wey get carpet, not to talk of polish wood? As for me o, a no fit.'

'Why do you keep a duplicate key then?'

'Na here a dey come read newspaper. Na dis be de only place wey man fit get peace for de whole office. And de smell na in better pass anywhere for Isale-Eko. Even boardroom no smell fine pass am.'

'Thank you, Mathias.'

But Mathias held the door open a little longer. 'Na you we oga go gi' dat job you go see. A sabbe when 'e like somebody. An' e like you too much.'

'Thank you, Mathias.'

And Sagoe shut the door at last and slammed home the ENGAGED bolt. Immediately, a light wraith of scented breeze fanned him about the neck and filled the luxurious furnishing of the ante-room. It was an automatic purifier device imported by the Managing Director on his seventh Economic Mission to Sweden . . . and Sagoe, sprinting on thick carpets to the pink bakelite seat of the inset alcove sighed with regret, thinking, this man and Mathias are wasted geniuses.

But, later, the inevitable aftermath.

Chief Winsala at his most hearty called at the Hotel Excelsior. He was installed in a deep armchair when Sagoe came, and at first, Sagoe pretended a total lack of recognition, but Winsala merely found this funny.

'Ha ha, so you are Sagoe. Sit down, come and sit down. What is the matter, don't you know me again?'

'I'm afraid not. I have only just returned to the country, that's why.'

'Ha ha ha, I can tell that. Your whole manner and behaviour indicate somebody who is young, reckless and johnny-just-come ha ha ha.'

'I don't understand.'

'You will, you will. Let me refresh your memory. You were our interviewee the day before yesterday morning.'

'Your what did you say?'

'Our interviewee. I am a member of the Board to which you came to answer our advertisement.' He lifted his glass, empty. 'By the way, I take schnapps.'

Sagoe apologised and called the waiter.

'In the mornings I drink whisky, in the evening schnapps. In the afternoon I don't drink at all, I sleep, ha ha ha ha ha.'

Sagoe waited patiently.

'Now let me see, now that we have made our acquaintance, I must tell you. You are a bad boy the other morning. A very bad boy. But that is the same with all you boys when you are just returning. England, or is it America in your case? Anyway it gives you high opinion of yourself.' He looked round the hotel and clicked his tongue. 'Hm, your father must be a rich man for you to be staying in such hotel.'

'He is in fact a millionaire.'

'Well well, is that so? I did not know we have millionaires in Nigeria.'

'He doesn't advertise.'

'Very wise. Very wise of him. And for you to be wanting to work too, that is very wise of you. Young man should be independent of his father, pursue his own course of life.'

Until the schnapps arrived, Sagoe listened to trite irrelevances. Where they were headed had become obvious, and Sagoe waited on him, docile, until after the schnapps when Winsala's manner turned brisk. 'Mr Sagoe, I am a straightforward man. I like to see pushful young men succeeding. Unfortunately things are always more difficult than one can wish. You yourself have seen the numerous number of clients who come to interview that job I think.'

'Were they many?'

'Oh yes. And yesterday even more. It's true, with independence all the *oyinbo* have been kicked out, but that is long time ago. Before, degree is something, but now everyone is having degree. Degree is two for penny, so everybody is rushing to fill all vacancy. No more degree passport.' He was long practised in the art and Sagoe did not see him signal the waiter, who arrived a short while later with another schnapps.

'Anyway, the thing is this. You yourself know that you are not experienced for this job. The editor told us at the meeting that you are really trained as . . . er . . . something like building or something like that . . . oh yes, surveyor.'

And he allowed himself a long pause; it was a mark of expertise, a deprecation pause, enough to let the victim's inadequacy sink in. Although where he got the surveyor idea . . . Sagoe shrugged. It did not matter anyway.

'And then of course, you annoy the Board very much especially our Chairman. But . . . er . . . matters can still be repaired . . . well, it is all in your hands, you get my meaning?'

Winsala signalled another drink. Then he spread out his hands and grinned. *'Se wa s'omo fun wa?'*

'How much?'

'There are four of us to be—seen to. If it was only me . . .'

'How much?'

He took the schnapps, laughing. 'The Englishman has not left much of his diplomacy on you. You are more like American, straightforward. That is how I am too. You know, I like the American, they are not like the English, too much cunny for English man, so so diplomacy but they are much more so wicked even when they are saying Yes please and No thank you ha ha ha ha ha. I like straightforward men, that is how I am made.'

Hidden inside Sagoe as in several others of his age was a traumatic centre of castor oil, and nearness to this vile colloid made schnapps the most revolting potion of his experience. Schnapps might be famous as the secret of the ageless old men of the Niger creeks and the only antidote for swamp rheumatism, but it was hard to think of it uncoiling down those aged guts; on their ricketty joints seemed much likelier, and Sagoe's insides turned every time Winsala smacked his lips.

'Just tell me how much.'

Winsala stopped running his tongue over the schnapps tail on his lips and became businesslike again.

'As you are new, we will make it something for drinks. Let us say . . . fifty pounds?'

There were many ways to dangle him, to draw him out on hope like the dribble of a senile chin and Sagoe ran over them one by one, eliminating them all finally as the schnapps odour overpowered him. 'Suppose . . . suppose I tell you that I had a phone call from the editor-in-chief, barely fifteen minutes ago, and that he said the job is already mine?'

Winsala sagged and his confidence vanished. Or did he? It was not impossible that it could have been a delusion. And now it was replaced by the laughing Winsala of the amorous episode, eyes shut and chair on its hind-legs and a full sixty seconds of this. 'My boy, it never does to try your elders. When a cub yields right of way to an antelope, first look and see if Father Leopard himself is not a few trees behind. I will tell you a secret and if you like we will bet it and see who is right. On Monday you will receive another phone call from your editor, telling you that the Board reject your appointment. You see, the final word is with us. Don't you know that I will have sense to talk with Nwabuzor before coming here? I know that he will be phoning you already. The job is there, but you have to secure it.'

This time Sagoe was so intent on the man's face that he saw the schnapps signal. The green waistcoated waiter appeared also to know his man, reacting almost before Winsala raised his face in the expert tilt. Again Sagoe was baffled, decided that Winsala would not easily be outfaced. But he could take no more of the man's castor oil and he rose when the waiter approached.

'I'll see what I have in the room.'

'That is more sensible. When the Sanitary Inspector looks under the bed he's looking for kola, not *tanwiji*.'

The smell of the new order followed Sagoe out, and he longed for a strong rind of lemon.

Sagoe went on the balcony, heaving in huge gusts of the lagoon air. It was turning dusk and the street lamps were just beginning to flicker in their eternal struggle against uncertain power. It would continue thus for half the night and then perhaps the duty engineer would find the faulty coil and take it out altogether, leaving the street in darkness for a month or more.

A long American car was parked almost directly beneath the balcony. Something was familiar about the chromium lines . . . in fact, it was more than that. The oriental cushions on the ledge behind the rear window, familiar symbols of a vulgar opulence; Sagoe recalled the place—the *Independent Viewpoint*. He had squeezed between its bumper and the wall when he left the offices. Chief Winsala's? Sagoe looked again at the vague shape in the rear whom he had thought the driver; the man was sleeping, his head fallen forward on his chest. The cap was unmistakable, the triangle flap of the *abetiaja* stuck backwards on his neck, unorthodox. Sir Derinola, Chairman of the Board.

Sagoe did not immediately connect him with the fellow member in the lounge, but the pattern remorselessly asserted itself, nakedly, and he felt an acute embarrassment that he should have witnessed this cruel exposure of men whose age demanded his respect. Sir Derinola slept peacefully and Sagoe felt on himself the covering of shame. He was the guilty one who had trespassed on secrets that should never be exposed. But how, how did it begin? Winsala had after all only asked for fifty pounds. It was a lot to him certainly, but to Sir Derinola, should it mean anything? Twenty perhaps to Winsala and thirty for Sir Derin. His mind re-tuned itself to the cold actuality of figures. There would be other boards and other opportunities, maybe twice a month. Incidental earning —sixty a month, non-taxable. It made sense. It was worth dozing incognito in an air-conditioned car while a front, a brazen clown like Winsala came up to do the bargaining. There must be other calls that night. The schnapps seemed to have stuck to his clothes and the sly head in the car below resumed his nausea. Winsala seemed the cleaner of the two, outfacing him and declaring himself for what he was. But Sir Morgue below. . . .

Sagoe went to his room and lay on the bed, staring at the

ceiling. He called room service and asked for a gin and tonic to be sent to him, and fresh lemon separately.

Once, once upon a long time ago, he was not even allowed the lemon after the weekly purgative. Egbo and he discussed the problem at Sunday School, scribbling on the desk in pencil.

'Better prepare. My mother is coming to your house today, and she does not let me suck lemon any more.'

'Why?'

'I don't know. But it will mean no more for you too.'

There was a long break. Egbo's guardian was lately married, and Sagoe's mother took it on herself to bring her up in the ways of children's ailments. Especially preventives. The weekly purgative was one, or at least fortnightly. Saturday was dreadful for Sagoe and now there was this threat of cenapodium without lemon, the horror of eternal nausea, of a tongue that for two days after slithered like a snail.

'What of alum?' Egbo wrote. It did not trouble him much because the teacher's wife was a little afraid of him. But Sagoe's mother was always around, and she had persuaded her that Egbo was a godsend for health experiments. 'Just try it on that little monster for a month and see what a difference it makes.'

Sagoe considered alum. 'Yes, that should work. Where to get it?'

'We have at home. Teacher keeps it in his medicine cupboard.'

'Is there enough?'

'Plenty.'

The desk had filled by now and they had no rubber. But the solution had been reached. And then Sagoe recalled a thought that had troubled him for long and it couldn't wait. So he tore off the edge of his *Pilgrim's Progress* and wrote on it,

'What about God?'

The teacher caught it. 'Out, Sagoe, and you, Egbo. Remove your infinitesimal bodies here and bring that epistle with you.'

He was clearly disappointed. 'What about God?' In a Sunday School the most idiotic child would find legitimate, even commendable explanations for such a question, so he declined to investigate. But the paper looked suspicious and he called for

87

their books. She sat next to them, Dehinwa, and she was resolute in her refusal to swap books in spite of threats of diabolical tortures after school. Their punishment however was light, two pages of *Pilgrim's Progress* to be memorised before next Sunday School.

Afterwards, there was the point to be settled. 'Do you mean, does God drink castor oil?'

'Yes.'

'He doesn't eat so he won't need it.'

'If I didn't eat for a whole week my mother would still dose me with it. In fact she would think I must have missed my last dosage.'

Dehinwa had caught up with them, but they ignored her. 'Cenapodium is worse. Mine is due again next Sunday. Egbo is lucky of course, he hasn't got a time-table.'

'Only when I have stomach ache or when I am spoiling the air too much. And even then, she has to seek support from your mother.'

Dehinwa asked. 'Is it you spoiling the air? You have to watch them, you know. My auntie does it all the time and she blames us children. But I can always tell. I always know when she is going to do it. She bends her buttocks to one side, after that, everybody scatters.'

Sagoe felt superior. 'My mother is more regular. Always after prayers every evening, very loud and prolonged. When the bombing is over she says, "Thank God," and we all have to reply, "Amen".'

Dehinwa said, 'Your mother has no shame. Even before guests.' Sagoe swiped at her with the bible but she skipped off lightly.

They had come to Egbo's door. 'Don't forget the alum.'

Egbo stopped. 'Now I remember. You know what the dispenser told me? He said they now make castor in round form, like a tablet.'

'True?'

'He showed it to me. Nearly round, like the egg of a lizard.'

Sagoe cheered up considerably for a moment then shook his head. 'No good to me. Mamma will say it can't work like the liquid one.'

'But if the dispenser says . . .'

'The dispenser will agree with her. You know he is all eye-service.' And Dehinwa tilted her head, scornfully, walked off a little.

The two boys stood pondering for some time, weighted by the hopelessness of things.

'Don't forget the alum,' and Sagoe quickened his pace, walk-right past Dehinwa. She trotted after him accusing, 'Just because I wouldn't change my book with yours . . .'

A stranger woke him up a short while later and Sagoe leapt up in alarm. 'Good God, what is the time?'

'Half past seven.'

'Oh is that all? I thought I'd dozed for much longer. . . .' He stopped short, and Bandele laughed softly. Sagoe reached a hand to the wall and pressed the switch. For a full minute they stood and stared. Then suddenly they gripped each other by the arms, not speaking. Kola burst in then and Sagoe flooded over, embracing him and shouting the common words he never thought to hear himself say, 'You haven't changed', and hearing in turn, 'Nor you.' Overflowing with joy he wrapped his arms around his waist and lifted Bandele a few feet from the ground and his head hit the ceiling one inch away. Sagoe set him down exclaiming, 'Good God, if it isn't Giant Alakuku. Not one inch shorter and still as solemn as British royalty.'

Bandele sat on the bed. 'You are the last to return. Sekoni beat you by three months.'

Kola asked 'Why have you been hiding? Confess.'

'I'll explain later. How did you know I was back?'

Kola laughed. 'You have a file or don't you know that?'

'A file? What is that supposed to be?'

'At the Foreign Office. Aren't you supposed to be a communist?'

'Well . . .'

'Egbo works at the Foreign Office. He told us you had come.'

'Why the bloody . . .' And he slapped himself on the thigh and laughed. 'And there was I sneaking in and out thinking no one knew of my existence.'

'Your dossier fills a whole filing cabinet—Egbo will tell you more about yourself.'

Sagoe scratched his head. 'But what of Egbo? He could at least have called on me.'

'Well, we all guessed you had your reason for hiding. So we thought we'd wait a week or two.'

'Well, it is nothing sinister, I can tell you. I just didn't want the family to know I was back. You know, thought I'd dispose of myself first, get a job or decide not to get a job, a brief courtesy visit and then finish. Every man to his own business.'

Bandele shook his head, 'That is not so easy.'

'Maybe not. But I intend to try.'

'Isn't Egbo here yet?'

'No, I haven't seen him.'

'We arranged to meet here at seven, give you a surprise. We got held up on the Ibadan road. Some horrible accident.'

'Come on, let's go down and settle at the bar. Have you cooked up something for tonight?'

'It's your night. You tell us what you want to do.'

The last step down the stairs and Sagoe sensed an unusual quiet in the room. It broke across their boisterous entry and Sagoe held back, recollecting now the visit of Chief Winsala. Their entry seemed timed for the middle of some shabby act. The bar was across the lounge, and a cluster of green waistcoat uniforms directed their attention to the scene.

'What is it?'

'Wait.'

Chief Winsala appeared to be asleep, and a waiter hovered round him poised for a cue. Suddenly it came. The wide agbada sleeve rose and swiped in his direction. Obviously the waiter had been expecting it. He retreated smartly muttering, 'But oga, make you answer me now.' The other waiters fed their boredom on the game, laughing out aloud.

It was obvious that this game had been going on for some time. Winsala's voice was thick. 'Don't come near me unless you bring more schnapps.'

'But oga, make you fust pay for the one you done drink.'

In front of Chief Winsala was a half-bottle, now lying on its side.

The role of a hotel greenbottle buzzing impecunious drunks was one he understood, and the waiter moved forward again. 'But oga, I beg now . . . I wan' close.'

Winsala bawled aloud, 'You are sheeky. If you sheek me I will get you sacked. I have told you I am still waiting for my friend. Now get away.'

Bandele, seeing Sagoe's face asked, 'Do you know him?'
'Wait.'

In the dim recess of Winsala's faith, Sagoe was returning
with fifty pounds, or half the sum and a promise of the rest.
With the same assurance he had seized his chance to order a
bottle of schnapps, then generously reduced it to half. But
Sagoe had delayed his return.

Tray outstretched, Greenbottle advanced, circled him but
Winsala seemed finally asleep.

'Enh? Abi 'e done sleep?' And Greenbottle tried to see the
eyes beneath the cap. Winsala's patience was rewarded, an
alert paw shot upwards and the tray flew up, caught Greenbottle on the proboscis and went clattering on the tile.

Greenbottle retracted wounded, underwent instant changes
of ugliness. The buzz of his outraged comrades swelled the
incident beyond proportion. It was the only sound that could
be heard, a slow gathering buzz of a swarm of greenbottles
disturbed on some rotting fruit. The ordering class in the
lounge turned their back, embarrassed to witness the humiliation that must follow. The waiters had quick feelers, a big man
was about to be rolled in manure and they waited for the first
stream of insults from the waiter.

The ball of indignation had been passed to him and Greenbottle took his time, warming slowly. He was no novice, he
knew exactly when the impulse would be lost and indignation
turned hollow, put on.

'A no fit take dat kin' ting from any man. I dey work here
das all, nobody fit beat me like horse.'

Behind him, a buzz of approval.

'A fit take dis case for police. Customer no fit push tray for
inside my face. I done day serve better person for dis place,
nobody fit trow tray for my face like that.'

Chief Winsala, his huge frame shrunken, his confidence collapsed, waited in deep fog, resigned to the beginning of a
shameful scene, degrading to a man of his position. To himself, for himself alone, a stream of belated saws came from his
lips, muttered silently while his head shook in self-pity . . .

Agba n't'ara . . . it is no matter for rejoicing when a child
sees his father naked, *l'ogolonto*. Agba n't'ara. The wise eunuch
keeps from women; the hungry clerk dons coat over his narrow belt and who will say his belly is flat? But when *elegungun*

is unmasked in the market, can he then ask *egbe* to snatch him into the safety of *igbale*? Won't they tell him the grove is meant only for keepers of mystery? *Agba n't'ara*. When the Bale borrows a horse-tail he sends a menial; so when the servant comes back empty-handed he can say, Did I send you? The adulterer who makes assignations in a room with one exit, is he not asking to feed his scrotum to the fishes of Ogun? Agba n't'ara . . .

'Make nobody come make big man for me here, because I no dey chop under am. Big man wey no respect inself, e no go get respect . . .'

Sagoe found that he had moved forward, picked up the tray. As he rose, there was a sudden flurry of cloth and he turned sharply in the direction of the main entrance. Beside the young palm shoot in a halved petrol drum stood Sir Derinola. And Sagoe was never never to forget the look upon his face. Beside the fright and his affronted dignity was marked the anguish of indecision. He had come up to see what caused the long delay and had entered at the start of the baiting. It was at first a strange kind of fascination, as if in Chief Winsala he saw his own fate, recognised the downward logic of the loss of self-respect. He had recognised the moment of rescue much too late, and as he postponed it, it got later still, and every step he took forward was retracted at the thought that Sagoe might return and see him with Chief Winsala. But above all, Sir Derinola was truly paralysed at the confrontation of a future image, and could not move to help. Now he saw Sagoe move forward, and tried to shrink back behind the palm. They gazed into each other, all subterfuge pointless. It was Sagoe who took his eyes away.

'What is the matter?' he asked pushing the tray back into the waiter's hands.

'E no wan' pay for in drink.'

'Then you should have called the manager.'

'Manager no dey. I no fit take dat kind ting. Governor-General self, e no fit beat me in execution of my duty.'

'You realise he is my guest?'

'Wetin e wan make I do? E done pass my time for closing. I tell am say I . . .'

'Put the drinks on my bill. And stop shouting at me.'

He put his hand on Chief Winsala's shoulder. 'Shall we go

sir?' He rose humbly, the bluff had all gone out of him. Bandele had come to support the man on the other side but Sagoe steered him round suddenly, 'We'll take the other lift.'

And with the corner of his eye he saw Sir Derin suddenly released, turn away from them and scamper to the lift.

Nwabuzor phoned Sagoe the following morning, incredulous. 'Did you bring with you some spell from America? The Chairman says I must give you that job. Honestly, what did you do to him? Just tell me, what did you do to him?'

6

'Mathias! Mathias! Come here, Mathias.'

The messenger looked round the door. 'Do you calling sir?'

'Mathias, are you still my disciple?'

'Oga?'

'I am broke. How well does the bartender know you?'

'Na my countryman.'

'In that case, you shouldn't find it difficult to get credit.'

'Oga I beg una o. Dat na different matter. When money matter dey for ground, nobody dey remember countryman.'

'Mathias, go now, and don't come back without the usual. Two.'

'Oga, I tell you . . .'

'Mathias, today is bible reading day. Go now.'

'All right o oga. I go try.'

His session with the editor had been painfully brief. Nwabuzor called him into the office and said, 'I want you to listen to this.' In his hand he had sheaves of foolscap which contained Sagoe's story about Sekoni. He had entitled it, 'Who Engineered the Escapade?' The facts were well tabled, nothing could be disputed.

While Nwabuzor waited for his call, he told him 'By the

way, your friend the white expert is gone. The one whose report damned the power plant.'

'What do you mean gone?'

'Simply gone. The Personnel Claims Board approved a claim of his on injuries sustained in the course of duty. Guess how much he collected.'

Sagoe shook his head.

'Eight thousand. Plus another two thousand lump sum compensation for the termination of his contract.'

'I see.'

'Don't start losing hope. It doesn't make your story useless. At least not that . . . There are various ways of verifying— if we want to.'

'But you don't want to?'

'That depends. Wait, I'll explain . . . hallo . . .'

Sagoe rose. 'I would rather not hear any explanation. That was two weeks' murderous work.'

'Sit down, sit down. Good, you certainly don't like waiting, do you? Hallo . . . hallo . . . this is Nwabuzor. I want to speak to the chairman . . .'

'Honestly I would rather just take it and leave it. You know this was quite a personal thing.'

'That is bad journalism, my friend. You'll soon find out. Anyway you've done your part, you've got us the story and the rest is up to us. Make that your attitude . . . hallo . . . hallo . . .' He covered up the mouthpiece. 'Quickly, pick up that extension on the table.'

From the other end came Sir Derinola's unmistakable voice, 'Is that you, Nwabuzor?'

'Yes sir. About the "revelations", can we use it now, sir?'

'No. File it away.'

'Do you mean postpone it sir?'

'No, we have already used it.'

'Oh I see sir.' And, obviously for Sagoe's benefit he said, 'So they agreed to deal, sir?'

'I don't want to talk about that on the phone.'

'Of course not sir, I am so sorry.'

'By the way, who worked on it?'

'It's the new features man sir.'

'You mean that er . . . that boy from America?'

'Yes sir.'

Sir Derin was silent for a long time. Nwabuzor spoke. 'He did a good job, didn't he sir?'

'Yes, it was satisfactory.'

Sagoe was astonished, because Nwabuzor was distinctly mocking. 'Wasn't it lucky we got him after all, sir?'

Sir Derin's voice was suddenly brusque. 'You forget I told you to employ him.' And he slammed down the phone.

Sagoe replaced the phone slowly, turned to Nwabuzor. The editor-in-chief waved him back to the chair. 'Well, that is it. Now you know.'

'Now I know what?'

'Shut your mouth, I shut mine. Plain and simple. You have got the chairman out of some nasty jam.'

'I have *what*?'

'It goes on all the time. You see, it is part of the mutual protection. Before we publish any revelation like that, it must go to our lawyers. And he in turn consults with the Chairman. It is out of our hands.'

'Go on. I am anxious to learn.'

'Well he lets the other side know what he has got on them. If they decide they can weather it, they say go ahead. If not, they say, Well, as a matter of fact we have been collecting certain things about Such-and-such a person on your side, and they send a copy along. Well I have a pretty good idea what Sir Derin had got himself into, but anyway, your copy came in the nick of time. They have done a swap of silences.'

'And about my friend?'

Nwabuzor shrugged as much as to say, What can I do?

Sagoe stood up. 'I hope you won't object if I send it to another paper.'

'Sagoe, look, I have been in this game for thirty years. Believe me there was a time when I held these ideals. I moved from one paper to the other, leaving in a flurry of righteous indignation. But look man, journalism here is just a business like any other. You do what your employer tells you. Believe me, Sagoe, just take my word.'

Sagoe took the manuscript. 'I am sending it to the other papers.'

Nwabuzor shook his head with the hopelessness of it. 'But Biodun you are in our employ. You used our time, this is our property.'

'Not if I resign.'

'No no, there is no need. Look, the other papers won't touch it, I tell you. The same process will take place and they will realise that a gentleman's agreement has been made over it.'

'In that case . . .'

'No, no, no, don't say things to make it worse for yourself. Just forget it. I know you think you owe some loyalty to your friend; believe me, you don't. In the end you'll find it's every man for himself.'

'That certainly is a large view to take of life. '

'It *is* a large view, and the only one. Look, your friend will get another job and you will soon forget about . . .'

The door slammed and Nwabuzor went back to his work thinking, he'll settle down.

Sagoe brought out his quarto volume and opened it at random.

'Come in, Mathias, any luck?'

Mathias entered with a sweaty bottle in either hand. 'E say e no wait till mont ending. Na up to dis week-end e gree give me for credit?'

'All right, sit down.'

'Make a open dem fust oga.'

'Thank you.' He waited until the beer had gurgled out, then passed the book to Mathias. 'Open it. Just open it anywhere you like.'

Eagerly, like one who was now accustomed to a treat, Mathias obliged.

'Good. Now drink and I'll begin.'

'. . . And silence is to the Voidante as the fumes of opium are to the mystics of the Orient. The silence of the lavatory in an English suburban house when the household and the neighbours have departed to their daily toil, and the guest voidates alone. That is a silence you can touch. In France, of course, the myth of sophistication is nothing but shallow and awkward posturing—like spawning toads. There I sought the fumes of silence in vain, till in the end, to escape the soul-debasing state of the hostel lavatories I would retire with a book and shovel into the nearby woods—there was this one redemption at least, the woods spread over acres. here I founded a little arbour where I contemplated regularly, read, or merely listened to the descant of Gallic birds. It was, I confess, cramped Voidancy, it lacked full comfort, total muscular relaxation. Worse still, the feel of a sudden wet blade of grass in the midst of my devotion made me leap in fear that a snake was trying to lick my balls. But the wet, heavy, bird-interpolated silence was a mystical experience, it made the risk of emasculation a minor thing. And now, my friends, I must tell you a shameful episode. Two hiking students followed me one day, curious to find where the daily combination of book and shovel led. It is still a revolting thought, that I was actually observed in this most individual function of man. But they proved interested pupils, purified themselves of the taboo by expending three day's budget in a single afternoon at the bistro. I granted absolution, and the wine made me generous and I made them full initiates into the Mysteries of Voidancy. Was the question ever resolved I wonder now? They were, I remember, converted to what, for me, was mere resourcefulness. In the humid soil and wet undergrowth they claimed, in sly concealed manipulation of creepers and shrubs lay the true Voidatory. Back-to-the-bush stuff, I shouted, Voidatory requires the art and science of man. Lighting must be muted on the eye. The air-purifier —for this is incense—must be selected for the right nuances in odour. The right books and paintings too, so that a desire to change direction of thought does not lead to frustration. Loudspeaker extension for selected music, not the vagaries of seasonal migration. For three days we were surfeited with Voidante dialectics. You are a bourgeois Voidante, they yelled—you know how the French love polemics—and I replied, and you are Voidante pseudo-negritudinists! You deviationist fools, can you not understand, atmosphere must be created as in a church? My book-and-shovel trips were mere expediency. But they threw Andrew Marvell in my teeth, hurled refrains of "a green thought to a green shade". Against their vision of virginal nature and arborial voidatory, my warnings of the snake menace proved ineffectual. It was gratifying to sow the seeds of Voidancy on the continent of Europe, but in a way, it was a small defeat, for I was powerless against their damned regression. . . .'

Solemnly Sagoe closed the book, and they remained in silent contemplation.

'I knew it Mathias, you are a natural. You are in fact, something of a clairvoyant. Not many people have fingers so finely attuned to their psyche.'

'If you say so oga . . .'

'I say so, Mathias. Silence. That was it. Silence. To have opened it at silence, that was the genius of it. Mathias, my good friend Mathias, you were predestined to save me from the madhouse, I am luckier than my good friend Sheikh. Now he, that is where he is going . . .'

'God forbid.'

'God won't forbid, Mathias. Do you know, I did not even know I was sold body and soul to Sir Chairman of this place, and now, after two weeks of St. Georging at the dragon, they tell me, no they don't even tell me, they rub my face in it, quite calmly. You belong to the Morgue, they say, now go back to work.'

'No take dat kind eye look am oga.'

'Because the good knight must be saved, they roast the Sheikh. Don't mind me, Mathias, I know I am feeling sorry for myself, and over nothing. People like Sekoni end up on the pyre anyway, but damn it, I didn't have to help them build the faggots.'

Mathias drained his bottle. 'Na so life be oga.'

'Silence, Mathias. Silence. I have known all kinds of silence, but it's time to learn some more.'

And the vows of silence. Above all else, the vows of silence must be kept. Against love, against need and the willingness to give. And remorse, even remorse proved powerless against such silence as bound Sekoni's father to a silent distance until death. A Christian girl! This sin, so heinous, so unfilial and blasphemous, no longer seared the memory of Alhaji Sekoni, but a vow was a vow, and pride propped his thirsted flesh when it would want to fall to love. Five years ago he had stood at the door of the Marriage Registry and implored the wrath of hurricanoes on the treachery of his blood, his *haji* mantle blown about his shoulders like the mane of Lear on an asphalt heath. And his desolation equally felt, equally unsolved. 'I will never, never open my mouth to speak to you. May Allah in his might strike me dead if I speak another word to you!'

And now bearing a stiff, manful back down on the pangs of separation, Alhaji Sekoni, nearly demented himself with grief and worry, made a home on the doorstep of the doctor. How is he, sir, tell me how is he? Will he recover? And remember that nothing need be lacking. If you want to send him abroad to specialists . . . no? Don't they say Switzerland has the best of everything? But doctor, surely there is something I can do, there is something I must do? What does he talk about? And who does he talk about? He mentions names? No no I only wondered . . . has he stated a desire to see anyone in particular? Did you say no? Only I hear that often they desire to see someone or other. There is a nurse with him all the time? But there ought to be . . . it will be so bad if he wants to see one of his er friends or . . . er relations, and we don't know anything about it . . . no no, he has no brothers or sisters . . . well, if there is anything at all, maybe a change of air, you are the doctor, what do you think? A change of air, a holiday is always good, isn't it?

The doctor understood whose need this truly was and the elder patient left then, already on the way to recovery. It was near the time of pilgrimage, and Alhaji Sekoni knew a cure beyond hope when his son turned his face, not to a London summer or a fortnight in Venice, but to Mecca. Sekoni's wonder-filled, miracle-seeking hands weighed heavily with hope and with history as they kissed the ruins of Old Jerusalem and not the Holy Stone . . . but what could Alhaji know of this . . . ? Through bazaars of spurious relics and souvenirs, leaving far behind him the madly running smocks of white thousands on their run of forty times around the black solid shrine and the death from trampling of four or five, Sekoni thrusting his fingers through the broken walls of Old Jerusalem, standing pitiless on his heritage before disturbing intimations, suddenly meaningful affinities . . . and he was awed, so wholly awed, beyond all concrete grasp.

Sekoni began sculpting almost as soon as he returned. His first carving, a frenzied act of wood, he called 'The Wrestler'. He had not asked Bandele or anyone to sit for him, but the face and the form of the central figure, a protagonist in pilgrim's robes, was unmistakably Bandele. Taut sinews, nearly agonising in excess tension, a bunched python caught at the instant of easing out, the balance of strangulation before release, it was all elasticity and strain. And the rest, like the act of his creation which took him an entire month and over, was frenzy and desperation, as if time stood in his way. Kola had an extension shed erected for him against his own studio, and watched with growing respect Sekoni turn the wood into some wilful spirit whose taming was a magic locked in energy. The face of Bandele was obviously a deliberate evasion, but it was inevitable. Only Bandele's unique figure could have come to such pliant physical connivance with the form. Kola called out Joe Golder who was sitting for the Pantheon canvas, and Golder the American stared long and silently at the sculpture and offered to buy it. Sekoni simply shook his head and continued to work. He worked now—it was the finishing touches— with uncompromising concentration, fluently, a contrasting delicacy to the earlier ferment, and with such sureness that Kola began to doubt his knowledge of the man, wondering if Sekoni had done any other thing but this all his life. 'Come on, Joe,' Kola said, 'let's get back to the Pantheon.' 'But won't he sell?' Joe Golder moaned. And impatiently, with a tinge of envy in his voice, Kola snapped, 'Oh damn your American acquisitiveness.'

And Kola found that he was indeed jealous. Unless 'The Wrestler' was one of those single once-in-a-life co-ordinations of experience and record, Sekoni was an artist who had waited long to find himself but had done so finally, and left no room for doubt. Certainly there was no self-doubt in Sekoni's hand, and none showed in this his first attempt. Joe Golder's verdict was the same. Kola struggled futilely with his canvas for a while, then gave up for the day, confessing, 'Sekoni's Wrestler has put me off. Let's continue tomorrow.'

'Put you off? Why? Self-identification?'

'I wish it were that. No. Just plain jealousy?' Exploding, 'Damn! You know yourself how long I have been struggling with this thing.'

'But you haven't finished.'

'That is not the point. You should have watched Sekoni at work. And then, the result. God, when you think that that man has done nothing but mess around with power stations . . .'

'Don't be so silly. You are a fine painter, Kola . . .'

'Don't give me that.'

Joe Golder rose and went up to the canvas but Kola stopped him. 'You can't see it yet. Oh I know some of it is fine. But look Joe, that thing, that something which hits you foully in the stomach, just below the belt, I have returned often in the night to look for it, to catch even the beginnings of it . . .'

'But how do you imagine you can? Kola, you painted this yourself so how do you hope to react to it the same way you react to a work by a different man?'

'I know that. But something really startled me when I watched that stuttering dark horse at work . . .'

'Oh, I think you are just jealous,' Joe Golder said.

'Did I ever deny it?'

Half-joking at first, Joe Golder made Kola's sullen fear no easier to contain by his feminine greed for Sekoni's sculpture. His blackmail was at first only tentative, then as he knew the complications which now drove Kola desperate, he became really irresponsible, selfishly dangerous.

'If you don't get it for me I shan't sit any more for you.'

'I'm in no mood for joking,' Kola said, and Golder replied, 'I'm not joking.'

But Joe Golder was not in the studio the following afternoon and Kola flew to the library and then to the Staff Club, but Joe Golder was in neither. He would not be in his room, but Kola looked just the same. A belated thought took him to the music room where the full trill of a tenor voice declared Joe Golder's presence.

He stopped as soon as he saw Kola. 'I have a rehearsal,' he said.

'You did not have one yesterday.'

'No, it's today, you see.'

And Kola shouted, 'Don't be funny, you know damn well what I mean.'

The Englishwoman accompanist looked from one to the other, gathered up her music sheets and said, 'Well, we had almost finished anyway, if you'll excuse me.' And Kola gnashed his teeth, knowing full well what the woman must be thinking of him, since everybody knew what Joe Golder was.

'Well, are you coming to sit?' he said when the woman had left.

'You get your friend to sell me the carving and I'll sit.'

Kola flopped into a chair. 'For God's sake what is the matter with you? Can't you see your face is healing so rapidly it will soon be useless?'

Joe Golder, American and three-quarter white, hated his face and on it he practised one horror after the other. Erinle in Kola's Pantheon, Joe Golder turned up in the studio one day with crinkled newsprint stuck raggedly all over his face, reward of afternoons of exposure to the burning sun. 'Just what masquerade do you think you are?' Kola, near-hysterical with anger.

'Your sun is more potent than I thought.'

Kola threw aside the palette in despair. 'Do you really think I will paint your face in that condition?' And he stopped, because even as he spoke, he was seeing Golder's face more intensively, seeing the different fierceness in its new character. When Joe Golder was ugly, he went the full range of transformation. His eyes revealed an unsuspected largeness, distending quite out of proportion. Sometimes the entire head would be worked as if by invisible cords below the smooth leathery skin like a terrified horse, and bordering on epilepsy. And he was being ugly from pique, self-despising as always that he could not take the sun like a full African negro. Kola, even before he began his canvas on the Pantheon, had remarked how well he would translate into one of the gods; when he at last began the mammoth task, Golder fell in place as Erinle only less obviously than Egbo as Ogun. And now, with the frizzled skin all peeling on his face, frizzled in little loops and curls with a few clean patches of arid land, Joe Golder had assumed an after-sacrifice fierceness, bits of slaughtered feather sticking to his face. Kola snatched up his brush again and squeezed more paint on to the palette, working furiously.

'You won't scrub your face?' he pleaded.

'Can't even bear to touch it. You cannot imagine how it hurts.'

'When will you give up trying to be black?'

'When I look three-quarters black. I feel like Esau, cheated of my birthright.'

'You look like Jacob with shop-soiled fur on his face.'

The following days were filled with near-despair; Joe Golder's face appeared to flake rapidly, a sudden breeze through the studio and a fragment of skin would gently disengage, float mockingly above the easels and after several triple turns in air, float gently through an open window while Golder looked on amused and Kola watched helplessly. Until a greedily large piece almost vital to the facial collage, a large piece frizzled sepia and Turkish slipper shaped freed itself from the cheekbone, then Kola lost control and attacked it, caught it on a brush point and flattened it on the painting where he left it, an outgrowth from Erinle's ear.

Then they would have to fight over the vaseline. Joe Golder, so scared of pain, he was really childish. But his face had been cruelly dried and some ointment would slow the flaking process.

'It hurts,' and he would shield his face against Kola's fingers.

'Of course it hurts. Who the hell asked you to go fry your face?'

And now this. Kola stared at the brittle skin, watched his appeal to Golder's better nature only arouse his instincts for baiting. Golder took the vacated piano stool and began to pick out the tune of the negro spiritual he had just been rehearsing. Kola moved swiftly to him and brought down the piano lid on his hands, sharply but not too painfully.

'Are you coming?'

'No.'

'All right. But I dare you to go into any night-club in town after this. Your last experience will be nothing compared to what you will get.'

Golder winced, recollecting, and Kola played fully on his fear of violence.

'Don't forget I know my way around and you don't. *Any* night-club, I dare you.' He turned on his heel and left him. Joe Golder hesitated. Ibadan without the music of the dives . . . he followed Kola to the studio.

7

And now Sir Derin was dead. Sagoe felt for strength in his legs, wondering why he felt compelled to go and see him buried. A big feature would be expected from him but it was not that. His photographer would be present and the funeral orator would gladly supply a copy of his speech—Sagoe could fill a centre spread without budging from the bed. But there it was, he felt a need to go in person. He raised himself on his elbows and looked through the window. The weather was no help. The rain had snuffed out the last flicker of life from the world outside. The air was dead. He heard a clatter of pans through the door and he knew that Dehinwa was back from work. The bitch. The goddamn bitch. She had woken him up with that racket on the pans—deliberately, he was certain. Still, he felt better; the sleep had worked some healing miracle.

The door opened. 'Oh, you are not dead, then.'

'What time is it?'

'Getting on to four. Do you want to eat?'

He stood up, testing one leg after the other. 'I can stand,' he announced.

'I said do you want to eat?'

'If you recommend it, yes. But first I must have a shower.'

Sagoe sat in the bath a long time, full of vague discontents. He heard, not wishing to answer, Dehinwa call him several times. And then Dehinwa thought, God he's passed out again, rushed to the door and flung it open. Sagoe was seated in the empty bath, staring gloomily at a length of rubber tubing in his hand. She squeaked and slammed the door while Sagoe chuckled to himself.

'But why a bath, Dehinwa? Why does a flat like this have a bath but no shower?'

'You've got the detachable shower in your hand.'

'This thing? This! This is a sprinkler, a dripper, a eunuch's secret. Don't you know what a shower is? I thought you went to a boarding school.'

'I did not build the flat.'

'Yesterday you did not build the roads, today you did not build the flat, and I suppose you did not build that nightmare wardrobe either.'

She kept silent and it irked him.

'In every new house that goes up. This jelly thing which never fits the tap. All the water comes out at the side—there it goes, I knew it. And then it bends over itself and blocks the flow. In any case it is too short. How can I get clean if I crouch. I need a strong down beat of water on my head, beating my drink lobes back into place. . . .' He stopped. 'Were you listening, woman?'

'I can just see you in your old age. An impossible old grouch.'

'Well, as long as you know what you are up against.'

'No fear, I do.'

'And the other thing you are up against. I hope you liked the look of it.'

'What are you talking about?'

'That which scared the hell out of you when you opened the door just now.' And he gave a high-pitched yell of delight, feeling through the wall Dehinwa's fierce silence.

'How a civilized girl like you comes to have such a dangerous repression I never understand. . . .'

'That line is for your American high-school girls, don't forget.'

'You needn't sneer at them. At least they didn't go round making their fiancés hold their groins in pain—in their very presence.'

'Apparently it wasn't just their fiancés, or were you engaged to them all?'

'So? But you watch out. One of these days you are going to find you've gone too far, and then you'll just get raped, girl. Raped in the good old-fashioned way. Now what will your mother say to that?'

A few seconds later Sagoe laughed, relishing the thought. 'Oh lordy lordy I can just hear you, I am pregnant mamma but it wasn't my fault. I got raped. And your dear mamma would say, Serve you jolly well right. Didn't I tell you not to move with that Northerner? By the way, you haven't told me, who is this Northerner you're supposed to be going out with?'

'A handsome Minister with a private yacht.'

'Talk sense. He can't be all three.'

'Some nosy woman whose Hausa ends in " sai gobe" heard your name and thought you were a Northerner.'

'I wish I really was so she'd conk out with a heart attack when we get married.'

'All right, all right,' Dehinwa said. 'I don't say such things about your family.'

'You are welcome to, dear girl. I hate their thin guts and I tell them so.'

'Leave mamma alone anyway.'

'You tell her too to leave me alone.'

'What has she got to do with you?'

'She came all the way from Ibadan just to protest against me. That's interference through interest. By the way I hope you didn't undeceive her?'

'No. Why should I?'

'Well, one never knows with you. Overcome by her misery it is just the sort of concession you might make. You are a big sucker for mother's tears, do you know that?'

'I think in fact,' after a hopeless wait for Dehinwa to take the bait, 'I must get your grandma to talk to you. Now she, she is the sort of woman who should be permitted a ripe old age.'

'Oh yes, I knew she would appeal to you.'

The grandmother had taken a long look at Dehinwa, inspecting her with great concern. 'Why are you so thin? You were plump when you first came back from *ilu oyinbo*.' She looked up sharply, boring into her eyes, then shook her head in relief and mischief. 'No' she chortled, 'I don't think so. But listen girl, I know this new habit of you modern girls, don't join them in the foolishness. If you are expecting a baby, have it. A child is a beautiful thing, have it. The important thing is to know the father. We have never been ashamed of children whatever your mother may say, and you are old enough.' Dehinwa was embarrassed, pointing to Sagoe. 'Grandma, at least not before him.' 'Why not? He's your man isn't he? He must be, to have come with you all the way to Ifo. Young man, I hope you are more sensible than she is. If there is a child, send for me and I will come and bless him.' She stopped suddenly and looked at both of them. 'What are you waiting for anyway? Why aren't you married? No no, don't drag me away. I just want to know. You should be married and giving me grandchildren. . . .'

Sagoe emerged from the bathroom, a towel round him. 'Your food is ready,' Dehinwa said.

'Sorry, I don't think I could swallow just yet. Keep it hot while I go for a walk.'

'All right.' Sagoe kissed her on the shoulder, nuzzled his wet face on her neck, then pinched her sharply and she yelled.

'You're the tightest arsed Confidential Secretary I've ever laid . . .'

'You've what?'
'. . . eyes on, damn you, tightwad.'

For four days the sun had remained hidden. 'I could do with some negritude,' Sagoe moaned, 'anything to keep me warm.' He recalled that it had been the rainy season when he returned from Europe and America. Instead of heat he obtained electric shocks—once as he touched the faucet of a bath with his toes and another time through a finger as he dialled a number on the phone. When he told Mathias he said,

'Na austerity measure. Government wan join three ministry together—Works, Electricity and Communication' and roared away at the idea.

And Sagoe had used it in his column, laying bets on which of the three ministers involved would kill the others for control of the new three-in-one portfolio. It earned him his first family delegation, a clever assortment of eleventh cousins whom Sagoe could not know. Pleading caution. Please, don't make enemies.

It would be getting near the time for Sir Derin's funeral. Perhaps the service was already over and the grim procession had begun. He resolved to walk. Even if he missed the grave-side rituals he would stand and watch the gravediggers fill in the soil, and perhaps add his handful.

Something hit him suddenly, a wet hand stretching up his trousers to his waist, a solid wall of mud.

'Rat! You filthy rat!' And he felt justly angry, finding in the act a great betrayal. Sagoe had passed the fifth or sixth abandoned car, and had begun as always to salute Rain the Great Leveller. And a bus it was which splashed him. 'Dirty double-crossing rat!' An impulse to run after the bus and ride it brought a mild relapse, a hundred grasshoppers flew in his skull and he leant on a lamp-post for them to settle back. The sight of his ruined trousers made him reckless when again he resumed his walk, stepping carelessly through mud and twisting his ankle on submerged stones. This is the day for getting drowned, said Sagoe. God is spring-cleaning in heaven, washing out his bloody lavatory. The sights that rode in the wash of flood were indeed of that nature. There was a film of oil, palm oil on a brown lake which had swamped a food-seller's shack, but Sagoe said, Castor oil of course.

It was hardly five, but already Sagoe had begun to encounter the night-soil men. Next to death, he decided, shit is the most vernacular atmosphere of our beloved country. It was hardly a month since Mathias gave him some news he could hardly credit. 'But oga, mout' no fit talk am, make you come see for yourself.' And Sagoe had gone, taking a cameraman. Mathias had passed the sight coming to work in the morning as his bus made a sudden, near disastrous swerve to avoid the spot. Round the corner of the Renascent High School it lay, some yards from the first bus stop entering Abule Ijesha. Sagoe encountered first the deserted night-cart and trailer; some distance behind, its contents were spread on the road. To reconstruct the accident—the enormous porthole had flown open and the driver had not stopped fast enough. Over twenty yards were spread huge pottage mounds, twenty yards of solid and running, plebeian and politician, indigenous and foreign shit. Right on the tarred road. Nwabuzor by some curious reasoning expunged his pictures from the page, said they would offend the general reader. 'But it is there,' said Sagoe, 'that shit is still lying there on a main road, in front of a school, in a residential area!' And five days later Sagoe returned to it in flagellating pilgrimage, took more photos to show Nwabuzor, who could not be persuaded to go himself—and still it reigned supreme, tyrannous. Diminished admittedly—dogs have peculiar tastes and some drivers were not quick enough and churned through it—but typhous as ever, unified in monochromatic brown.

Through the side-streets of Yaba the night-soil men continued to pad on a gentle trot around the little windows set low in the walls of back-houses, faceless janitors, pail-surmounted silences, short-broomed swathings flitting dusk to dawn, the cherished emblems of a vintage air. And Sagoe indulged in a vision of Sir Derin passing beneath an arch of shortened brooms towards his grave, but the vision passed as Sagoe thought how the sight of these men profaned true Voidancy.

It was drizzling again. Sagoe felt suddenly tired and hailed a taxi. He had just begun to feel relaxed when he caught sight of the neck of the taxi-driver, its muscles glistening with water, bunching like P & T cables in oiled insulators. For which party did he thug when he wasn't driving? And then, with sudden premonition, Sagoe's hands flew to his pocket. No wallet. He recalled now seeing it on Dehinwa's dresser, and meaning to pick it up. Trying not to be obvious, he felt his pockets one after the other. No money anywhere. Not a penny.

'Where you wan go for, Obalende?'

'To the police station.'

He knew these individualist taxi-drivers. They preferred personal settlement to stopping at the first policeman and laying a charge. The taxi-driver looked round sharply, made a wrong assumption. His manner became instantly servile, ingratiating.

'Oga mi, hm, so even Nigeria Police no fit arrest this foolish rain.'

For a moment Sagoe nearly betrayed himself. Then he understood and ceased to worry. 'What,' with just the edge of menace in his voice 'is the matter with your windscreen wiper?'

That confirmed it. 'Sah? You mean the wiper, sah?'

Sagoe did not condescend to repeat his question.

'Oga, na dese foolish firms o. Na today today I take this car commot for service, then rain begin and look my trouble. De ting no gree work.'

'You have no speedometer either.'

'Enh, oga mi, you see wetin man dey suffer. Sixteen pound ten na in den charge me for service. Unless we Africans drive all dis foreign firm commot . . .'

'Stop!'

'Oga, enh, you say make a stop?'

'I said stop. Stop!'

'Ha, oga, make you no vex now. . . . I beg you oga I still get case for court for driving wit one light . . .'

'Are you deaf? Stop right here!'

The man stopped, a jelly now, and convinced also that he had lost hope of a pardon by his delay in obeying the officer. He prostrated right inside the car, wringing his hands for pity. At the least he was sure, an OFF THE ROAD label. They carried a dozen on them, these police sons of bitches.

Sagoe got out. For a long time he stood looking at the driver awkwardly prostrated in the car. Then he turned and walked away without a word. The driver waited a short time, then drove away with a sense of miracle. In his hand was still the crumpled five-shilling note which he had prepared to pass on in one of the many practised sleights of hand.

Round the corner was the cabinet shop which had caught his eye as the car flashed past. The shop was just beside the disused cemetery of Alagomeji, an untarred road between the two. By Appointment, Cabinet Makers to Her Touchy Highness Dehinwa, Confidential Secretary etc. etc.—on that, Sagoe declared, he would lay his money. On the wardrobe handles was the same petrified flower motif.

'Yes, my friend?'

'No no, I don't want to buy anything.'

'We get everything. If it is furniture of any kind, and we can make to order.'

'No, I just wanted to look.'

Side by side with wardrobes, desks and cabinets were coffins, some flat on wooden tiers and two upended to reveal ornate brass workings on the lid. He looked across to the cemetery where there were glass wreaths, many cracked or broken, sealed into concrete slabs, and he looked back at the glass handles of the wardrobes with the dead flower beneath them, and recognised now from where the carpenters' inspiration had been obtained; with it came a sense of exorcism. Just the same he made a mental note to do something about Dehinwa's taste.

Sagoe had walked the entire length of Carter Bridge before he knew it, his tiredness completely gone. Not today the post-card lagoon and hair-oiled Nat-King-greasy-Cole hair ripples, not today the petrified palm trees and the glazed shore. The lagoon was a trough of shea-butter churning, and cockroach huts of ako stalks circled the water edge in uncertain nibbles. The bridge was deserted, he noted with relief, thinking again how such a day seemed to be created specially for drowning, looking instinctively into the water, and half expecting a floating body, water-logged beyond salvation.

And then it cleared like a miracle. Or perhaps it had stopped raining a long time on the island itself. But as he left the bridge the air lightened very rapidly, the sky opened into a tourist sunset, opened out loud and riotous for death to come at Sagoe rather like a rude child, its sticky tongue hanging out. As he stood looking in at the wine section of the French shop window, wondering how on earth he could stare at such a rich display and be unmoved, he caught a reflection of death in the glass and turned, exclaiming, 'What a joke!'

A battered car—it looked like a nineteen forty-five Vauxhall—moved so slowly that the two immediate followers often knocked their shins on the rear bumper. It was the greatest farce ever enacted before death. For the car was moving with an open boot and the turd which stuck out so disgustingly was the coffin. The procession was—he had an urge to count them—a mere eleven. They were clumsy and their grief seemed true. It was incredible—since all eleven were men—but you could swear that they had all been shedding tears; in fact, a few of them still did. The two who led the procession were unnecessarily awkward; their shins hardly left the bumper. They walked on either side of the jutting coffin, a rude, vulgar work, rougher than any he saw earlier at the Alagomeji Cabinet Works; it was ornately gilt in the cheapest tinsel and shone with wax polish of a rabid red. It looked like the perfect tongue of a cola-nut addict.

God-forsaken fools, Sagoe kept muttering, why could you not at least tie the coffin on the roof? Not that it matters much to the dead man, but need you make death quite so ignoble!

In white jacket and trousers, each item a consistent misfit, with tennis shoes that lacked laces and collars sunken in part, each mourner looked furtive, guilty, as if in the back of his mind was the thought that more should have been done for the dead man. They pronounced it themselves a shameful trudge to Ikoyi cemetery, and the dead man stuck out his tongue at them, tottered inanely, and dared the mourners to let him fall.

Sagoe blinked hard. A white man appeared to be at the wheel. He fell in step, hardly thinking, with the odd man at the rear and they moved down Moloney Bridge Street, towards the short bridge, a near-symbolic bridge because of its situation, separating the living from the dead. And among the dead Sagoe included the suburban settlements of Ikoyi where both the white remnants and the new black oyinbos lived in colonial vacuity.

It was only another minute to the rout of his adopted procession. A rumble of hearse wheels was unmistakable, and the tread of a thousand feet raised a tremor in the earth which Sagoe felt in his feet and wondered if the others felt. Especially the driver at the wheel, driving so funereally. Sagoe wondered if he should move forward and warn him of the other train and urge him to quicken speed. He did nothing, preferring to watch what would happen if the two should meet at the bridge. And they did. And with the automatic respect of the poor for opulence, Sagoe's cortège stopped, while the other, a mile of car and human mourners, filed slowly past. Forty cars at least followed the hand-pulled hearse, and all cars were piled high with gory carnations. The hearse itself was smothered in wreaths and the mourners carried the extras on their arms. Thank God, said Sagoe, for our orgiastic funerals. If he ever freelanced he knew where to go on lean days. Weddings also, yes, and child-naming, and engagements, and cocktail parties, but a funeral with its night-long waking, its outing, its forty days turning over of the body, its memorial service only a few weeks later, its second turning over of the body, its sudden irrational remembrance feasts—a man could spend his entire life just feasting on a dead man. And many did.

In one of the leading cars, a face was screwed in painful concentration over a sheaf of papers—the funeral orator, beyond a doubt. Again Sagoe felt let down by his boot coffin mourners. If they looked foolish before they looked moronic now. Immersed undoubtedly in their grief, it required more than this to remain still while a four-mile-an-hour five-mile cohort passed in self-repeating glory. They failed to be indifferent to the pageant which passed before them, their squirming indicated unease, and each took refuge in examining the tennis heels of the man before him. The twisted bumper served the foremost two.

But neither did the other masque, Sir Derinola's final imposition on his countrymen, dare to divert its gaze from the preceding windshield, or their thought from hopes for their own funeral, that it might come somewhere near this glory of an upright son of the land. That for Sir Derin's three-hour traffic hold-up, they might boast six. Half the following train of Sir Derin passed before a policeman came to the rescue of the boot-coffiners, held up the crowd and allowed their sparse line to dribble through the final bridge. At the cemetery, separated by a hundred graves or more, the two bodies accepted now a common destination, passed through to the final expunction.

Sagoe joined Sir Derinola's train and pushed his way through, battling firmly until he reached the massed wreaths. Openly he took a glass wreath and two fresh ones, muttering, the glass one for the Holy Ghost, the rest for son and dad; you owe me that at least, Sir Morgue, I am certain you do not mind.

With difficulty he fought his way out again, in time to see the other men struggling to free the coffin from the boot. Sagoe gave the wreaths to the nearest of them saying nothing. Only then did he notice that the driver was not a white man at all, but an albino. He stayed on only a few minutes later and then, filled with a sudden revulsion for his role—for only now did it leap consciously to his mind that he hung around them because he saw a story in this for his page—he turned and left them, just as the albino approached him, perhaps to thank him for the wreaths.

He walked fast, barely short of rushing, from the cemetery. On his head the words beat hard off loudspeakers everywhere as the orator read his panegyric to a thousand heavy mourners. Sagoe fled, pursued by silences that left the world only such noises as

. . . his life our inspiration, his idealism our hopes, the survival of his spirit in our midst the hope for a future Nigeria, for moral irridentism and national rejuvenescence. . . .

8

Run, poor negro, run—the refrain to a truly bad poem Sagoe had read in an 'identity' journal and long forgotten, now raced through his head, beating chimes to a hysteria that had gathered beneath the balcony of Hotel Excelsior. It began just behind Oyingbo market where vocational idlers sheltered briefly from the rain, emerged to filter through incautious wares, picking off a bare existence. The hunt picked them up on its way. Then the touts joined in. And the watch peddlers rammed suspect 17-jewel instruments down deep pouches and swelled the running ranks—run, poor negro run—that versifier too had made a christ of his fugitive and this scum of Oyingbo was no mean substitute. Pontius Pilate on point duty faltered only for a moment but his sense of duty won. He turned a starched rear and continued to wash his hands in the stream of traffic. So the crowd bore through him, swarmed into the car park, slipped on wet tar and rose muddy and gay, snatched a handbag or two from sheer opportunity and blacked the grounds before the squat lumpy factory that was Hotel Excelsior.

Sagoe leapt off the bus and joined the throng—Run, Barabbas, run, all underdog sympathetic. Run, you little thief or the bigger thieves will pass a law against your existence as a menace to society. Sagoe followed them . . . run, Barabbas from the same crowd which will reform tomorrow and cheer the larger thief returning from his twentieth Economic Mission and pluck his train from the mud, dog-wise, in their teeth.

The youth chose by compulsion, made one violent line for the dubious safety of the lagoon.

Ole! Ole-e-e-e-e-e!

Lagos staged such pursuits daily, the unfortunate snatcher and a bored crowd. It was a moral demonstration and the prospect of indiscriminate beating was an incentive. The boy, man, he was hardly one or the other, appeared to be speaking. He had made other attempts to speak but as he checked his headlong flight a new crop appeared to sprout from beneath his feet and fear sped him again on his course. So now he was shouting to the lagoon,

'But I take nothing . . . I swear I don't take nothing. . . .'

He was deceptively the symbol of purity that morning—in the absence of the sun, his soft silk *dansiki* and tapered trousers flowed hurtfully white on the grey morning fall. And he was good-looking too. When they brought him back, naked except for his black underpants, he had indeed the lean, lithe torso of one of the not-so-holy companions of the Agony. Sagoe stretched the comparison no further. Dressed in his white *dansiki* he would be above suspicion in any company; in flight he presented a shaming spectacle of injustice. He was however an awkward, even ungainly runner, or perhaps it was fear. But compensation there was in the pools of white silk which swirled round his armpits, sped his lean shanks fast to an imagined refuge. Even his return was far from ignominious. He had lost his silk but he was silent, the fear had died off his face and his sparseness rebuked the weighted figure whose hairy paw was stuck so clumsily in the thief's fisherman briefs.

Blood would have come on the outward chase. Barabbas had a good start on his pursuers, and a driver, his car pointed at the fugitive's route had taken a hand. The grim concentration of this man's face left no doubt at all, his aim was to crush the thief's legs as he came past his bonnet. Barabbas leapt! New menace in the engine noise pierced his diffuse terror then. This might be Lagos and daylight, but he could be killed.

'That driver meant to kill him!' Sagoe cried out involuntarily.

'Kill the bastard!' a man shouted beside him.

By some strange, imprecise, unthinking agreement the flee-ing youth could be killed. The carelessness angered Sagoe, but it excited him also. And it was not merely that he wanted the crowd to learn a lesson—it was doubtful if they were capable of that—but he had become used to a thinking which required the sharp, violent focussing of dormant problems. Like the casual barbarism of such a crowd, their treachery against those who were momentarily below them in daily debasement.

He ran into the hotel, ran all the way upstairs and onto the balcony. Now he could see over the heads of the pursuers, see Barabbas just elude an attacker who now lay briefly on his shoulders, his back and scattered legs coming to a belated rest on the ground. Sagoe cheered, but sport though it was for most, the crowd wasted none of their cheers on the thief's elusiveness. Barabbas's legs had lost all doubt. Like sand-elves in *Ogboju Ode*, the mob materialised with every step and every sting of a stone or the passing breath of a near miss made him begin to wish for a merciful release.

'But what have I done, enh . . . what have I done. . . ?'

It was after this attempt to plead his case that he submitted to the verdict of his tormentors and headed for the sea. The crowd now blocked Sagoe's vision from that height and he remembered the roof garden. Winded and panting after a run up four flights of steps, he checked himself as he reached level floor. A man was there, his hands lightly rested on the rails. But what amazed Sagoe was that the same man had stood a short way from him on the lower floor. He could not mistake him; it was not merely because he was an albino, Sagoe could not mistake the kaftan, the fez cap and dark glasses.

From below . . . 'Don't let him take to water . . . don't let him take to water. . . .'

A thief, that is, a common thief, is a superman. He can leap from the sixth floor of a building and hold his breath while he swims the entire length of the lagoon. So no one doubted that he would escape if he made the water.

Barabbas jumped down the eroded slope towards the water and slipped the last few feet gracelessly on his arse. He was quickly up, skirting the lagoon where the land formed an overhang below the bank so that he was invisible to everyone for some ten yards. Eyes turned towards the other side where he was bound to reappear. When he did, he paused and calmly stripped himself of his martyr's vestments. A little island, just big enough to take one man broke the water some distance from the bank. Barabbas, holding his clothes above his head, waded towards it and sat there out of reach. His meaning was plain. At the first signs of danger he would jump into the water.

'In fact the boy may be innocent.'

The voice was so close to him that Sagoe jumped nearly out of his skin. The stranger had come nearer and was standing next to him. Sagoe hesitated, decided he would be civil.

'I don't think so.'

The albino was silent some moments, then he said, 'I see you don't remember me!'

Sagoe looked at him, finally shook his head. The albino had turned to the scene by the lagoon. 'We can all take fright if we are accused wrongly. It can happen to anyone. Is that not a possible fact we must consider?'

'The crowd hardly ever mistake their man, but he may be innocent.'

The crowd was parting to let a man through. 'Perhaps a policeman,' said the albino. 'The thief is hoping for that, otherwise he would not leave the place.'

Irritated now by the man's continued presence Sagoe said, You seem to know a lot about thieves' habits.'

'Oh, yes,' the albino said.

Some bargaining was obviously in progress between the newcomer and the thief. Then the man shouted at the crowd, told them to disperse about their business. There was a disappointed murmuring and they moved back a little. For some moments Barabbas watched the manoeuvring. Reassured at last of the man's authority, he left his perch and climbed confidently into his custody.

The crowd made way for them. The man's hand was hooked into the boy's pants, the only firm hold on a sweat-slippery body. His late pursuers seemed to have lost interest; there were pockets of jeers but they failed to be popular; threats of the earlier chase were now resolved in a subdued curiosity; for the most of them it was the first glimpse of the thief.

Sagoe could not forget the face of the leg-crushing driver, and recognised it now among the crowd, visibly thwarted and as yet unable to accept the failure of his blood-lust. The man pushed his way to the front, stationed himself so that Barabbas would pass directly by him. As the pair came level he cried, '*Omo ole*' and clubbed him in the face. And then restraint was forgotten and Barabbas, torn from his protector, was cast upon the eagerness of a hundred awkward blows. Without thinking, Sagoe spun back and made for the stairs hoping in some vague way to do something to save the boy. Only then did he realise that the albino had disappeared. At the end of the first flight down, Sagoe stopped. He had a sudden sense of certainty, inexplicable, and he returned to the roof garden, waiting for the albino to reappear among the crowd.

. . . I hit him! Ha-ya that was a good one, right on his face . . .

. . . *Ole! E ṣi'gbati fun yeye!*

. . . did you see that? Right on his greedy stomach by God . . .

. . . just lend me your stick. *Alakori* . . .

In a minute the albino had reappeared and seized the boy. Together with the other man they protected him against the crowd, the albino especially with a stream of abuse, unsparing. Nor were his opponents silent.

'Father of bats!'

'Thieves always stick together.'

'Are you shy? Remove your dark *gaga* to that we can recognise your face.'

Loud derisive laughter accompanied every abuse, but none of them actually offered to touch him. . . . Were they short of

117

firewood at home? Your mother forgot to bake you properly. . . .

He pushed Barabbas into the lift and clanged the doors to his opinion of their mothers' profession and their own sex diseases, caught, he reminded them, from their sisters. The defeated authority pushed off a last lone try for a swipe at Barabbas and the lift took off.

Sagoe ran down to the lounge floor, stood in front of the lift to see where they would take the boy. Outside, the mob remained to howl disappointment. Soon they would melt off in twos and threes and hang around the markets bored until further diversion could be provided—like a wedding procession or a motor accident.

He stood aside as the lift stopped and the men came out. Sagoe again hesitated, recalling now the albino's attempt to impose his companionship. The man broke aside and accosted him. 'I feel ungrateful because I have not come to thank you for your gift to our departed brother.'

'I don't recollect . . .'

'At the cemetery two weeks ago. You brought wreaths to our burial.'

Of course. The albino at the wheel.

'I wanted to say thank you, but you left very quickly.'

'You must have a good memory for faces.'

'Not really so. I have seen your photo on your newspaper column. I recognised you on that day.'

'Ah, of course.'

'Was he your friend? Our dead brother, I mean.'

'No, I didn't know him at all.'

The man was puzzled. 'You did not know him? But . . .'

'Please, don't make something of it. I took it from the other funeral which happened to be glutted with the stuff.'

'I see. You are a man of God.'

'I am?'

'Yes. And now please, Mr Sagoe, if I may I would like to come and speak with you at the office.'

'Any time. You know where it is?'

'Yes. I will like to hold important discussions with you.'

The man shook hands and left and Sagoe wondered, what does he think? He had not smiled once since he first met him, had betrayed nothing now through his dark glasses. Who were they anyway, the brethren of the battered Vauxhall and the protruding corpse? As for the albino's part in the rescue of the thief, there was a cool efficiency about him which left Sagoe's nerves a little chilled. Albinos always had, for him, an unsettling effect, seeming not to share with him a normal physical consistency. . . . Sagoe watched the man recede into the lounge, selecting a dark corner of the room by instinct until he could see only the white flesh on the back of the albino's neck as the man drew out an arm-chair. It dived forwards and settled fitfully above the back rest, flitting as he spoke, a pale bat in the corner gloom. Sharply Sagoe silenced his imagination and resolved to forget the man until he should seek him out.

9

In the safety and sense of Bandele's house, Osa always, for Egbo, turned into a senseless but necessary pilgrimage. Within reach, reassuring presence of sounds in an atmosphere which demanded less of himself, less of resources into which a man must needs drill, risky like an oil-well; it could be dry and he would find it out at the moment when his presumption most needed it. There was greater diffusion in for instance the blaring gramophone which lined his way to the office, in the senseless hoot of taxis, the curses of the irate trader and the haggler, in the bureaucratic replica of it all in files and minutes and diplomatic jargon.

Perfunctory doles towards the Union of Osa Descendants . . . messages between the old man and himself . . . all these had built up ties, surreptitiously . . . delegations too, to feel him out, sent by Egbo Onosa as he knew quite well destiny, they always said, you were destined . . . all these and much more . . . his own overwhelming need to retain that link with some out-of-the-rut existence . . . illicit pleasure at the thought that a kingdom awaited him whenever he wanted it, a kingdom through its daughter whose face he could never recapture and he wondered if she had been a bit like his aunt, a restless wind whom the creeks had spawned . . . a subtle thrill of power. It all availed him nothing. The core he had barely touched and he felt it elude him. And this was not now a question of conscience but the progress of wisdom, and for a man himself, merely a question of drowning, for Egbo, resolving itself always only into a choice of drowning . . . like the darkness of the grove and then the other water, the water of the suspension bridge, seeing for a fleeting moment water indeed suspended, a bridge of clear water suspensions. And he only plunged again into the ancient, psychic lie of still sediments, muttering, how long will the jealous dead remain among us!

'Why do you continue to brood?' Always Bandele knew exactly when he flogged his mind over the decision at Osa. 'You brought yourself to the point of a choice, that had to happen, you know.'

'Even that choice is a measure of tyranny. A man's gift of life should be separate, an unrelated thing. All choice must come from within him, not from promptings of his past.'

'You continue to talk of the past as if it has no place with us.'

'It should be dead. And I don't just mean bodily extinction. No, what I refer to is the existing fossil within society, the dead branches on a living tree, the dead runs on the bole. When people die, in one sense or in the other, it should not matter what they were to us. They owe the living a duty to be forgotten quickly, usefully. Believe me, the dead should have no faces.'

'You and Sagoe should get together,' Kola said.

'He is a politician.'

'Meaning? You tell me what new African doesn't spew politics.'

'You see? You don't even know what I am talking about. Can't you get it in your head that your global or national politics don't really count for much unless you become ruthless with the fabric of the past.'

'So what are you complaining about?' Kola asked.

'Nothing. Nothing as far as my head goes.'

'But otherwise. . . ?'

Impatient now, Egbo cried 'Is it so impossible to seal off the past and let it alone? Let it stay in its harmless anachronistic unit so we can dip into it at will and leave it without commitment, without impositions! A man needs that especially when the present, equally futile, distinguishes itself only by a particularly abject lack of courage.'

'Which brings us back to Osa, not so?' Bandele, intruding quietly.

'I am speaking generally now.'

'Sure, sure.' And he laughed, rising to answer the now persistent knocking on his door.

He was back some moments later, waving foolscap sheets before him. 'You see, a present from my students. Yesterday was the deadline but this is the first essay to arrive. Everybody wants to arrange the universe to suit his whims but where does that get me, the other man?'

'No good looking at me,' Kola said. 'I didn't carry us on a Mungo Park excursion down cannibal creek.'

Egbo said, 'I merely say that the dead should be better tucked away. They should not be interfered with because then they emerge to thrust terrifying dilemmas on the living. They have no business to make impositions on us.'

'But there was never any question of an imposition.'

'And I repeat there was. To be manoeuvred towards a choice —never mind by what forces or circumstances, never mind how tenuous the forces . . .'

Kola interrupted him. 'You deliberately throw your resentment to the winds. Throw it on your own head where it belongs.'

Another student interrupted with knocking and Bandele groaned. 'More essays, I guess. By the way, we'd better get moving or we'll be late for Joe's thing.'

'What time is it supposed to be?'

'Nine. Is Sheikh coming?'

'Sheikh?'

Egbo looked round to discover Sekoni sitting motionless by the record-player. 'You know, Sheikh, sometimes you are the most non-existent person in the world.'

'What time is it now?'

'Nine.'

'Let's go. We can continue arguing in the interval.'

But Sekoni had been toiling and he burst with a sudden effort at the threat to the closing of the theme, 'In the d-d-dome of the cosmos, th-there is com . . . plete unity of Lllife. Llife is like the g-g-godhead, the p-p-plurality of its mmmanifest . . tations is only an illusion. Th-the g-g-godhead is one. So is life, or d-d-death, b-b-both are c-c-contained in th-the single d-d-dome of ex . . . istence . . .'

He paused for breath, and Kola stood up, 'Come on Sheikh, let's argue this on the way.'

'No no' Egbo cried. 'He hasn't finished.'

'The recital will be if we don't hurry.'

Bandele returned, flung a new batch of essays on the table. 'Are we going? What do we do about Simi?'

'I'll wait for her here,' Egbo said.

'That means you are going to be late.'

Egbo laughed. 'Well that depends on when Simi comes, doesn't it?'

'And you? I suppose you'll be holding out like mad.'

'I am practically here already. Haven't moved near a woman for weeks.'

Bandele reminded him gently, 'What of Owolebi of the squelching oranges? That was only a fortnight ago.'

'I had forgotten her,' Egbo confessed.

Kola bawled out aloud. 'Forgotten her already? She whose banks were bared. . . .'

'Oh get out.'

'Maybe Egbo found it wasn't a woman at all.'

'Yes, now I think of it you never mentioned her again.'

'You're right. She wasn't a woman, she was just a matriarch symbol . . . and now will you get going?'

'Try at least to make the second half. Joe always sings "Sometimes I feel like a motherless child" towards the end.'

'Bandele will you get that ineffectual artist out of here before I . . .'

'I'm going. You make sure you come.'

'I always do.'

Owolebi? One of many accidents, and the event of the visit home had pushed that right out of mind. Not so Simi. But Egbo doubted if there was ever any waking time when Simi was wholly absent from his mind. For the loss of his 'orphan virginity'—this was how he set it apart from the normal loss of innocence—'woman, you took my orphan virginity, what more do you want!'—this loss came with his first consciousness and fear of sinning. And Fear. Fear itself he thought he had dispersed among the clouds on his first flight, and this knowledge of Fear never again returned until the night in Simi's bedroom when he had felt a terror of the senses, not daring to relive the revelation of the night, for his body was in that instant gelled to the earth and heavens, and the pull of life from within his sensuousness he felt as the rending of heavenly vaults and upheaval in earth's core. No single man had the right to feel what he felt, to command rebellions of the ordered cosmos in the withering of his boastful rise amidst talcumed brambles. And he, only after all a schoolboy, barely cleaned of the schoolfarm sod in his fingernails . . .

Egbo stirred in his sleep, but he had only slept briefly.
  'My dear . . .'
  Suddenly alert, Egbo asked, 'Who touched me?'
  'What?'
  'Somebody touched me.'
  'You are a very funny boy,' said Simi.
  'Funny? Do you believe in God?'
  Egbo could not control the wandering of his tongue. He moved, realising it, towards the big, inevitable dare of life, daring even as he shrank and cowered, daring by his deliberate blasphemy divine revenge on his assertion of the past hour.
  'Why do you ask such a question?' Simi asked.
  'Do you believe in God?'
  'Of course. Doesn't everybody?'
  'Some don't. In my last year in school I nearly didn't. But then I found that whenever I wanted a thing badly enough, I was always full of genuine fear that this Power might thwart me.'
  'Did you persist in what you wanted?'
  'Oh yes. That is how I come to be here.'
  Simi understood after a while, began to stroke his neck with increased gentleness.
  'But what I was going to tell you is this. . . . Some goodness has gone forth from me. . . . And now I will deserve it if God rises and strikes me dead.'
  'But why?'

'Why? Do you mean you don't know who said that?'

'Who did?'

'No, let me not draw you into this. Although I suppose it doesn't really matter. The words had already come into my mind anyway, and the thought is as sinful as the deed. Speaking them out is the lesser crime, isn't that what they teach you?'

'I don't know.'

At that moment, all Egbo desired was to return to his host. He had had no suspicion of such areas of the senses and could not think to know this terror again, to reach the gulfs that bared beneath his feet the threat of sublimation. Desire was an alien thing, Egbo could not remember its existence. He looked towards Lagos again, to the single rented room, to the ledgers in the office and stale buns on monthly credit. Best of all, for that jostling, dangerous cycle ride to the office across Carter Bridge.

'What are you doing?'

'Putting on my clothes.'

'But why?'

'Why? To return to my host of course.'

His voice went suddenly small as she took the clothes back from him. 'You mean . . . you er, expect me to stay here all night?'

'If I had wanted to sleep by myself why should I have brought you here?'

There was no more bluster left, Egbo was whining for pity. 'But I am exhausted.'

'I told you not to overwork yourself.'

'Well, that's too late now, I must get some rest.'

Simi's voice was soft in mockery. 'What is the matter? That was only the beginning. We have still to get to know each other. We have all night, and tomorrow. You don't have to leave for Lagos until late afternoon.'

'Who has such time? But, you mean . . . you actually expect more of me? And where on earth do you think I will get the strength?'

'But you are such a funny person. Do you think you just sleep with a woman once and leave her like that? Don't you know that is only the beginning for her?'

'O-oh, so you want to kill me altogether. You are not interested in the fact that I am probably knobbled for another year.'

'Oh. Where is my filled bag on Warri airfield, enh? So, so, you don't know anything you see . . . come, leave me to show you . . . you see, you don't know anything at all . . . you must leave yourself in my hands.'

And Egbo, astonished at his flesh, unbelieving that from somewhere within him could come again this new pylon of power, in the same night, barely two hours after his first initiation. And after this, the second time, Egbo felt he was like the quarry at Abeokuta when all the granite had been blown apart and nothing but mud-waters of the rain fill the huge caverns underground.

The long, slow train journey to Lagos, Egbo had begun to fasten upon it as the hope of restoration; some balance in his life was upset and he boarded the train that Sunday afternoon feeling distinctly hollowed out, weak, nervous and apprehensive. Someone must know, someone must have born witness to his night of fantasy, when the sorceress Simi took him by the hand and led him into paths and byways of the most excruciating ecstasy. And Egbo was looking into the faces of the passenbers one by one, wondering which of them sensed his transformation. But they only stared back and a woman with four Sunday-school dress children continued to ply him with boiled yams and maize which he declined with diminishing courtesy. And the ticket inspector came and demanded his ticket, but not even he seemed to know.

Egbo never ceased to thrill to the dark rumble of the wheels as the train passed through the bridge at Olokemeji, and to look out at the rocks overrun by Ogun river at its most aloof. The bridge spanned the Ogun where the boulders appeared like those rugged Egba ancients in conclave. They were far-flung toes of the unyielding god, Olumo black of Egba. Always for Egbo, the god expanded through the forest from his seat at Ikereku, his colossal feet thrust through the soft underbelly of earth, for he had come to rest and his tired foot submitted to the soothing run of the waters of Ogun. Egbo deserted the train at Olokemeji, the sweet and heavy dark liqueur smell of coal smoke had turned him drowsy, and Lagos was far and the offices stale and unplaced in these new proportions of life.

Today he would hear that rumble from below the bridge,

for this was what he wished. He walked forward along the rails while the train filled with water and took in ballast, and slid down the slope onto the river banks, pursued by displaced stones and moss and the burden of knowledge of loss and gain, weakened by mysteries of the celebration.

Perhaps after all Simi could weep, for the light-filled waters in rockpools were the weave of Simi's eyes. So Egbo lay on the rocks and waited for the train to run him over with that deep rumble, below here it would sound like the laughter of gods, or of their bottomless menace. Drowsily he reassured himself in scattered mumbles that he could still take a lorry and join the train at another station further down, or even right up to Lagos. The train was not much fun once it was dark, in fact; he decided he would do the rest of the journey by lorry. . . .

He shook off sleep and took off his clothes. It was good to bathe in Simi's tears now that he could, for those eyes looked like eyes which never wept. His swimming was brief, Egbo found he had never known such weariness and he dragged himself back to a rock and stretched out to dry. Soon after the train passed him over, but the chaotic thunder of its wheels flung from girder to girder, from rock to rock, and raising tremors in the pools of Simi's griefs were part of wild dreams that had begun to toss him on the rocks. The train passed into the distance and Egbo was left alone among the rocks, and the closing forest, naked in the coming dark.

In the middle of the night he woke and could not tell where he was. In the middle of the night, groping around in nowhere, no stars, no glow-worms that he could see, the other bank had held the course of rushing bright waters now they were turned black, black as the deep-sunk cauldrons of women dyers and the indigo streams from *adire* hung up to dry, dripping like blood in the *oriki* of Ogun, *to to to to to*. And where was the light of Simi's skin and where were sloes on the bed of the river, and where were light-grains in the toe-grips of Olumo's ponderous nails.

So now, for the first time since his childhood ascent into the gods' domain, Egbo knew and acknowledged fear, stood stark before his new intrusion. For this was no human habitation, and what was he but a hardly ripened fruit of the species, lately celebrated the freeing of the man . . .

And he was remembering the wrung cries of his love-making now . . . In darkness let me lie . . . so now he laughed. In the great yawn of the land the river's run stilled, turned a black choking tongue, he laughed, for the words were hardly dry on his tongue . . . in darkness let me lie . . . cry also . . . in darkness cry; did not his teacher always say, what makes a small boy laugh will make him weep?

He had loved darkness, silent stagnation. But not this roar of deadness and the blindness of its path. Overslept in caverns in the dark dwellings of an avenging God? By whose remote design? Whose Siren stole the touch of teething breezes!

Till he grew bold with fear, and angry, truly angry. What mean trick was this? Whose was the dark-sheltered laughter spying on his plight! And his anger mounted, seeing only the blackmail of fear.

If this be sin?—and he knew that his weakening had come from this so he ended it. If this be sin—so—let come the wages, Death!

And he lay back upon the rocks, and slept.

And morning came, baring lodes in rocks, spanning a grid-iron in the distance; it was a rainbow of planed grey steel and rock-spun girders lifting on pillars from the bowels of the earth. Egbo rose and looked around him, bathing and wondering at life, for it seemed to him that he was born again, he felt night now as a womb of the gods and a passage for travellers . . . Remember your pledge, he prayed, remember your pledge, for I survived this night. Remember my terrors of the night.

He left with a gift that he could not define upon his body, for what traveller beards the gods in their den and departs without a divine boon. Knowledge he called it, a power for beauty often, an awareness that led him dangerously towards a rocksalt psyche, a predator on Nature.

And he made it his preserve, a place of pilgrimage.

'Come,' Egbo said, 'and I will show you a wonder.'

He was alone in the house, Bandele had gone for his lectures and a shy girl stood at the door. She was perhaps nineteen, and she held out sheets of lined foolscap, covered with large unfeminine scrawl. Without taking the essay from her, Egbo wondered how such a frail, nearly fragile creature came to have such monstrous handwriting.

'I only came to leave my essay.'

'I happen to know about that. You should have submitted it yesterday, shouldn't you?'

'Can I just leave it on the table, please?'

'Your tutor is not in.'

'I know.'

'Aha, so you waited until he was out, did you?'

The girl tried to push round him into the house but Egbo filled the doorway with his body. 'Well, will you take it then, if I can't get in.'

'No, thank you. I am not going to help any lazy student.'

'Your friend is no better. We won't get these back till the end of term.'

'O-oh, a disloyal student, enh? How dare you talk of your tutor like that? I will tell him to fail you.'

'Tell him. He knows it's true. If he could he would bring his bed into classes and lecture lying down."

Egbo bowed solemnly, 'I must say I agree with that perceptive observation on my friend.'

'And now may I leave my essay?'

'After that remark, of course.'

Egbo watched her place the essay on the table, waited until she was again on the doorstep, then: 'Stay and talk to me.'

She stopped, frowning.

'Or are you not allowed to do that?'

'There is no question of allowing. But I can't stay, thank you very much.'

'Why not? I am drinking alone, which is bad. I am even lonely, which is worse.'

'Don't bother to try that one on me. It won't work.' She was grown up all of a sudden.

'Good God, are you students that sharp?'

'We are not total fools, you know.'

'All right, all right.'

She waved gaily. 'Good-bye, then. Enjoy your drink but don't get drunk.'

Egbo watched her going off, and all of a sudden he was filled with a great sense of deprivation. He had gone to sleep half-drunk because Simi had not turned up after all, had woken up wondering if Simi truly fulfilled his growing needs, if Simi did not remain unchanged while he . . . he climbed out of bed and stared at the stubble on his chin. There were lines now on his forehead, and only a month ago Simi pulled five white hairs from his head. The fact impressed him enormously and he had stretched them out on a black sheet of carbon. How had he aged so quickly? Twenty-eight and white hairs on his head!

Egbo hurried after the girl. 'You know, you never asked me what the wonder was.'

'What wonder?' She looked at him with a remote amusement.

'Don't you remember? When I opened the door and saw you standing there . . . '

She stopped. 'Oh yes. You said, come and I will show you a wonder . . . something like that.'

'And you never even asked what I meant.'

'I thought at first you were mad.'

'Is that so?'

'Or that you were rehearsing some lines in your head.'

'That is more charitable. And now, will you come with me and see what it is.'

'No thank you. What do you take me for?'

'A coincidence.'

She frowned. 'What is that supposed to mean?'

'Simply that I was thinking of revisiting a shrine of my own making, since I got up this morning I have thought of nothing but that. It's some time since I last made the journey.'

'Well, how does that . . ?'

'Wait, child, I'll get to you.'

'Who are you calling a child?'

'Please . . . don't interrupt now. You see I was just wishing that I could go there with someone, up till now I have always gone by myself. Guarded it jealously. A week ago the thought would have been sacrilege, but now . . . well I can't explain it just like that. I only know that just before you came, I wished I could take someone along.'

'Why me?'

'Why not you? You will do as well as the next person.'

'Oh?' She gave a mock curtsey. 'Thank you for the honour.'

'Well, shall we go? I have to get out the car.'

'Oh, a drive in a car. Is that supposed to impress me?'

'Blast you, girl, and your memorised responses.'

'Thank you, wolf, and your spontaneous designing.'

Egbo stopped, unable to contain his delight. 'You certainly show spirit. In fact, I think you are a very delightful person. Most students I know are not.'

The girl began moving again towards the lecture buildings. 'Well, will you come?'

'I have work to do. Our exams are very near.'

'Finals?'

'No, not yet. But equally important. For me they are.'

'You are a very serious young woman.'

'One needs to be in this atmosphere.'

'Come for the drive anyway. I promise you we will not be long.'

She had turned grave. She seemed to be considering other things, not him at all, and she was worried.

'Perhaps you do not trust me?'

Without looking up, she shook her head. 'No, it isn't that.'

A need to commit the sacrilege—above all, Egbo was aware of this. Perhaps secretly, even for a long time, he had longed to show someone this retreat, the last stronghold of that initiation, to share the trial of his night below the bridge with some human sympathy. And Simi could never be that one. Although the direct cause, Simi never once in all that time appeared to be part of this retreat. Her response would be profane, seeing nothing of the different phases of its character, from bright quick running water to a burial-ground of gods, large granite gravestones above blue-grey lawns of water. She had surprised him once, and then he understood, learning to leave Simi in her own environment for there she was infallible, the one and all time queen. For Simi it was four walls, a radiogram, a rich carpet of Kurdish pile, not crumbling pine needles in the forestry reserves, beside thick columns of ants, beneath the whistle of the wind through cone-gathered pines and wet surmounted globules from rain-tree secreting brown golding gum crystals. Once he made Simi a necklace of these dried crystals and she only said, 'You are a funny boy.'

The girl was asking him 'What do you do?'

'Foreign office. And they only employ men of sterling character.'

'And what is sterling character?'

'Well, that is a little complicated, but it boils down to this—

you may spend your nights in a brothel as long as it is indigenous, but you may not speak to the daughter of a foreign ambassador.'

They drove the twelve miles to Ilugun, on a road that coiled and uncoiled on itself, and Egbo repeated silently, I will show it to her only as a stranger, and never again, never once after that. Admitting also, it is not strange for me to need companionship, to be truthfully without designs. And it was what she sought also, just the impulsive companionship, she was so wilfully independent. 'It is a condition,' she continued to repeat, 'you must never call me after this.'

'Of course not.' She looked up quickly, disbelieving his assent.

'You needn't take it so lightly. Anyway how could I expect you to? You already have your degree so it is all the same to you whether I burn my time or not.'

'You are not very fair.'

'It has happened to my friends, I know what I am talking about.'

'All right, all right, have it your own way.'

At Ilugun they stopped and Egbo bought fresh game, newly roasted on little fires. From beneath his seat came his constant companion, an empty keg, and Egbo began to crawl, looking on both sides into the bush.

'Is someone supposed to meet us here?'

'Yes, but he doesn't know it. Just wait for him to come down.'

'Come down from where?'

'From the god's neck. The Lord of the spiral rib, the palm.'

She was so amused she could not stop laughing. 'Better not laugh to his face,' Egbo cautioned, 'unless you do not intend to drink of his milk.'

'It's you,' she said, 'lugging that great demijohn around with you.'

'Be prepared, always be prepared for the god's descent. Along these tracks they do not know what water is. The palm wine is what comes down from the tree. In the towns water has been invented, even alas in villages. But the palm wine tapper in these wilds stands alone with nothing but air between him and his god. He dares not dilute the sacrament.'

She clapped. 'A marvellous lecture, very inspired . . . stop, stop, that's one.'

'A keg of wine, roast game, a book as the enigmatic thou beside me in my wilderness . . .'

'You like Omar Khayam?'

'I know and like but that one tetrastich—that is the name, isn't it?'

'But what do you mean, enigmatic?'

'If I knew that I wouldn't call you that, would I?'

The path had almost disappeared, but Egbo beat aside the tall shrubs and creepers, swinging the heavy keg from side to side.

'It will serve you right if it slips and breaks.'

'Palm wine does not betray its own, believe me.'

He stopped. 'Watch.'

'Are we near the river?'

'That is some yards to that side. This is something I want you to see.' He appeared to measure his distance from a tree, and satisfied, he parted the bush at a point, 'Follow me. Carefully this time. I don't like to leave a path.'

'What is it?'

'In a minute.' Always he felt this guilt of selfishness. A hundred times he had felt, I should bring Sekoni to see this marvel, and promised, next time I will. They came into a part of the bush which seemed untainted by human breath and there he showed her the desolate cathedrals, ignored now by the fat whitish ants who built them. There were new ones rising slowly from the ground, the structure rose almost before their eyes, swarmed by hundreds of soft white palpitations, busily suckling little hills alive.

'Like a lot of busy monks,' she said.

'It seems so senseless, since they only leave them in the end. Come this way, I will show you the masterpiece.' He parted the leaves some distance away and stood, waiting for her approval as if he unveiled to the world a work of his own creation. 'It is, isn't it,' he asked almost with anxiety, 'the Mother and Child?'

Built spathe form, a broad cowl moulded two figures, uncanny in their realism, like fluid faces in the sky; the wind had given it a rough grain finish and it rose a brown sepulchre amidst dew greenness. The cowl formed an alcove, within it the Mother and Child. A third plane rose behind them both, obelisk, tall against the homage of tassels in the lightest breath.

'Perhaps now I will bring the Sheikh.'

'Bring who?'

'The Sheikh. His real name is Sekoni. He sculpts.'

'Yes, you ought to.'

'If you are not afraid and can stay until the shadows lengthen, you will see it darken behind the pair giving greater depth within the alcove.'

They walked then towards the river, waded through the rockpools to a smooth porpoise back which was Egbo's favourite bed. Egbo looked towards where Olumo brooded, unseen behind twenty miles of intervening forest. 'Don't flick your blasted toe,' he said, 'I have a guest.'

Eating now, she grimaced and said, 'It is not well roasted.'

Egbo took huge draughts of the wine, and held the keg for her while she let it gurgle into her throat. 'Careful, careful,' he warned, 'that thing is untouched by hand or water.'

She watched it run down her chin and onto her chest, sticking the dress to her skin and hurriedly Egbo looked from her small breasts, feeling the tremor in his heart.

'I have never had palm wine which tasted like that.'

'You don't get it by staying in the library.'

And this turned her solemn again. 'Yesterday, no, even this morning, if someone had said I would be sitting in the middle of Ogun, drinking palm wine and eating half-roasted meat...'

Egbo looked at her for a long time before she asked, 'How did you ever come to find this place?'

And Egbo told her of his night of terror beneath the bridge. She sat, disturbing the pool with her feet, her head bowed as the words poured from him, and he relived his passage of darkness.

'And you have never brought anyone here? Not even the woman, Simi?'

'No. It was . . . a night of discoveries and I made them alone. Like waking in the morning and feeling in me a great gift, accepting it without seeking to interpret. I come here often to draw upon that gift and be reprieved. I find I need it more than all my friends, they are all busy doing something, but I seem to go only from one event to the other. As if life was nothing but experience. When I come here I discover, it is enough. I come here, shall I say, to be vindicated again, and again and again. Some day I may find that once has been sufficient.'

'What happened this time that you needed this . . .'

'Vindication? No, it is still too early to talk of that.'

'Don't think I don't understand. Some men turn to other men to be reassured.'

'That is it, to some extent. Their inadequacy is greater than mine.'

'You are not inadequate.'

'You have a gentle nature, but you are wrong. Who dares be adequate?'.

'One can be. It is necessary to be.'

'Not even when you get your first-class honours. Not even when your assumed sophistication settles truly and becomes a part of you.'

'At the least then, wholly self-reliant.'

'Yes, I believe I sense that in you. Like coming out with me. You chose so wilfully, damning your natural suspicion and uneasiness.'

'No, no, you mustn't believe things like that.'

'Because they aren't true? Oh, it is a mark of lonely people and I was full of respect.'

'No, please don't let us talk any more. I don't like your way of putting things.'

'Another bull's-eye, you see. Your instinct serves you right. To continue as we began, we might end by revealing too much of each other.'

'Yes, anything you like, but we must talk of something else. Tell me about the Foreign Office and your diplomatic files, tell me about anything, anything . . .'

Egbo drew her to him. The hardness was only an outside crust, only the stubborn skin on her self-preservation and it gave in his eager hands. The centre pure ran raw red blood, spilling on the toes of the god, and afterwards he washed this for her, protesting shamefacedly, in the river. And Egbo confessed, not since that night of Simi, have I been so nervous, so fearful of the venturing.

She said, 'My exams are next month. You must not try to see me again.'

10

Bandele paused, latch-key in hand. 'I forgot to warn you. I have a guest and you may not like him.'

'For the privilege of escaping Lagos,' Sagoe said, 'I will accept any torment. Who is he?'

'Some journalist hitch-hiking through Africa. Has the most formidable array of camera equipment I ever laid eyes on.'

'English?'

'No, German, but he thinks he is American.'

'Oh?'

'You will probably find him unbearable. I do.'

'If the worst comes to the worst I can go and stay with Kola.'

'I won't advise it. He is grown manic over the Pantheon. Quite unbearable as a social animal.'

There was a stampede of elephants on the stairs, a yell of 'that you, Bandili?' They sensed a leap from the fifth step down and a crash just behind the door. There was a few seconds' fumbling with the knob, filled with sounds which exhorted them to be patient, won't be a minute, what's wrong wirra godamn door, but the door opened suddenly, a pink oval grinned over them, a hairy pink wrench pumped their hands, slapped their backs—how ya bin you son-of-a-gun—tore the bags out of their hands—that your friend from the Foreign Office?—and shoved them into the sitting room with a beer in each hand.

Then the same zoo rushed up the stairs bellowing, 'I had begun to think you weren't coming back tonight how did your friend like America wanna talk to the guy diree ever get to Chicago?'

'Is this a practical joke?' Sagoe demanded.

'I don't know.'

'What do you mean you don't know?' But Bandele only shrugged and sipped his beer. 'Well, this is your house isn't it? So now you keep a private jester.'

'Met him on the compound with Joe Golder.'

'And who the hell is Joe Golder?'

'Sorry, American lecturer, history. You'll run into him some-time. Anyway the next thing I knew Joe Golder had made off and left that clown on my hands.'

'You invited him to stay with you?'

Bandele sadly shook his head. 'Don't remember doing that. But he's here.'

Peter came down again much in the same manner as before. This time he introduced himself formally, 'I'm Perrer. Hi!'

'Are you American?' Sagoe asked. He had no choice but to remain seated. Peter had placed both hands on the arm-chair rests and thrust his face right into Sagoe's. Then he busied himself mixing up all the accents.

'Yeah. Wall, not really. I'm German but I use 'merican passport. Just gonna get m'self a zrink. So soree couldn't come down wi' ze others to Lagos, burra had a date wiz a Minister. I'm a journalist, you know, reckon Bandili told you. Did you paint ze town red last night? Fabulous guy your Minister, real feller of a guy. Invired me to spend a week-end at his country residence.'

'You going?' Bandele's affected indifference amused Sagoe enormously.

'Sure, felt real honoured.'

'Which Minister?' Sagoe asked.

'It could be any. A bit of overseas publicity, gratis.'

'Until the result though, then they'll find they've been mis-quoted.'

'And then it's—Drive them out drive them out who the hell do they think they are how dare they abuse our sovereign integrity with neo-colonialist neo-capitalist reactionary misre-presentation deport the bastards Nigeria we hail thee . . .'

The refrigerator shuddered with unaccustomed violence and Sagoe remembered that Peter was still with them.

'Your friend's a sure funny guy. Wassat he was shouring just now?'

Sagoe spoke under his breath, 'That you seem to me a graft of emptiness on dregs of crushed Aryan bestiality.'

Peter was laughing. 'First you shout so the whole house is shaking zen you whisper so a guy can't even hear one word.'

'That's my nature,' Sagoe confessed.

'So how's life in ze Foreign Office.'

'No spies lately, how about you?'

In a way, Peter reminded him of Chief Winsala, the way he laughed. 'Bandili, your friend is just aboure funniest guy I seen in Africa. You reckon I'm a spy, Bandili?'

'No, I don't think you are a spy, Peter.'

'He ain't like you. Bandili is so solemn but your friend is just aboure cat's whiskers. Couldn't guess in a hundred years he worked in ze diplomatic service.'

'I admire your perception. I don't work in the Foreign Office.'

'Bandili, dig that, ain't he just about ze . . .'

'You were mistaken, Peter, this is Sagoe and he works on a newspaper.'

'But I thought you wuz expecting your friend from the Foreign Office.'

'His plane arrived late. He will be here later.'

Sagoe was puzzled. He looked at Bandele but was silenced with a signalled promise of a later explanation.

'So you're in ze profession!' And he walked over and pumped his hand. 'Well I must confess I really feel at home now.'

Bandele winced.

'Damn your instant implication of life-long familiarity,' Sagoe muttered, turning his face away as the compost vent of Peter's mouth hit him fully. He pushed his way up saying, 'I'll just go up for a wash.'

'How we spending tonight, Bandili? Let's go and celebrate your friend's acquaintance as a fellow-journalist.'

'Actually, I've been asked to some sort of party.'

'Very good. Ve all go.'

Bandele looked very sad. 'Ah, you don't know our families here. It is really a family thing you see.'

'So you take me, huh? I am vun of ze family. I feel I am a Nigerian. I really feel at home you know zat? I don't feel no different from nobody. Already I make so many friends wiz people in ze street, eat at ze roadside shacks just like a common Nigerian.' He stopped, seeing Sagoe take the back-door out. 'Where's your friend going? Hey, that ain't the way to the bathroom. You wanna go upstairs.'

'It's O.K.' Bandele patiently explained. 'He only uses the shower, in the boy's quarters.'

'Gee, that's a reel guy, your friend. A reel guy. You know I like ze sort of guy who don't go for no ceremony. Ha, Bandili,

I gorran idea. First we go to zis party, zen we go to some dive and look up some tarts, what you say?'

'Sure, Peter.'

Peter, after experimenting variously, settled on the whisky and thrust the bottle in his mouth. 'Just whar I like about Yankees. You know when I go to nightclub here people always looking at me cos I drink from bottle. Americans don't waste no time on glasses, zey all zrink from bottle.'

Bandele sighed, mentally writing off the bottle because he would not offer what was left of it to anyone he called a friend. Sagoe had come back into the house muttering, 'That damn fool didn't let me remember to take soap and towel.'

Before he reached the top of the stairs, Peter was after him. Too late Sagoe tried to lock himself in the bathroom but the key had fallen to the floor. Desperately, since the door was now sealed with Peter's wide frame, he turned into the cupboard and made to begin shaving. Furiously he lathered his chin and upper lip so he would not have to open his mouth, wondering had the fool overheard him at last?

'Say, thought you might like a swig while you're shaving. Don't you wanna swig?'

Sagoe shook his head.

'What's zis? Ah, after-shave lotion. Ho ho whisky much better for rubbing on ze skin, you gorner have a drink? Whas merrer c'mmon let's get high. I always get high before I meet my family. Family's always square you know. Reel square.'

'WILL YOU TAKE THAT BOTTLE FROM MY FACE!'

Bandele chuckled to himself and braced for Peter's descent.

'Say, your friend's a sure touchy guy. What's eating him?'

'Ask him.'

'I guess I just don't know what he got so sore about. What the hell, enh? I just offered him a zrink zat's all.' He helped himself to another mouthful. 'You gonna drink, Bandili?'

Bandele shook his head.

'C'mon man, let you and me git reel high.'

'I'm already on beer.'

'Zat's okay, you zrink some visky and chase it wiz beer, yes? C'mon guy whas marrer wiz everyone?'

He thrust the bottle in Bandele's hand and Bandele took it but not quite. The bottle crashed to the floor and Bandele returned calmly to his beer.

138

Peter was up in a broad flash. He picked up the mop and stopped in the doorway of the bathroom long enough to say 'Your friend sure acts crazy. What's he gone and wasted good liquor for?' He sounded truly aggrieved and began to mop the liquor, incessant in ideas for painting first the town, then the night itself, red.

In the garage Bandele stopped. 'You are sure you want to go to the party?'

'Anything to get away from Peter. God, in five minutes that man reduced me to an apprehensive jelly.'

'O.K., let's go.'

'What will he say when he finds we are gone?'

'Oh he'll find us an excuse. He's pretty thick-skinned.'

'What was that business about planes?'

'Only to get rid of him. I said a friend who had been on foreign service in Canada was returning with his family and would be staying with me.'

'Is Egbo coming?'

'He is hardly out of here now. Some little girl has really done for him.'

'I don't believe it.'

'You'll see for yourself.'

'No, I don't believe it.'

The drive was choked with cars at the big party and Sagoe said, 'let's return the car and walk back.' Bandele shook his head.

'The dogs will bark at us. Or bite if they think we are stewards.'

'Yes, I gather they are snobs. What do they do to cyclists?'

'Depends. Stewards get by. Two short barks for lecturers; it means—Commies.'

'I am impressed.'

In the dashboard glow, Bandele's face was dry and straight. 'That is nothing. If you drive any of the bigger models they lie on the road and let you kill them.'

A buzz of wit, genteel laughter and character slaughter welcomed them from the drive and they entered the house of death. From the direction of the punch bowl, a shrill voice—it was a strange dialect of some British tribe—'and then she developed a sudden interest in the madrigal group, so John said, better see what's going on.' General titter, then a deep

139

voice intoning, 'I did think her departure to London was very sudden,' and right on cue again, measured titters.

'Will we ever get through to the bottles, think you?'

'We only need push slightly and they'll withdraw.'

'Wait a minute. I see black faces—are they Nigerians?'

'Appearances deceive, come on.'

Among the bowls of tit-bits—groundnuts, popadums, meat-on-the-stick, and the inevitable olives, Sagoe saw a bowl of fresh fruits and made for it shouting 'To hell with patriotism, Bandele, there is no fruit in the world to beat the European apple.'

'You are deluded,' Bandele said, 'but go find out for yourself.'

Sagoe returned in a fury. 'What on earth does anyone in the country want with plastic fruits...hey...hey, wait a minute Bandele wait a minute. . . .' He was only now seeing the decor of the room and his tongue went click-clicking as he spun slowly in a circle.

'What is the matter? Oh, still on about the fruits?'

'To use Mathias's favourite expression, O-ko-ko-ko!'

From the ceiling hung citrous clusters on invisible wires. A glaze for the warmth of life and succulence told the story, they were the same as the artificial apples. There were fancy beach-hat flowerpots on the wall, ivy clung from these along a picture rail, all plastic, and the ceiling was covered in plastic lichen. Sagoe had passed, he now noticed, under a special exhibition group of one orange, two pears, and a fan of bananas straight from European wax-works.

'I feel let loose in the Petrified Forest. What's the matter with those who live in it?'

'Nothing.'

'Have they petrified brains to match?'

From the area of the truffles, 'I tell you I had to give up my leave on her account. Nephritites simply cannot stand Africans. She's such a sensitive cat. Who was to look after her?'

Bandele gently removed Sagoe's fingers from his arm. 'I heard. I don't need a tourniquet.'

'But did you hear? I mean, did I hear aright?'

'Yes, yes, just face the drinks table.'

'But who is the black fool listening so sympathetically. Who is the bell-boy in the tuxedo?'

'Don't talk so loud. That is the new Professor. It's his party.'

140

'. . . I tell you she positively breaks out in rashes. Simply allergic to Africans. Oh she is such a dar . . . ling.' And again the Professor nodded with understanding.

'But if she were talking to a fellow white I would understand. . . .'

And gradually, beginning from his fingertips Sagoe felt a strange excitement. A crawling sensation over his skin of a dubious and dangerous anticipation.

A woman approached. 'I think,' Bandele began, 'this is where you pay for your drinks. You should have put on a tie.'

'What do you mean?'

'The hostess approaches. Good luck.'

'Good evening, Bandele,' the woman said, 'I didn't see you come in.'

And the excitement grew until Sagoe found he needed a pee.

'I was very late, I'm afraid. I have only returned from Lagos.'

'You mean you drive on that road at night? It is very dangerous, you know . . . those madmen. I always make my husband take the driver if he simply must travel at night.'

'I was determined not to miss your party.' Bandele said, and Sagoe nearly dropped his drink.

'Isn't it sweet of you to say that. Who is your friend?'

Sagoe sharply forestalled him. 'We only met on the steps, didn't have time to introduce myself. I am Edward Akinsola, you must be the hostess,' humming inside him . . . bells on her fingers, Big Ben on her toes, and she shall have B.O. in spite of her rose . . .

She extended a hand—gloved. Gloved elbow length. 'How do you do? We haven't met before have we?'

'No I don't think so.' Sagoe took the glove . . . what have you got inside it, woman, a slithery fish?'

'You must be new in college, of course.'

'I have just arrived from America.'

'A-ah, the States. That explains it, of course.' Sagoe stared and waited for her to explain what explained what, and she obliged. 'Americans are so informal, aren't they?'

Sagoe, caught off-balance, felt outraged. But she beat him to a possible retort asking 'Have you started lecturing?'

'No, I have been doing some research' . . . and to begin with, research me why your bulbous navel sprouts an artificial rose. . . .

'I forgot, lectures are over in fact. Mostly exams and things at the moment.'

'Indeed,' said Sagoe, 'exams and things.'

She smiled sweetly, 'Ayway you will need the time to settle down first. Always a difficult thing to settle down after one's student days I am sure. I always think it is terrible for students to be put straight to lecture, very difficult to re-adjust. Bandele, bring him to us for tea won't you?'

'With the greatest pleasure, Mrs Oguazor.'

'Did you manage to find something to eat, by the way? It was only a buffet supper. If you hurry you might get some . . .'

. . . the plastic apple was nice thank you . . . but Sagoe only simmered, silenced, and to make it worse, Bandele was chuckling as the woman turned her back and left.

'What the bloody hell do you find to grin at?' Sagoe exploded.

'You. That was touché.'

'I don't see what was so bloody touché about it.'

'Don't feel so bad. You didn't do too badly yourself, only, for people like that, you really have to be prepared.'

A concentration of clucking in one corner of the room, just by the stairs. All the women had somehow sifted together and stood waiting for something. Sagoe turned to Bandele to ask if the party was over when the professor himself approached them.

'I thought Ceroline was here.'

'She was a moment ago.'

'Oh der, end the ledies are wetting for her.'

Just then Mrs Oguazor herself emerged from a group and came to the professor.

'Ceroline der, the ledies herv been wetting for you.'

'I know. I was just looking for you to tell you we must go upstairs. Will you handle things at this end?'

'Ef cerse der.'

'Ah I see you've met the *new* lecturer'—and Sagoe distinctly perceived the exchange of understanding—'I have asked Bandele to bring him to tea; he is not yet used to things here.'

From the marionette pages of Victoriana, the Professor bowed. The contempt in his manner was too pointed for any error, and it was with the greatest difficulty that Sagoe refrained from looking down to see if his fly was unbuttoned.

'Cem en der,' and the Professor took his good lady's hand, 'we mesn't keep the ledies wetting.'

Caroline accorded Bandele another teaspoon smile and they watched her diminish in little rustles.

'I told you, you should have put on a tie.'

'Have I disgraced you?'

'Oh yes you would have done, irreparably. But you forget you told the lady that I didn't know you.'

'Of course. Just as well. I have a sixth sense for these things. Though I'd better not risk your reputation.'

'It's ruined, don't you worry. The politeness is the barest they can manage for me.'

'Why do you bother to attend their party, then?'

'But don't you enjoy just watching people sometimes, especially when you know they can't stand the sight of you?'

'That's a queer taste.'

'Not so queer as theirs. Why did they invite me?'

'If I may presume to say so, there didn't seem much strain between them and you.'

'That is what is known as civilisation. We are all civilised creatures here.'

The hall was clear. The women crowded the foot of the stairs, awaited the final summons for ascent. The men, house-trained and faultless, had created a Men's Corner at the opposite end of the room. A few did require manoeuvres by the professor, but his suggestions were imperceptible. Coffee came and cigarettes were counter-offered. By tacit understanding, their backs were turned on the stairs until such time as the women would have completely disappeared. It was all so gracefully managed that Sagoe was lost in admiration. The Professor was whispering to them that the ground-floor lavatory was all theirs, but Sagoe had found it much earlier. Excitement loosened him in short drips like a dog, and in some strange perverted manner, he felt a tingle of excitement fan out in him until it seemed some event must happen suddenly or he would die of heart failure.

The stairs movement took unnecessarily long, sabotaged by the efforts of a young girl in the middle of the floor, patiently explaining a point of disagreement to two wildly gesticulating gloves. Some moments earlier she had been engaged in animated conversation with some male guests, but they made a graceful departure when Mrs Oguazor appeared and coughed lightly behind them—no more word was needed. The girl was however ignorant of signs. And when Mrs Oguazor finally explained the point, her reply was

'Oh later perhaps, thank you Mrs Oguazor.'

The interval had grown quite embarrassing before Sagoe caught the first words from the pair.

The girl was saying, 'But I don't feel like going.'

And the hostess, her sweetness dissolving slowly down her face, 'Mrs Faseyi, you are keeping the others waiting.'

The girl's voice remained a patient whisper. 'I assure you I don't want to go upstairs.'

'My dear, you are being very awkward. All the ladies retire upstairs at this point. They are waiting for you dear.'

'But I don't want to go.'

'These details of common etiquette cannot be really strange to you. And if they are, simply watch the others and follow their example.' She had grown more terse.

'I used the ground-floor toilet about ten minutes ago. I don't feel like going again so soon afterwards.'

'The point is not whether or not you. . .' Her voice pitched suddenly high and she caught herself, glanced quickly round. The few men who had looked round quickly obscured recognition with huge puffs of smoke. Sagoe cast aside all sense of decency and moved nearer to eavesdrop, while the women turned positive backs on the girl's disgrace. Mrs Oguazor tried syrup once again. 'My dear, the point is this, all the ladies have to go upstairs. Perhaps you'd like to adjust your make-up or . . .'

'But I don't use make-up.'

'Surely you will want to freshen up, Mrs Faseyi. And anyway if you don't come, you'll be left alone with the men.'

'Oh I don't mind at all.'

'You are being impossible, Mrs Faseyi. And from you of all people. I don't understand why you choose to upset everyone in this manner.'

Her eyes opened wide. 'I have upset someone?'

'Now come on, that's a good girl.' Commanding now, she took her arm. 'Come along now.'

The girl arrested her rush by placing a friendly hand on

Caroline's shoulder. 'You take the others. But don't leave me alone too long.'

This should have been the end, and a few days before it would have been. But this was her first social evening as the Professor's wife, and the scene—it could no longer be disguised —had become public. And she, a rare species, a black Mrs Professor was faced with the defiance of a young common housewife, little more than a girl, in her own house, publicly, and the code of etiquette was on her, Mrs Oguazor's, side!

'You will come with us at once,' said Caroline, 'or don't ever expect to be invited to my house again.'

And the girl said simply, 'Oh, I understand that.'

It was the women who came to the rescue. Mrs Oguazor was prepared now to leave, but the hall had lengthened in the meantime and the distance was bare and endless to where they were herded. Across this desert loped salvation, the gaunt Mrs Drivern, wife of the gynaecologist.

'I think we've waited long enough, Mrs Oguazor.' She seized the grateful woman by the glove, threw a proud hump at the outcast and trooped ahead of forty-odd moral supports to the forced sanctuary of supped ladies.

Sagoe said, 'Is the girl's husband here?' And when Bandele nodded he asked, 'What do you bet I pick him out first time?'

'Nothing. That would be no guess.'

Sweat had broken free on the neck of a husband. Nothing kept him earthed but the desperate wish that the floor might open and swallow him. His motions became palsied and his palms clammed on a cigarette until it snuffed out.

'He'll take off,' Sagoe said. 'The earth won't swallow him so he'll take off. On the wings of his bow-tie.'

'He is already framing his apology. I know Ayo.'

And they heard his glass rattle on a table, and Mr Faseyi squared his back, turned to reveal the resolution of a man on trial, dissociation from a wife's conduct—by instant reparation.

Simultaneously, Bandele and Sagoe set off for the floor centre.

'You have to live with them. Better keep out.' And he firmly pushed Bandele back.

But even Sagoe was too late. Kola was just coming in with Egbo when the scene began and had remained watching from the door. They saw him walk briskly to the girl who stood so starkly isolated, talk briefly to her and then begin quite crazily to do a slow High Life to the ballet music playing softly from hidden loudspeakers. Sagoe retrieved his glass, saying with mock disgust 'This place is crawling with Sir Galahads.'

The record was Popular Pieces from Famous Ballets and the pair merged their slow high life to the contribution from Swan Lake. In the corner Faseyi sweated, thrown, irresolute. This husband would wait but a tightening of the back warned him of a watchful Professor and he stepped forward.

'Fash!' It stopped him. He turned and was relieved to find that it was only Bandele. 'Ah, hello, sorry just leaving.'

'With the dancing just beginning?' And then Bandele produced his brainwave. 'Or do you have to go and lock in the boys?'

'Enh. Sorry . . . I . . . what did you say?'

'Stop pretending. Everyone knows you've got the warden job in Shehu Hall.'

'Enh, what's that? Enh? Where did you hear this?' He became a rotor dog, a wet bone at both ends of a whistle. 'You mean you heard something . . .'

'Oh come off it, Fash . . .' And then the record was snapped off. The Professor gravely laid the pick-up aside, wasting no glance on the dancers' profanity.

Sagoe was not drunk but he felt that excitement again. The Professor was returning to his group, the dignity of his home restored, protected in an armour of righteousness.

'Jolly good.' Above the hush Sagoe's voice rang out startling, 'Let's have a juju or a twist instead.'

It halted the Professor in his stride and the Men's Corner went silent with indignation. Glasses stayed in the air as when the toastmaster has fallen flat on his face. It was the silence that follows a bounced cheque, the silence—felt Sagoe—of a makeshift voidatory.

The Professor moved at last, his face set so that each guest began to ask his neighbour, 'I hope it wasn't you who brought him,' and sighed, disappointed that the candidate had not lost his chance of nomination to some committee.

By all appearances however, J. D. Oguazor was dismissing the whole episode from his mind. A new Professorship called for new virtues, like—magnanimity. His face appealed for calm, dignity and restraint in face of barbarous provocation.

The company responded, the chatter was slowly resumed. Egbo joined Kola on the floor and Sagoe followed almost immediately, but the husband drew Bandele back, began to question him about the wardenship. All rumour, Bandele insisted, but rumours from important quarters.

Finally he invited Bandele to lunch.

Lecturer Grade III Adeora managed to discover where the President of Guinea had lunched when he visited the university, then recounted an intimate conversation they had together shortly after that lunch. 'Yes yes. Had lunch with him. Capital fellow.'

Nnojekwe asked the Professor for fatherly advice on when he should take his annual leave, then praised the brass chandeliers on the four walls. 'Chandeliers?' asked the Professor. 'Oh, oh yes,' Oguazor, scared to be ignorant, failed to perceive the trap. 'Very expensive they are bet Caroline wanted them so badly.'

And Nnojekwe drew him out a little further, then returned to his group to transmit Oguazor's latest.

From Dr Lumoye, '. . . this is really confidential, you know, but did you know one of the girls is pregnant?' Gasps of horror. 'Second year student, came to me in my clinic and asked me if I would help her. Man, that kind of thing I don't do, that's what I told her. I advised her to wait out the remaining weeks and go home and let her parents handle it.'

'That's the last thing she'll want. Most of them can't expect any sympathy from their family.'

'Well she won't get *that* kind of sympathy from me I tell you. I'm not risking seven years for someone else's pleasure. If I tasted of it myself I would at least have something to show for it . . .' And the laughter rose genteel above the champagne bubbles.

Professor Singer was playing with an ash-tray and Oguazor beamed on him. 'Do you like that?'

'Rather nice, oh yes indeed, rather nice.'

'Got them for my wife's birthday. Six of them. And those chandeliers on the wall.'

'Sorry . . . er . . . what did you say?'

'The brass ones. Useful things to herve around the house. I am a rather prectical man with presents. And Ceroline is very fend of chendeliers.'

147

Professor Singer spent the rest of the evening trying to locate brass chandeliers on walls.

In the house of deaths where brains were petrified for Dehinwa's wardrobe handles, Sagoe looked up again and discovered clusters of green grapes and black draped from wall brackets and dripping with the shine of evergreen synthetic leaves.

Dr Ajilo denied that he took prostitutes home. Never further than his garage, he swore, but Oguazor was just behind him, and he was not amused.

'Those madrigals. Useful grounds, you know, then the husband began to suspect the late rehearsals . . .'

'They say Mr Udedo can't even pay his electricity bills. What does he do with his money?'

'Who is Salubi going with these days? That boy is morally corrupt I tell you. He doesn't even keep off the students.'

'Wen of these days,' Oguazor was saying, 'the Senate will charge him with meral terpitude.'

A scarf of a man aimed himself at Bandele and found himself alone with Sagoe. 'Hold him off if you can,' Bandele muttered, dissolving instantly in the crowd. Sagoe was now fully in the power of his excitement. He achieved the weightlessness of a true Voidante after an enema—the company was castor to a Voidante psyche.

'You must be the turnip,' was Sagoe's salute.

'I beg your pardon?'

'The turnip. The turnip is missing. I've seen apples and pears. Even plastic mistletoes although I won't ever look that way if I see Ceroline standing under it. Would you?'

'I beg your pardon.'

'I said, are you the turnip?'

'Who are you, I don't believe I understand you.'

'You don't? Don't you speak English?'

'Ha ha. I should think I do indeed. English all the way and not ashamed of it.'

'In that case I beg your pardon. Wrong person.'

'That's all right. I did think it was all rather strange. My name is Pinkshore.'

'Pinkshawl?'

'No. Pinkshore, ha ha. Are you new in college?'

'Yes and no. I am the Professor's son-in-law.'

Sagoe felt his duty was now ended, Bandele had safely disappeared and he lost interest in the man. But Pinkshore now appeared to adopt him, following him every step around the hall. At first he thought he had acquired cultivation value as the professor's son-in-law, but this was a mistake. Pinkshore knew all about the professors and deans and registrars and the chancellors vice pro and real and senate councillors and chairman and their families down to the most intimate detail and he knew the simple fact that Professor Oguazor had three sons and one five-year-old daughter only and the daughter gave him much sorrow and pain because he could not publicly acknowledge her since he had her by the housemaid and the poor girl was tucked away in private school in Islington and in fact was Oguazor's favourite child and the plastic apple of his eye . . . so it was obvious to him that Sagoe was an impostor who had come to steal the silver and it was a good thing to perform small services for this new black élite which he secretly despised but damn it all if the asses are susceptible to fawning and flattery let's give it them and get what we can out of them while the going is good.

So Pinkshore stuck to Sagoe and there was no dodging him, He became quite an obsession and Sagoe ran out of the most sadistic schemes for getting rid of the plague.

And suddenly Pinkshore appeared to wilt. An animal noise came from his throat and his eyes popped in alarm. He retreated three rapid steps, bumping into a small gathering and Sagoe gathered his senses back to the immediate and understood why. In his hand was another of the apples and his hand was pulled back to send it after its brother. Vaguely he recalled that his hand had gone through a similar motion within the past . . . but time was now diffused for him—he could not recall the actual start to the ejection act. Two bright refractions indicated the flight of Pinkshore's glasses and the Shawl curved to pick them up. Before he straightened the apple was through the window and Sagoe picked up a pear from the next wall fruit-bowl. Pinkshore reeled, drunk on astonishment as Sagoe from whisky and euphoria.

'What . . . what the devil do you think you are doing?'

'Feeding the dog.'

'Are you trying to be funny? That was the Professor's property you threw out of the window.' Sagoe sent out the pear.

'Are you mad? What right have you to throw away those things?'

'What things?'

'The decorations. And don't pretend you don't know what I'm talking about.'

'They are fruits—not decorations.' And he threw out the bunch of bananas.

'Stop it or I'll report you to the professor.' And Pinkshore moved in on him.

'If you come nearer, I will call in the dog.'

'Don't try to clown your way through this.'

'Clown? So that's all it seems to you. Look out if you like, only watch out for the tip of your nose. He's savage.' He decided to throw the bowl as well but the hostess was upon him now. He raced her to the first words, and won.

'Before the party ends, may I offer my congratulations to you for the appointment of your husband to a professorship?'

'That is kind of you but would you mind telling me ... ?'

'I see now why it's a tuxedo party. That kind of event deserves nothing but mourning dress.'

'Just tell me who you are and why you have been throwing the decorations through the window.'

'But I told you, madam, I am the UNESCO expert on architectural planning.'

'Frivolity,' and she gave the dead stare, 'does not amuse me.'

'He must be drunk, Mrs Oguazor,' said Pinkshore.

'That is a lie, you anaemic Angle.'

'To what department do you belong sir?'

'Architecture.'

Very sharply she retorted, 'There is no department of architecture in the university.'

'I am hardly surprised madam. Just look at the buildings, enh? Work of amateurs!'

'Will you please . . .'

'Of course your own house is very charming. Obviously an outside job.'

She swung on starch and Sagoe knew she was looking for her husband. For Pinkshore it implied a sentence of failure, and a situation like this seemed built for him. He planted his indefinite frame before Sagoe and began, 'Look here, my friend. I think you're a gate-crasher.'

'Of course he is!' and she swung back.

Suddenly Sagoe asked, 'Do you keep hedgehogs?'

Pinkshore retreated in fright. 'Because'—and his smile was benign—'my neck is tickling from poisonous spines.' He looked round the guests studiously, nodding each time with discovery.

Pinkshore whispered, 'We had better get help, Mrs Oguazor. I think he's mad!'

'Ha you think so, enh!' He snarl was manic, straight from the last bullet of the 46th floor last-stand films. Pinkshore yelled aloud and fifty heads turned in their direction. Sagoe saw the Professor apologising his course through glass and smoke and he began to consider retreat.

'On second thoughts, madam,' he bowed. 'I will retrieve your plastic cornucopia. If this butler of yours is right and they are decorations, the dog would not have touched them. He's a real choosy bitch.' And before Mrs Oguazor could guess his intentions, he raised her hand and kissed it.

Oguazor arrived just then. 'Congratulations, Prof,' he fawned on him. 'Many happy returns of today.' Sagoe hesitated, then decided his host was not really of ministerial rank and so he wouldn't kiss his hand. He contented himself with two vigorous pumps of Oguazor's hand. And he bent with a speed which suprised himself, sniffed the plastic rose which decorated Mrs Oguazor at the navel and sprang up again holding his nose to heaven in aromatic bliss.

'Like real, Caro. Like real.' And he shot from the room like mad.

He walked rapidly, half-expecting some form of pursuit but unable to tell why. A neighbouring dog began to bark and he stopped. His heart was pounding and the excitement was not quite over. He began to retrace his steps, making no resistance at all to the madness that urged him on. Round the back of the house, squeezing between the shrubbery that fenced off Oguazor's home, he slipped suddenly but recovered, looking down he saw the cause, it was one of the plastic lemons he had thrown out. Sagoe picked it up. He skirted the house bending low in the shadows until he found the window. They were all there, undoubtedly they were discussing him. Pinkshore leant out from time to time to see if any of the fruits were lying about in the garden. Sagoe closed his eyes saying, Pinkshore, really you shouldn't tempt me. And he counted five to give him what he called a sporting chance. But Pinkshore stood there still, a little to one side now, saying something to the Oguazors. The fruit was light and Sagoe crept nearer saying, Winds be still . . . and flung the lemon. It took Pinkshore full on the mouth, soft, wet from the grass and sudden. His brain spinning instant solutions found mysterious terror—witch-moth, bat shit, murder, knobkerry, death, africa at night . . . . Pinkshore, ignorant of the fact, levelled up with his assailant by passing out on his hosts.

PART TWO

11

The rains of May become in July slit arteries of the sacrificial bull, a million bleeding punctures of the sky-bull hidden in convulsive cloud humps, black, overfed for this one event, nourished on horizon tops of endless choice grazing, distant beyond giraffe reach. Some competition there is below, as bridges yield right of way to lorries packed to the running-board, and the wet tar spins mirages of unspeed-limits to heroic cars and their cargoes find a haven below the precipice. The blood of earth-dwellers mingles with blanched streams of the mocking bull, and flows into currents eternally below earth. The Dome cracked above Sekoni's short-sighted head one messy night. Too late he saw the insanity of a lorry parked right in his path, a swerve turned into a skid and cruel arabesques of tyres. A futile heap of metal, and Sekoni's body lay surprised across the open door, showers of laminated glass around him, his beard one fastness of blood and wet earth.

It helped Egbo not at all that he fled to the rocks by the bridge until the funeral was over where unseen he shed his bitter angry tears, or Sagoe locked in beer and vomit for a week and Dehinwa despairing of his temperature, battling to keep him quiet while he bawled you're wetting me all over with your goddam tears. And he would only rest when she agreed to retrieve his Books of Enlightenment and read to him from a random page.

'. . . I remember at this period of my childhood, and the door of our huge sprawling guaranteed eternal dug-out, a portrait in colour of a pair of supra-human beings, ethereal, other-existential in crowns and jewels, in wide fur borders, gold, velvet and ermine, with orbs and sceptres and behind them, golden thrones. These images in my child's eyes, and—

lest any ideological significance be attached to the portrait's location, these portraits were present also in the parlour and in the bedrooms, for my people were staunch royalists—in my child's eye, these two figures could be no less than angels, or God and his wife. It was a critical phase in my introspection and if I had been in this country where all the facilities are available, I would undoubtedly have graduated into a full-time schizophrenic. For it became an obsession with me, the limitations on this delicate, unreal pair. Did they, or didn't they? As in a séance, the solution came with blinding simplicity. In one session of a purely Voidante nature, I realised finally the attitudinal division within this human function. They would be Voidantes; but Christ, never the other!

To shit is human, to voidate divine.

This was the Birth, the concrete formulation of Voidancy . . .'

To Bandele fell the agony of consoling Alhaji Sekoni, his vow violently cancelled for ever and penance insinuating its vague salvation into his knotted grief, confused, so confused he sat and watched his mind dissolve round notions of penance, some penance sought, some penance required and he could not know what it was, unless this, the loss was the penance, but Alhaji Sekoni could not say or feel . . .

And Kola's brush raised itself again and again, faltered and worked blindly in spasms of grief and unbelieving . . .

Egbo, returning late at night from the river, met Bandele sitting in the dark, the suit he wore to the graveside still on him. Startled to find the death-still figure in a room he had thought empty, he moved at once to the switch, but Bandele's voice stopped him.

'It's me. Don't switch on the light.'

'Bandele?'

'Yes.'

'Oh, I'm sorry.'

'There is a note for you on the table, a girl brought it.'

Egbo took the note and went past Bandele towards his room, leaving him seated rock-like in the dark.

It came from the strange girl. 'I remember' she wrote, 'You spoke of a sculptor friend of yours called Sekoni. I am sorry about his death. I would come if I thought you needed me, but I am sure you would rather be by yourself. I am very, very sorry.'

She signed it but he could not read the name. And for the first time, it occurred to him now, he did not know her name.

A fortnight after the funeral they all met again, listening listlessly to another group of wandering players and the long wail of a horse-tail bow on a string and a sound-box of calabash.

Across the floor, an albino sat slanted like a leprous moonbeam without the softness. Freckles on his face like poisoned motes, dark scabs, and they floated on sheer phosphorence of the skin. Kola, busy on his everlasting serviettes, blurred the details, dissolving chicken grease blobs in sallow depths of the man's cheek and eye hollows. In the end he relegated him to a brooding speck on a cabaret of wild whoops and fire-eaters. The drumming had turned brisk for the floorshow, it was the familiar beat that announced the guttural entry of the witchdoctor in foreign films on Africa.

'I have never solved the mystery of that rite,' Kola said. 'The fire-eating certainly looks convincing.'

Dehinwa cast yet another apprehensive glance at the albino. 'Who does he know here? Why does he keep looking this way?'

Without looking back, Sagoe asked 'Do you mean the albino?'

'You've seen him too?'

'It's me he wants. I don't know how he discovered my haunt.'

'You? What does he want with you?'

'I'd like to know that too. But I am not really in the mood.'

. . . *oyekoko moniran . . . oyekoko moniran . . . oyeroba, oyeroba. . . .*

'In the States,' Sagoe said, 'there was a group who called themselves the Authentic Cobra Maidens of Kokokabura. If I didn't look back I would think they were exactly the same gang. Same war-yells, same tone of gibberish, same clowning. The only difference is the costume, in the States they really go to town.'

. . . *oyeyeye moniran . . . yiaooow!*

157

'I wish,' Egbo prayed, 'the rain would start again and snuff it out.'

Over his calloused soles, his glistening arms, over his war-painted body the fire-eater ran the flames and he let them linger.

Now he was taking the torch round to demonstrate the heat. He passed by the albino and the man shaded his eyes in discomfort as the torch was whirled round, caught and thrust suddenly at him. Kola shouted 'Look at him, quickly', but the flame had gone to the next table and a man lit a cigarette from it.

'What was it?'

'Too late now. You should have seen the albino against the flames.'

The man had recovered and was his street-neon pallor again. He sat like a drowned cadaver, sitting bent as if he would quarrel with gravity.

'He is not a bit like Usaye,' Kola remarked. 'Usaye is soft, quite beautiful in fact. When she is seventy she still would not look like that albino.'

'But she did repel you at the start. You said so.'

'Only very little and that soon passed. She is cast in a wholly different clay, she is quite an astonishingly formed thing, I never quite get over her. But that man looked like yellow bark soaked eternally in *agbo* and boiled tough and arid.'

The pirouetting fire-eater leapt up suddenly and slipped off the edge landing in a small puddle beside a banana clump. His acolytes rushed to help him up, his torch a sorry drip, belching dark smoke and the smell of kerosene. His paints were running, designs which he had perhaps copied from the film of Tarzan's Adventures with the Authentic Cobra Maidens of Kokokabura.

'The night-club salesman of Sango,' Egbo announced, 'has defected to more watery deities.'

But they all felt a little like that, flat. Sekoni's death had left them all wet, bedraggled, the paint running down their acceptance of life where they thought the image was set, running down in ugly patches. They felt caught flat-footed and, Kola thought, not a bit like the finished work tonight, more like five figures from my Pantheon risen from a trough of turpentine.

Dehinwa alone was certain of it—they should not come here. Habits have to change when memory becomes unbearable, and Sekoni had been too much a part of a union they took so much for granted, and these were the physical facts, inescapable, like meeting at the Cambana nearly every fortnight and at the Mayomi in Ibadan the following fortnight. These were the accidents that grew into set habits, reminders among several more of Sekoni who was more oppressively with them now than the strain of his stuttering intensity ever was.

'He's coming,' Dehinwa hissed between her teeth. Sagoe turned round and met the albino with faked cheerfulness. What did the man want anyway? 'Well well, I wasn't too sure it was you. So, you finally ran me down enh?'

'It was not easy, but at last I found your messenger . . .'

'Mathias?'

'Yes, that was the name he gave me. And he told me that this is your favourite place for passing the night.'

'Sit down, sit down, take my chair. It's all right, I'll get another.'

And, almost imperceptibly, Dehinwa shrank as the albino took the chair next to her.

Sagoe returned with a chair and the man began speaking almost at once, in a tone which mixed deference with a great degree of his own sureness. 'Mr Sagoe, I will not disturb you more than necessary, but, as a newspaper man, you can help me.'

He dug into the pockets of his kaftan, bringing out a wallet. From it, he extracted a plastic envelope in which was an old faded piece of newsprint. Through the browned plastic, it was evident that the cutting had probably resided long in a book, folded in sharp edges. Alarmed then at the fragility of the important document, its owner wisely found it a plastic envelope, and now it could be viewed and read without fraying the edges or eroding the precious words.

Sagoe held it to the light and read. He looked again at the albino and passed the envelope to Bandele. In turn they all read it without comment, looking only at the man before them with some mixture of wonder and scepticism. They all waited for Sagoe to deal with this. The stranger was after all, his man.

Sagoe took the cutting from Dehinwa and returned it to him. 'How long ago was this?'

'Nearly six years.'

'Perhaps I should ask first, why did you want to see me?'

'Why? As a newspaper man and a man of God, you can help us.'

'Us?'

'Yes, my church. When the great event happened to me and I rose from the dead my life no longer belonged to me. I offered it to God.'

Bandele said quietly, 'The cutting does not tell much, will you tell us some more?'

'Yes, I know. It is no more than a news item, and indeed what more could it be, except between me and my God. I fall dead in the streets of a strange village. The kind people bury me the following day, only, as they are lowering the coffin into the grave, I wake up and begin to knock on the lid. That is all that is open to the eye of mortal witnesses.'

Egbo found that he was trying to guess the albino's age, but it was impossible.

Lasunwon was thinking how it happened everyday. Why, only the other day, some poor man woke up in a mortuary, how careless these doctors can be, Christ, what a horrible thought.

Kola, his mind was full of fantasies—what should one make of this stranger's timing, so soon after Sekoni's death? . . . and yes, now doctors even talk of 'apparent' death, what does it mean then, death or no-death, for instance, Sekoni, as he was lowered into the grave, suppose a sudden knock was heard and Sekoni stammering, lllet me out, lllet me out . . . and Kola found he was boring into the man's face as if he thought to see the Sheikh's face de-metamorphosed from the albino's . . . from the face of mottled yellow chewing root wrung of all living juice . . .

Dehinwa longed for Sagoe's arm to cling to, thinking, I knew there was something unnatural about him . . . as if he had no natural blood . . .

Sagoe started suddenly, as a new thought struck him. He looked sharply at the man but did not speak. The albino continued.

'I do not know what I was before I died, or where I came

160

from, but what really frightened the villagers is that before they put me in the coffin, I was like you, like all your friends, black. When I woke up, I have become like this.'

Sagoe remarked, 'The paper says nothing of that.'

'How could they!' the albino replied, 'would they believe it? Do you? In the short time I was put in that coffin, to change into an albino! But they all said it, and the nurse of the Rural Health Centre where I was first taken. She told me with her own mouth.'

Lasunwon burst out, 'What a horrible fate! You know, there should be safeguards against this sort of thing. It could happen to anyone. Just think of it, to be buried alive!'

The albino's face hardened, but only Sagoe who was next to him noticed it. 'I was not buried alive. I was dead.'

Lasunwon laughed now. 'Surely you don't believe you actually died. If you are alive now you couldn't have died. A coma perhaps or something like that, there are medical explanations for that sort of thing.'

The albino turned to Sagoe, 'What I want to do is to invite you to the service in our church. I will like you very much to come, because it is a special service.'

Bandele said, 'But can you say . . . can you recollect— what you felt? You understand, during that period when you —woke and began to bang the coffin.'

'I will like to tell you, but everything has appropriate time. A matter like that, how can one talk of it in this place, where life looks cheap. But if you come next Sunday to my church . . .'

Egbo's eyes had never left the man, they gleamed with morbid intensity, seeking like the rest to extract from his face the essence of the man's experience. The albino stood up.

'I invite your friends also to come, they also can help us.' He left, bowing courteously to the group.

'But your church, where is it?'

'Ah, I forgot, you don't know that. But it is not possible to describe it, so I shall send someone to guide you.'

'You know my house?'

'No, but we met somewhere before, at the Hotel Excelsior, where a young man was being chased as a thief. Can we meet you there?'

'All right, what time?'

'Our service begins at eight in the morning. A guide will be there from seven-thirty.'

'All right. I'll be there.'

'Please, don't forget, you can help us and so can your friends. If you all come I will be honoured in the service of the church.'

The man was hardly out of hearing before Lasunwon broke out, 'He doesn't really believe that, does he? Is he really thinking he died?'

Sagoe said 'It wasn't even that, I was thinking. What occurred to me was that cutting needn't refer to him at all.'

Bandele nodded. 'Yes, that is true.'

'You are right,' Lasunwon cried, 'and that business of a change of pigment made it even more fishy. Surely the newspapers would have mentioned that.'

Kola said, 'Yes, that is pretty hard to swallow. In fact it is a right fish-bone across the throat.'

'Well, what do you think then,' Sagoe asked, 'is he a washout?'

'He has me curious,' Kola admitted. 'Is he just another of the local prophets?'

'I only met him about six, maybe seven weeks ago when he rescued a pickpocket from a howling mob. Also at a funeral. But he could be another of our locals getting a new slant on publicity. That item for instance, he could have seen it in some old newspapers and cut it out for future use. It's good business these days, religion.'

'Just the same . . . well, what do you say, Bandele, shall we come down?'

Bandele groaned. 'You mean another hundred mile drive next week?'

'I will do the driving.'

'But I still get the bumps.'

'Come on, don't be so damn lazy!'

'Why do you want to go to such a thing?' Lasunwon demanded.

'Curiosity, among other things.'

'You are just a lot of religious gawpers.'

'And you,' Kola said, 'are just devoid of any imagination.'

'Of course I am, we can't all be artists, can we?'

'When you try to sneer, Lasunwon, you become singularly ugly.'

'Oh, I know, I know, I suppose sneering is another art. We poor lawyers can't compete with artists.'

Bandele, quietly, 'Enough, enough. What is the matter with you two?'

'I am just sick of his eternally superior airs, that's all. As if there is anything special in scratching a few figures on paper. No imagination!'

'Oh I see, that is what hurts. All right, you do have imagination. You have a water-logged, ponderous unimaginative imagination.'

'And you are just a time-waster, you are the most useless member of society and you know it.'

Egbo said, 'Careful now, Lasunwon. Where would you place bum journalists like Sagoe?'

'There is nothing much wrong with him except for his lavatory brain.'

'Just a minute. Is that supposed to refer to my Voidante philosophy?'

'Is that what you call it?'

Bandele was laughing inside. 'You had all better keep off Lasunwon tonight. The man is spoiling for a fight.'

'What has got inside him anyway?' Egbo said.

Sagoe said, 'Kola touched him on a raw spot.' And it acted almost like a button, starting him up all over again with increasing vehemence.

'Yes, I don't deny it. And it is not the first time either. What is he anyway that he goes round giving himself some special status in the universe? And I don't mean just him, it's the whole tribe of them. Everyday somewhere in the papers they are shooting off their mouths about culture and art and imagination. And their attitude is so superior, as if they are talking to the common illiterate barbarians of society.'

'Perhaps, Lasunwon, the trouble is you don't understand what they are saying.' Bandele's light mockery was red pepper to the raw in Lasunwon. 'Not understand what? But they don't say anything. Gibberish, nothing but gibberish. Like that Sekoni and his infernal Dome . . .'

And he stopped, remembering too late. Kola had leapt up shouting 'You vile-mouthed bastard!' but it was not really necessary, Lasunwon sat deflated, longed to take back the words, while Egbo thought, but why not, why not. Why does he stop because the man is dead? And he had never known such passion in Kola. Kola risen, a quivering rain-drop on the roof-edge, and then, collapsed into his seat, his face buried in his hands.

12

'My name is Lazarus,' said the man in lace-fringed robes, all white, 'My name is Lazarus, not Christ, Son of God.'

A little shack by a brown lagoon, a thatch and beer-case splinter hovel, with spliced palm rods for doors and windows, uneven beams and deep thatch roofing. It could have been a mill with those whitewashed narrow planks and the steady hum, like grinding corn, of liturgical refrains which sifted through the walls while they waited until the prayers should end. At last the voice of Lazarus succeeded some dragging of rough benches and in they went, eyes glued to the man at the crude lectern. They sneaked into a rear bench, but a man rushed up and led them out again. And now they noticed what should have informed them upon entry, the neat rows of shoes by the door.

'My name is Lazarus, not Christ, son of God.'

They took off their shoes, covered in confusion at the distraction they caused and the attention to themselves. Coolness through Egbo's toes made him look down, the floor was glazed concrete and trowel arcs of the rough and ready workmen still showed. There was still one ignorance for them to display. Dehinwa, about to turn again into the bench, found herself led respectfully to the other side and now they saw that the men sat separate from the women. Their guide cleared a bench for her with a wave of the hand and did the same on the other side. So they were seated at last, and Egbo wondered if the revelation which Lazarus had promised for this

Sunday would be worth his increasing unease at the intrusion.

'It is true that Christ was raised from the dead, but that is Christ the Father Christ the Son Christ the Holy Ghost. He raised himself, for he is the Father who raised the Son, the son who raised the Holy Ghost, the Holy Ghost who raised the Father. But I, who was re-baptised Lazarus, the good Lord raiseth from the dead.'

Drenched in morning dapples through the thatch roof, Lazarus looked sicker than they had ever seen him.

'My brothers, this is the tenth day of the death of our brother, this is the day when we perform the outing of his death according to the traditions of our church. And those who are grieving will surely ask, did not the Lord Jesus promise resurrection? This man was an apostle of our church, a God-fearing man, why is he not here today?

I am the resurrection and the life. He that believeth in me shall not perish, but shall have everlasting life.

A man rose from among those who occupied a bench near the altar, separate from the main body of the church. He stood with his eyes somewhere on the corner of the roof, and it would appear that he quoted without prompting, from memory.

Lazarus nodding emphasis, 'I am the resurrection and the life . . . And I, Lazarus, give you this assurance, from the personal confirmation which I was given by the Lord. For the hand of God descended on my head, and the light of the Lord poured a new life into me.

'It is my duty, as you all know, when an important member of our church dies to reassure you . . .

Be of good faith; the Lord is with you.

'. . . that before you were born, before I was born, long before our great great great grandfathers were born, the Lord Jesus Christ defeated death . . .

Where is thy sting, where death thy victory?

'He wrestled with death and he knocked him down. Death said, let us try *gidigbo* and Christ held him by the neck, he squeezed that neck until Death bleated for mercy. But Death never learns his lesson, he went and brought boxing gloves. When Christ gave him an uppercut like Dick Tiger all his teeth were scattered from Kaduna to Aiyetoro . . .'

And they saw death in hiding, shrunken in the full sun of

the congregation's laughter. Bandele, glad already that he had come with the others, laughing the strongest, silently.

'. . . even then do you think Death would give up? Not so, my friends, not so. Death ran to his farm, took up his matchet and attacked Christ from behind. Christ dodged him like an acrobat, and then he brought out a long shining sword of stainless steel and he cut Satan's matchet in half. But he did not want to kill him altogether, so he gave him small tiny cuts all over his body and Death was walking about in bandages from head to toe like *ologomugomu*. My brothers, they had many more fights, but Death knows his master today, his conqueror whom he must obey. And that man is Christ.

'As you all know, my concern for a long time now has been that we must build something better to honour this man who thrashed death for our own sake. It was in this connection that I went, shortly after the death of our brother, one of our devout and energetic apostles, into a house of sin and immorality. For wherever the business of our Lord takes us, even there must we unhesitatingly go. The man whom I went to meet is among us today . . .'

They were the strangers and a hundred heads turned round and studied them fully.

'. . . praised be the Lord. He has come to help us. By the power of God we shall build this church, fit for the dwelling of our Lord, we shall raise it on the foundations of faith and the goodwill of our friends.

Sagoe hissed, 'That man is suffering from optimistology.'

'As I was talking with him, one of his friends—he also is here, praised be the Lord,' and the heads turned round again, 'he is here and the others too, to help us in this task. And when I showed them the mark of death upon me this man said, "Surely you don't believe that you died?" '

Lasunwon, offended, was ready to leave the church, so Egbo held him by the wrist, hissing, 'Don't be an ass!'

'It is from the words of this brother that I want to choose our text for today. For did not the Lord Christ himself say the same sentence, only in different words, when he heard of the death of Lazarus?'

And promptly on his cue the verse feeder recited—*Our friend, Lazarus sleepeth.*

'Brother, let us hear it again.'

Our friend, Lazarus sleepeth.

'Again. Sing out the message of hope!'

Our friend, Lazarus sleepeth.

'My friends, Our friend Lazarus sleepeth, but I go . . .'

. . . that I may wake him from his sleep.

'Grief, dear brothers, is a natural thing. Grief and sadness are our portion on earth. Even Jesus Christ, the Son of Man, was overcome by grief. When he came to the cave where Lazarus was laid, a cave with a big stone on its mouth, the cave in which they put Lazarus for four days now so that even Martha the sister of the dead man held her nose with a scarf when the Son of Man asked her to remove the stone. She made fun-fun-fun with her nose and said,

Lord, by this time he stinketh; for he hath been dead four days.

'Yes, my brothers, the lot of our human life is death and corruption, but the Lord, if we believe in him, will save us from despair. Brother, remind us of the message of resurrection.

I am the resurrection and the life; he that believeth in me, though he were dead, yet shall he live. And whomsoever believeth in me shall never die.

'I wish to give you this message then. Grieve, but never despair. For Christ also became like you and me, like the eleven apostles who carried our beloved brother to his grave, but you must understand these two words of divine pity.

Jesus wept.

'He did not despair, he did not lose hope but . . .'

Jesus wept.

Lazarus paused.

Then he gave a sign, but it took the next man to him tugging at his coat to recall the verse feeder from concentration. He sat down.

'Yeah though I walk through the valley of the shadow of death . . . It was in that valley that I felt the hand of God. I dreamt that I was walking through a field of cotton, cotton wool which was just floating up from the pods. But there was no sound, all round me were cotton pods bursting softly, at my feet a carpet of cotton, in the air, in the sky, bursting pods that made no sound. The cotton wool pressed out gently like small pillows with the wool coming out when your head presses it. Everything was white. The trouble was that I could not find a way out. After a while I began to be frightened and I began to shout, calling on the cotton farmers to come and show me a way out. But I could not even hear the sound of my voice. I began to run here and there. I began to look for a way out of this thing because they were increasing all the time and I know that soon I would be unable to breathe. Already I was having great difficulty brushing them away from my eyes my nose and my mouth. And then suddenly, they stopped. All their movement ceased and the air cleared a little.

'I was tired. My throat was dry, perhaps from the shouting or perhaps I had breathed in too much cotton wool, I do not know. I ached all over and my head seemed about to burst open. So I said, I will rest a little. If these things start again I will wake up and run. I lay down, it was the softest bed I have ever known in my life. But just as I was falling asleep a very old man, old and wrinkled with a long white beard appeared suddenly out of nowhere and he stood looking at me. I could not move. Then he took his stick and began to prod me and in that moment I could hear again. "What are you doing here?" he asked. I said I was tired and resting. He smiled and said, "Good, very good. I am glad you use your eyes. You could not have chosen a better place to rest. I hope you are comfortable?" "Oh yes," I said. "I could sleep here for ever." The old man smiled again a terrible unnatural smile, my brethren. Because I saw inside his mouth and it was stuffed with cotton wool. No tongue, no teeth, just cotton wool. He said, "I am not surprised to hear you say that, everyone who comes here thinks that he can sleep for ever." Then he began to go away and I remembered that I did not know my way out. But he came back himself before I called him. He said, "I forgot to ask, your father owns this farm, is that not so?" I said No, that I had no idea who owned the farm. "O-oh, you have no idea who owns the farm. And did anybody give you permission to sleep here?" Before I could open my mouth to ask forgiveness, he landed a blow with his stick. I struggled to get up but before I was on my feet he gave me a good dozen, hitting me without caring where the stick landed. I began to run. I saw the impressions which his feet had made on the cotton and I followed them, but this old man had no difficulty keeping just behind me, beating me cruelly with his walking-stick. And then the footprints came to an end. In front of me was a huge gate and I could see the top of it, but the end? It was nowhere. Neither to the left nor to the right, it was nowhere at all. And the old man stood now with his cotton-filled mouth open in a big laugh, watching me to see what I would do. I ran up and down and he just stood there laughing at me, just to show me I could not escape. And then, suddenly, the cotton wool started blowing again and this old man said, "You see what you have done?" And he resumed his flogging. This old man showed me no mercy and the cotton wool poured down heavier than ever. I turned round to him to beg for mercy but I received such a blow on the mouth and my head that I thought I was finished. My mouth swelled from the blow until it became nearly bigger than my head. And in great fear of death I began to cry "Help me, someone, in God's name help me!" There was no help anywhere. I ran back and tried to jump on the top of the gate, but the cotton wool made me slip, and this old man beat me while I was down. "In the name of God help me or show me the way out of this place!" My voice was failing, the cotton wool drank my strength and drew me down, soon it was up to my knee and still this old man showed me no pity. Like a lizard I tried to climb this gate, which had no foothold, no scratch or nail of any kind. It was smooth and it was black. "Show me the way out in heaven's name, save me in God's name, for the love of Christ save me from this place." I fought with the cotton in my mouth and in my nose. The falling wool soon hid this man completely and I saw neither him nor his stick, and soon I could not hear him laugh and I could not hear my voice, but the blows remained more cruel than ever, the cotton was weighing me down, weighing me down, it had climbed to my neck and each fall dragged my arms back into this dreadful silence. And I cried, "Save me," but no sound came. "O God, deliver me, O God, deliver me . . . O God deliver me . . !" '

Lazarus, his eyes dilated, was lathered in sweat. He was clutching the rest of the lectern and the sweat ran onto the Bible, the terror of death seized him again and spread, and encircled the congregation. His wild eyes scraped the walls like a blind beetle and came to rest staring straight through the open door into sunlight . . .

'. . . yes, it was just like that, as I face this door, so did I look up suddenly and see that gate open before my eyes . . .'

Flooding him again with the sense of a miracle. And Lazarus shut the Bible, saying simply, 'Brothers, help me to thank God.'

A man rose from the front bench and led the congregation in a long prayer. And it was the prayer which unwound them, slowly. A hymn was called after that, but it was at a much later stage in the service that that church was fully itself again.

The front bench seemed to contain the authority during worship. Another man rose from it and spoke to the church.

'My brothers, it is a terrible day for us, when we the Apostles of the Lord, we to whom he has give all the burden and task of the church, baptising, marriage, confirmation, when we who carry most of all the burden of death on our shoulder, that the day should come when it is our turn to supply the next load for the grave. It is a thing which grieved us too much, that we should have been visited by the hand of death, and bury one of us. But death is no respecter of persons. The doctor in hospital he die. The rich man, he die. The poor man, he die. God does not take bribe. He is a man of impartiality. Jesus Christ himself, he die to prove to us that we must expect no favour. Brother Ezra was our oldest man. On his wise head we rely on for so many advices, so many of our problem that we have to deal with. He guide us well through all the trouble times. Since this church was founded by our Brother Lazarus, we are the foundation members who have been try to settle all quarrel, listen to the problems of our members and endeavour to do our best according to our poor wisdom of our disposal. It is a terrible thing for us that now we look around, Brother Ezra is not with us today. But we give thanks to God.'

The Verse Feeder did not stand this time, but spoke with the same up-gazing concentration.

The Lord giveth and the Lord taketh away; blessed be His name for ever.

'We hope that he has gone into a land of peace.'

Amen. From the congregation the deep sighed rumble, *Amen.*

'We pray that he is sitting on the right hand of God.'

Amen.

'We hope that God will teach us to profit by the light of his shining deeds to life.'

Amen.

'And that when it is our turn to die, God will say to us, What is the matter? Ah-ah! Don't trouble me my friend. Don't you know the man who is long time here before you? Go and find Brother Ezra. Wherever he is sitting, sit down by his side.'

Amen. Amen O God, Amen. Amen.

'Yes, my brothers, God speak to us. God has give us a sign.'

Allelujah!

'God has promise us, and he has fulfil his promise.'

Allelujah!

'Brother Lazarus said unto God, where shall I find an apostle for the man you have taken? Which of my congregations must to be the twelfth Apostle in thy service? But the Lord shake his head. He said, Look outside the church, go ye into the streets and into the byways. And Brother Lazarus obeyed. For did not the Lord say unto us,

Behold, I shall come to you like a thief in the night.

'Brother Lazarus find the appointed of the Lord, and he said, Lord how shall I know if it is he? And the Lord tell him again.

Behold, I shall come to you like a thief in the night.

'But still the doubt remain in Brother Lazarus's mind. Because you see, this is a young man. He is a very young man chosen of the Lord. How, say Brother Lazarus, can this young man carry the burden of the congregation? How can he follow the path of thy way?'

And he took a child, and set him in the midst of them. And he said unto them, Suffer little children to come unto me.

'And in his name, unto the service of the Lord our God, I ask you to receive our brother Apostle, a sinner who is born again, a sinner who is wash in the blood of Christ and has choosing the path of righteousness.'

He went to the door by the side of the table that served for altar. The congregation, curious and excited, strained with impatience. He separated a curtain, the most elaborate thing in that church, a much-worked, silk-ornamented curtain. From between silk portraits of two saints, a frail young man emerged, stood hesitant.

Lazarus, now recovered, rose and the front bench with him. The Memory Reader began to intone in winded bursts—

And when he had called unto him his twelve disciples, he gave them power against unclean spirits, to cast them out, and to heal all manner of sickness and all manner of disease.

And as ye go, preach saying, The Kingdom of God is at hand.

And when ye come into an house, salute it. And if the house be worthy, let your peace come upon it: but if it be not worthy, let your peace return to you.

Verily I say unto you. It shall be more tolerable for the land of Sodom and Gomorrah in the day of judgement, than for that city.

For it is not ye that speak, but the spirit of your Father which speaketh in you.

Lazarus went forward and received the boy. There was a sharp intake of breath from the rear bench and Sagoe's constricted voice, 'But that is the shop-lifter.'

'Who? You know him?'

'The thief they chased at Oyingbo.'

This boy did not look like a thief, he was purity itself among the other apostles, a toughened medicine ball eleven. A plain white smock reached to his ankles, a straightforward bag with holes for arms and another for the head. Someone brought a bowl of water and held it out. Over it Lazarus offered a prayer. Then he led the novice to each apostle.

'Receive him, brothers. Receive him for the flock into the service of God.'

And Sagoe fisted himself on the head. 'Idiot! Those are the eleven men who walked behind the coffin.'

'Where?'

'The funeral. The same day Sir Derinola was buried.'

They all embraced him while Sagoe continued unsettled like a man tormented by ants. 'But what has he done to him? Brain-washed him? There is little left of *that* Barabbas. As if a wet astringent sponge has wiped flat a face of eczema.'

A hiss from Dehinwa on the other side, 'Quiet!'

'The apostles,' said Lazarus, 'are the servants of the flock. Their appointed tasks are deeds of great humility, for they follow in the path of He who chose them.'

The novice knelt, and began to wash the Apostles' feet.

'We baptised him Noah,' said Lazarus, because we fear that the Lord may have forgotten his covenant with earth. Look outside brothers, look out and see the great deluge. Our farms, which brought a small revenue into the church treasury, have been washed over. The church itself has to be repaired all the time and we have been flooded twice. The very foundation of our church is shaking from erosion. Brothers, if mankind forgets its duty to God is it not foolish to expect God to remember his covenant with earth? And yet I give thanks to heaven. For this morning, for the first time in four Sundays, there is sunshine in the world. It is a sign and I give thanks to God for this. It means that he is pleased with what we are doing. Our Brother Noah has brought us a sign of forgiveness from God. Brothers, raise your voices and praise the Almighty!'

Praise be to God.

'He cannot hear you.'

Praise be to God!

'The vaults of the heaven are high. You have not reached him!'

Praise be to God!

'Brothers praise him!

Praise be to God!

'And His son in the Highest!'

Thanks to His Son our Jesus!

'And the Holy Spirit!'

Descend O Holy Spirit!

'Allelu . . .'

Allelujah!

'Allelu . . .'

Allelujah!

And Lazarus turned to the Verse Feeder on the wave of elation, prompting, 'Woman, why weepest thou . . ?'

Woman, why weepest thou? Whom seekest thou? Go to my brethren and say unto them, I ascend unto my Father, and your Father, unto my God and your God.

'Why seek ye . . .'

Why seek ye the living among the dead? He is not here but he is risen.

'Well brothers, is Brother Ezra dead?'

He lives!

'I say, is Brother Ezra dead?'

He lives on in the Lord, praise God hallelujah!
'Will he live on in Brother Noah?'
He walks among us!
'Rejoice brothers. Receive him to your hearts!'
Hallelujah!
'For He has given us a child . . .'

> *For He has given us a child*
> *Allelu Allelu*
> *For He has given us a child*
> *To keep us on His path*
> *Allelu Allelu*
>
> *For He has given us a guide*
> *Allelu Allelu*
> *For He has given us a guide*
> *To light us through the dark*
> *Allelu Allelu*

Through stamping, leaping feet and a thunderous ferment of handclaps, Noah washing feet that won't keep still, accompanied all the way by the Apostles who are tossed from each wave of ecstasy to the task of clearing a path for Noah and tossed back again, Lazarus weaving back and forth. His possession was the violinist's, alien in a group of *agidigbo*, as if it was not he who would not submit his body completely to communal joy but an ordered force keeping him separate in his own spiritual capsule.

'Receive him, Lord' he shouted from time to time, 'receive him, Lord!'

> *For He has given us a sword*
> *Allelu Allelu*
> *For He has given us a sword*
> *To rid Him of His foes*
> *Allelu Allelu*

There are bells ringing wildly and the white-robed women who appear to have no hand at all in the running of the church come into their own at last, running up and down with hand-bells, going everywhere. The result is a Witches' Sabbath, clangorous and weird. From time to time they seize Noah and dance with him and the Apostles are attacked with sheer noise of bells at their ears and the bowl of water has to be replaced again and again so often is it upset by white exulting phantoms. Even the children are caught in it. The wide sleeves of women's surplices flutter incessantly, turn them into misproportioned moths around the frail flickering candle that was Noah.

Lasunwon gave a sudden laugh and said, 'If he was as old as the other apostles they wouldn't chase him so much.'

'You must admit he's not bad-looking.' It was Dehinwa. 'Move over. Everybody appears to be mixing so I thought I would join you.'

Sagoe said, 'Hadn't you better join them and try your luck?'

'No, dear, I won't stand a chance.'

And then, before they knew it, the bowl was beside them and Noah knelt by the bench. 'This is past a joke,' Lasunwon said.

This time, the Apostles formed a tight determined barrier against the women's ecstasy, and their gyrations were confined to the upper part of the church. Not only that, but a new towel was produced for the visitors, and with touching meekness, Noah began to wash Dehinwa's feet.

Sagoe whispered, 'Are you thrilled, dear?'

And she said, 'At least he has gentler hands than yours.'

Then it was Sagoe's turn, then Bandele. Lasunwon was writhing and cursing himself for the foolish impulse which brought him there.

'But what,' Bandele asked, 'is wrong with getting your feet washed?'

'I just don't like it, that's all.'

'We can't complain,' Kola said, 'what with the preferential treatment.'

When the bowl came to Egbo, the Apostles pleaded and protested, but Egbo, silently firm, refused to have his feet washed, offering no explanations, only negative gestures of the hands and his head.

The bowl was taken away and the Apostles led the way out. A woman had been taken by the spirit and she began to prophesy but this did not disturb the dedication of Noah, borne forward now on its own triumphant power. Two of the prophets stayed with her and the others preceded the surge of a jubilating mass.

They had noticed the huge cross as they came in, and now this cross was lifted onto Noah's shoulders and buoyed by bells and songs, by joy-pent power on a driving wind, they began to circle the church, stopping at the door each time to offer a brief, silent prayer. When Noah looked tired, the Apostles merely took the cross from him and made one round with it and he recovered his strength. It *was* a heavy cross, and as they stood outside some distance from the door, Lazarus said, talking to them for the first time, 'That is one of the few gifts which we have for the new church. When it is built, that cross will surmount it. One of our members, a carpenter, made it for the Lord. His wife made the embroidery of the vestry curtain with the picture of two saints—did you notice it?'

The seventh station had been passed when an Apostle ran from the church and beckoned Lazarus. From inside Egbo heard the agony of the possessed woman, the scream of foreign tongues and her fight for breath. Through the briefly opened door, her strength was mounted against three men and a woman, but they withstood more than a flabby woman; forty demons strove within her and her inner sights misruled her body. Even before they left the church she had folded sudden like a foetus, leaping taut in the air and breaking herself on the ground. In the grip of her unnamable torments she was all steel springs and lathe bent double. She was a worm, an insect, a snail, a scorpion. She frothed at the mouth and brought forth huge dribbles. And she would grovel like a snake and strike like one. Egbo left before the others; he had seen too much like her and could never like it. *Esu. Sango.* Similar throes of a scotched boa. At such times Egbo longed for the other possession, the triumph of serene joys and sublimated passions. The young maid of *Ela.* The transfigured wrinkles of *Orisa-nla.* Inertly rendered bodies and unearthly exultation in the eyes, and on the skin. Deft whispers of the godhead, numinous presence, flooding the medium's sympathy; in such communion he would partake, not in the woman's violation of the body.

Sagoe continued to shake his head. 'There are moments when I don't believe this is that young thief, you know. It is hardly the same thief, but perhaps he was too scared at the time.'

Lazarus nodded with satisfaction. 'I am glad you find him changed. I was anxious to hear your opinion.'

Egbo said, 'I cannot like the new apostle. He looks submissive, not redeemed. I find his air of purity just that—air. There is no inner radiance in the boy, only a reflection from the spill of zealot's flames.'

Lazarus listened, open-mouthed. 'You are mistaken. That youth has received the holy spirit of God.'

'I do not like apostasy,' Egbo said. 'He has the smooth brass face of an apostate.'

Bandele spun round, 'What was that twisted idea?'

Kola said, 'I agree with Egbo. If I painted him, it would be as Christ.'

'You mean to say Judas,' Dehinwa corrected him.

'No. I meant Christ the apostate.'

'Wait a minute. I think we ought to get our definitions clear.'

'No need,' Egbo said. 'Kola is only trying it on. But don't start hanging your notions on mine. When I said apostate I meant the straightforward Judas type.'

'And I meant the Jesus type. And that is just how I would paint Noah.'

Bandele said, 'I suppose it was too much to wait until you got out of here before pronouncing your blasphemous ideas.'

'Are you turning hypocrite in your old age? Since when did you recognise the term?'

'It isn't that,' Bandele said. 'But do you have to state it now with Lazarus at your elbow?'

Lazarus, who had half turned away and with Sagoe observed the progress round the church now faced them and said, 'Please don't think I mind. After all every man comes to God an unbeliever. Our task is to show him the light.'

Another of the Apostles came again and spoke urgently to Lazarus. Lazarus disapeared with him into the church saying, 'I shall come back. That afflicted woman requires my presence.'

When he had gone Sagoe said, 'I agree with Bandele. All that talk could have waited until the man was gone,' but Egbo only repeated, 'I do not like apostasy.'

'Neither do I, but so what? I was at Oyingbo when the boy was being chased and believe me, even then he was not such a sorry spectacle as this. He seems to have turned soggy clay in the hands of Lazarus.'

'Let's all go home,' Dehinwa pleaded. 'I don't like all this.'

'Well, I don't know what Lazarus wants, but my editor could use a centre spread on a prophet with a difference, for the Sunday edition.'

Bandele looked at him, 'Is that all?'

Sagoe turned, 'What do you mean, is that all?'

'Never mind, it's not important.'

'No go on, what did you have in mind?'

'Nothing.'

'Why don't you go ahead and paint him, Kola? Then I would use the painting in my feature, give it some kind of dimension. . . . I don't know how exactly, the idea is just winging its way into my brain.'

Kola shook his head, 'No. I might paint him, but not on the Cross or any such waste of time. I was thinking of him as Esumare. Intermediary. As the Covenant in fact, the apostate Covenant, the Ambiguous Covenant. When Lazarus called him Noah, I thought about it then. He does possess that technicolour brand of purity.'

'Yes, yes,' Egbo murmured. 'And it is just as vaporous.'

Bandele was mocking, lightly. 'Sagoe has his story, Kola has filled another heavenly space on his canvas, what are you getting out of this, Egbo?'

Egbo turned angrily on him. 'What are *you* getting out of it?'

'Knowledge of the new generation of interpreters.'

Sagoe exploded. 'You sound so fuckin' superior it would make a saint mad.'

'Just be careful. When you create your own myth don't carelessly promote another's, and perhaps a more harmful one.'

'Whose turn is it now?'

'Lazarus. Don't carelessly promote his own myth.'

'What is that supposed to be?'

'You see,' Bandele said. 'You haven't even tried to find out. He asked you here didn't he? Have you thought why? Or do you believe in that bull of the church building alone?'

'What else does he want? Publicity, of course. All the local prophets want publicity. It's good business.'

Bandele shook his head. 'I saw his face when Kola mentioned painting Noah as Christ.'

'So did I,' Sagoe admitted. 'But why not? If he wants to be

a kingmaker instead of king it only does credit to his intelligence. I tell you, the man gets more interesting.'

'Why don't we just go home, Sagoe.'

'Woman, don't interrupt . . . wait. You know, I've just thought, what are you willing to bet that all those so-called apostles are ex-convicts or similar lower depth characters.'

'Your brain is running riot again.'

'No, no. Lazarus and his "resurrection". Founds a church, turns thieves into apostles and calmly awaits the second coming . . . hm, it isn't likely but still . . . dammit, the man is intriguing.'

'Like a piece of crossword is intriguing. Or a murder story.'

'Please, Bandele, just stow your susceptibilities for the moment. The man asked me here to use me and I earn my living from using others in turn. This is a thing I see stretching for weeks, one feature on each of his disciples, and a big blow-up for the man. As I said, he is a gold-mine.'

'What did you make of his death experience?'

'Did *you* believe it? Well did you?'

Bandele pondered for some time. 'It didn't matter whether I did or not. But at least one thing was obvious, this man did go through some critical experience. If he has chosen to interpret it in a way that would bring some kind of meaning into people's lives, who are you to scoff at it, to rip it up in your dirty pages with cheap cynicism, or Kola to . . .'

'Keep off me, enh. I don't know what bee has been buzzing in your bonnet lately but you keep off me now. Damn it, Bandele, what's going on anyway! You have become so insufferably critical and interfering.'

It was almost as if Bandele was a long praying mantis. Visibly he retracted into a hole, feelers trodden on like an incautious ant; and he only said, 'None of you minds much what suffering you cause.'

Kola said, 'I knew I had to come. All I wanted was the link and here it is. Right here. I wish a rocket would shoot me to Ibadan now, with Noah.'

Egbo said, 'Does that mean the Pantheon is complete at last?'

'From the moment I saw Noah I knew I must take him back tonight.'

'How do you think you will manage that?'

'If I tell Lazarus I want to paint his latest saint and present it to the church you think he will object? I can do better than the carpenter's wife's embroidery.'

'You will have to show something for it,' Egbo said.

'One hour's work. I can paint something acceptable to Lazarus in a half hour.'

'What about what Bandele said—suppose he's right and Lazarus wants him on a Cross?'

'Then he can paint his own damned Jesus.'

Sagoe was thoughtful. 'I wish he would. I wish he would. It would make an unbeatable scoop for the paper if I could be present from the redemption right through the nurturing of yet another Christ.'

'It would be sensational,' Dehinwa mocked.

'Look, woman, don't take over Bandele's role, you hear? As for Lazarus, if my editor approves, I intend to go to this resurrection village of his, see if any of them remembers.'

Dehinwa teased him, 'Why bother? You are not really interested in truth.'

'Only in certain aspects of it. For instance, if I find Lazarus is a fraud through and through, is it any business of mine to tell his congregation? That is a point on which even Bandele holds a strong opinion. Only some aspects of truth are of any lasting significance. Suppose tomorrow Noah becomes Christ and Lazarus can prop him up successfully, whose truth requires me to tell the truth? Mine, you see. My—as Bandele would put it—my cynicism or my take-it-or-leave-it approach settles that.'

'In any case, what does it matter? The flock would still believe what they want to believe. Wasn't it your paper which tried to pull down a Christ not so long ago?'

'Can't remember. Must have been before I came back.'

'He was the boldest of them yet. He said he had come to enjoy himself at this Second Coming, not to suffer. The papers waged a most vicious attack on him.'

'Did he survive it?'

'He's prospering more than ever. Big transport business and a bakery and a big harem which has survived two suits of seduction.'

'And they attacked him?'

'Viciously.'

'You see. The world cannot stand prophets of joy. Everyone is in love with agonies.'

'No,' said Egbo, 'not agony, just the fact of sacrifice. Ritual immolation.'

'You have a blood mentality, that's your trouble. After all, what is more logical? He did choose suffering the first time, and we accept his right of choice. So why shouldn't he choose pleasure now and we accept it?'

'I ought to find out if that Christ is still in business you know. Stir up a competition between the two. Survival of the fitter turd . . . that's four pages—with pictures.' And Sagoe kicked chunks of earth into the Lagoon.

'Another centre spread, just pictures and captions' and his toes stuck tons of type and smacked them neatly onto more pages of the lagoon. The placid stretch appeared to incense him. 'Block that space!' he shouted, and the shingles whipped the water. 'Small news items to whet the readers' appetite,' and Sagoe continued to pock-mark the surface and his story spread in infinite ripples until he gasped in sudden pain and clutched his toe.

'The type-setter has broken down,' and Dehinwa gave him her shoulder for support as he stood on one leg. 'Serve you damn well right.'

In spite of the small group which stood alienated by the side of the lagoon, oblivious of their presence, a ripe field of corn swept past again and again, pausing for prayers at the door. Then the breeze would swell once more, white sails and light raffia sails on mushed earth, and a hundred hands lifted Noah and the cross till they felt themselves routed and grounded superfluous.

Bandele broke his silence. 'I would not have been curious to hear Lazarus if Sekoni had not recently died. Deep inside me, I suppose that was why I came.'

Egbo looked into the darkness of the deserted church. 'What did you think Lazarus could tell you?'

Bandele shrugged. 'I was curious. It gave me a strange feeling to sit opposite him at that table and hear him claim that he had died.'

'We should go now,' Egbo said, moving towards the cars.

'You go on,' Bandele offered, 'I will say good-bye to Lazarus.'

But Lazarus was just coming out, and he accompanied them

to where the cars were parked. 'I hope,' said Sagoe, 'the woman prophesied a philanthropist for your church.'

Lazarus looked far more solemn than when he left them. 'No, she was not prophesying today. Nothing was in it of the future but of the past. She had visions into the past because she saw me walking with a faceless companion, and she says it was Death.'

'I have been meaning to ask,' Bandele said when they had driven some distance from the church, 'have you had news from. . . ?'

'Home? The lagoon reminded you also. No. And newspapers terrify me.' Egbo laughed shortly. 'I thought I had buried it, but it isn't true. I am haunted often by the feel of that old man's fingers on my face and his blind eyes, and I wake up thrashing the sheets.'

They drove on for some time and Egbo said, 'I have thought about it often and if it happened again, I am not sure I wouldn't stay. My rejection of power was thoughtless.'

'You think so now?'

'If you seek to transform, you must not be afraid of power. Take Lazarus.'

'I haven't been in this area before.' Kola, speaking from the back.

'There are a number of such lagoon villages all over the place. Some of them you can only reach by canoe.'

'And they are part of Lagos?'

'I imagine so.'

'I am coming back later,' Kola announced, 'to talk to Lazarus about Noah. If he agrees I will take him to Ibadan tonight.'

'He won't object,' Bandele said.

'Trouble is, I'm afraid I'll get lost. I haven't much sense of direction.'

'I'll come with you,' Egbo volunteered.

'Good. That leaves only the danger of the car bogging down.'

'We will have to come while it is light.'

13

The stroller thought Sagoe was loitering. But it was a light from the house which stopped him on the doorstep, bent to the keyhole, listening for sounds. Humming, 'I make out nothing but that mean nothing,' Sagoe walked right round the house. Peter might be asleep but he could hear him rushing down the moment the door was opened to ask about his health or suggest a nightcap together. Then he considered attempting a straight run upstairs and to bed, but he could see Peter catching him at the door and offering to read him a bed-time story. Sagoe was still pacing when this man approached.

'Hallo.' It was a white face. The faint light from the house ringed his flattened nostrils. 'Are you in trouble?'

'No. Simply have nowhere to sleep, that's all.'

'God, that's funny.'

'It is? I am glad for your sake.'

'Oh I suppose it isn't really funny. What I meant is, I seem to run into that sentence every other day.

Sagoe squared. 'Listen, you . . .' But the man stopped him gently. 'It is true . . . I hear it quite a lot. I am American, you see, and that seems to be the free hostel sign for every American tramp in the country.'

For days now Pinkshore had aroused his periodic dislike of white faces. Not even the memory of Mrs Faseyi's defiant form, contemptuous of the embarrassment of her own people and indifferent to the shock and indignation of her husband's, not even she could redeem the white race since that party. It was in fact only with a supreme effort of recollection which tore his drink lobes across the ligaments that he was able to think of her consciously as a white girl. And this man's manner Sagoe found particularly insolent, with grease.

'Well, I am not an American tramp.'

He smiled. 'I have yet to meet an African who isn't being insulted about something.'

'I have yet to meet the American who doesn't think his insolence should pass for heartiness.'

'Good God. When I set out I only planned to walk—where did I go wrong?'

Sagoe found himself muttering, 'Oh, just take off. Your face is antipathetic to the state of my drink lobes.'

'Sorry, didn't catch what you said.' Sagoe made no reply, and began to wonder if the risk of Peter wasn't preferable to this. 'You know,' the stranger said, 'I find you fellows a most unfriendly bunch in this country.'

'Yes I know. Americans expect to be loved. . . .'

'No please, please . . . not that. Anything but that.' Sagoe felt he had been betrayed into making a cheap remark.

'Look, my name's Joe Golder. I lecture in African history. I suffer from insomnia so I'm taking a walk.'

Sagoe nodded and bent again to listen at the door.

'Well, if you are locked out come on. Come over and have a drink.'

'No thank you. I've stayed reasonably sober tonight. I don't want to spoil it.'

'Well, coffee then. But do come and talk for a few minutes. It is some distance but I can drive you back.'

Sagoe considered it, decided that he did require thawing. Walking alongside him, he noticed and was surprised that Joe Golder was quite small. He had appeared bigger. But his whole body covered him in an air of full athleticism. And he had an unusually compact looking head on the shoulders of a white man. Sensitive too, Sagoe felt. Fools like Joe Golder, they come to Africa to be hurt.

'You haven't much of an American accent.'

'Oxford, I'm afraid. Five years in Oxford took care of that. I haven't missed it. I am not a very American man.'

'You should trade your birthright with one German I know . . .'

'Not Peter!'

'Yes. You know him?'

And Joe Golder's face vanished beneath a hard, gnarled leather mask. 'It is *that* you know. That and nothing but that all the time. Because I am American, every buffoon who comes here with an American accent or passport makes for my house. I have changed flats half a dozen times in the two years I've been here. They are told, we have an American lecturer and next thing I find them on my door step, or even in my sitting-room all ready to camp. I leave the house for them, I send them to the consulate but it makes no difference, tomorrow there is still another wide boy—even girl—waiting after a class. You know, I am a misanthrope. I do not like human beings. I like to be alone, what is wrong with that?'

Overborne, Sagoe could only mutter, 'A few people are quite like that.'

'And some of them think they are doing me a favour. One, he said he was a psychology student from Arizona, come to finish his Ph.D., he sat in my flat until three in the morning, and he was still trying to decide whether he would stay or book in at the hotel. Pity you haven't a telephone, he said, I will need to make so many appointments. . . . And when they stay your house is not your own. You come into your flat and you find a stranger there, you'd forgotten all about him. You understand, I am not a philanthropist. I don't like to be taken for granted.'

Sagoe had for some time now been giving the encounter his whole attention. But he decided he would continue with the walk. So now he said, 'But why don't you simply tell them to go and not bother you?'

'I admit I like to help people, it's just that I hate to be taken for granted. I am not obliged to help anyone. I can shut myself up in my flat and tell them all to keep out. I like my peace. Because I like to help people I hate to be taken for granted.' He appeared to be calming down somewhat, as if ashamed of his reckless outburst.

'I am sorry,' he announced. 'I have a habit of recollecting things as if they are just happening. It is a bad habit. When I am in company and I remember something unpleasant, I try to take flight before it assumes control of me.'

This time he was silent for nearly half a mile and then he spoke again.

'I am a very sudden person. My moods change. Sometimes I am a perfect host. And then I come in one afternoon and ask the man to pack his bags. Once I even broke off in the middle of a lecture just to run home and throw out some musician who had been staying for nearly a month.'

'Did you remember something he had done?'

'No. I just suddenly wanted him out. I remember driving so stupidly that I landed in a gutter, so I left the car there and ran the rest of the way.' He laughed. 'I value my time, you see. I may laugh with a colleague one moment and turn my back on him the next.'

'How do they take that?'

'Different ways. Some like to call it a pose.'

'That doesn't worry you, then?'

'I don't bother with fools, why should I? I am not a social person. I don't attend their parties or their meetings. I value my own time and I resent to the point of fanaticism even one second of it which I give to another man. If I waste a whole day myself just sitting in my flat doing nothing, that's my own business, but let me do the wasting myself.'

Lights were out in most houses. Some dogs barked very close, and remembering Bandele's analysis of their code, Sagoe picked up a stick.

'For the dogs? They don't bite.'

'I'll make sure they don't.'

'Are you afraid of dogs?'

'No. But I've been bitten before.'

'I was too, but that was different. In my own home town, where a white fool set his dog on me.' He laughed and seemed to anticipate Sagoe's puzzlement. 'Oh, you are taken in like others. I am negro. One-quarter negro in fact.' He smiled then. 'I wish it were more.'

'I met a lot like that in the States.'

Golder was surprised. 'You've been in the States?'

'For quite some time.'

'I am surprised someone hasn't brought you along then.' He climbed to a falsetto. 'You've been in the States? Oh you simply must meet Joe Golder. A most cha-a-rming little man. He has a most ma-a-rvellous tenor voice.'

'You sing?'

'You would have found out sooner or later. Unfortunately I love to sing, and I think it is true I have a good voice—best tenor in the college, some say. But usually it is the women who say that. And most of these tired housewives will not understand that I join their opera group to sing, not for the sherry and tittle-tattle afterwards.' He was growing excitable again. 'And I have a piano in my flat, so they think it a good idea to drop in for a short rehearsal. And it does not matter that I say no each time, they believe they can wear me down with trying. Look, if there is one thing I cannot bear, it is some female voice singing in my flat. It is an insufferable intrusion. I am very jealous of my privacy, I cannot tolerate any fool invading it and they so love to take you for granted . . .'

After they took the last turning into a fresh, barely made wheel-track, the nature of the silence had changed. It was no longer mere cessation wrought by a sleeping community, but a deadening load, a third oppressive companion on the walk. It came from the matted bush, and the dank of lopped palm bases, uprooted but alive, from a black blanket of toads' spawn on a shallow stream. Even across the cawing and the disturbed pauses of the toads, it was there. Sagoe smiled the smile of a contented Voidante immersed in perfect silences.

'You are smiling,' Joe Golder intruded suddenly.

He came back to his presence, but soon lost him again.

'You are a silent person,' Joe Golder said.

'Hm?'

'I say you are a silent person. You don't say much but you keep smiling to yourself.'

'Do I?'

'Yes. What were you thinking?'

'On the metaphysics of Voidancy.'

'Oh yes, thank you very much.'

They walked on in silence and Sagoe wallowed in it. He was growing steadily vacuous. Soon his mind was quite empty —a mistake it seemed, where Joe Golder was concerned.

'What are you thinking?'

He made no reply.

Indifferent to Sagoe's state of beatific passivity, Joe Golder became an insufferable intrusion. Sagoe wished earnestly that the man would shut up. He could not understand that any human could appear so sensitive and yet remain outside the octopoid lethargy of the night. Golder continued to intrude on the spell with his drum of tribulations until they reached the flats.

He lived in the newest block of flats, the furthest from the college centre and the tallest. And he had, without any diffi-culty, secured the top flat—nobody seemed to want it but he.

'It is eight flights of stairs, so take it easy. I hoped the labour would discourage callers.'

'How did you get the piano up?'

'Same as for one flight. Hard work, but I persisted.'

As he inserted the key in the lock, 'I have no friends. You will hear a number of people say Joe Golder is their friend, but that is only their conceit. Strangers come up to me and say, 'So you're Joe Golder, I met a friend of yours only yesterday . . .'

'Often it's only a manner of speaking.' Sagoe was becoming irritated, with reason.

A picture of an elderly woman confronted Sagoe and the rest of that wall was covered in books, all elegantly bound, similar.

'I once worked in a library. In Paris. Have you been to France? You have? Most of the books which the library threw out I took. And they often sold others cheaply, I bought them. Had them rebound. It did not matter what they were, I simply took them. Next to music, my passion is books.'

The room had such a fastidious air Sagoe could not immediately sit. And in spite of a light metal and canvas chair, a Design Centre coffee table, low, with white Formica, in spite of the cubist designs on tiny cushions, Sagoe had stepped into a remote world, ponderous, archaic. There were two candlesticks on the piano, with red candles . . .

'For heaven's sake don't make a joke about Liberace. All the Americans who come here do.'

'Liberace is dated,' Sagoe said, inspecting the ornate designs.

An oval antimacassar was spread on the piano, on top of it, another framed photo, both parents. 'Yes, they look completely white, don't they, but my father is half negro. One of the passing ones you see. He took his wife away before I was due. But I seemed all right and he came back.'

'What happened then?'

'Nothing for fifteen years. And then the past caught up with him.' He remained silent for some time. 'He's dead now. Suicide.

'You may be horrified when I tell you I drove him to it. I was so ashamed of him and I did not hide it. I spat on my flesh to his face because it came from him . . . I was young . . .'

There were a few fussy pieces on the piano, and a figure of Buddha. 'Jade?' Sagoe enquired. Golder said he didn't know. On a shelf, the three brass monkeys.

Golder had a fake mantelpiece. 'It goes with me when I change flats. Built it myself. I have rather peculiar tastes, there are somethings I cannot do without in a room."

The lampshade on the piano was a peculiar criss-cross box of black-painted wood and there was a similar creation, purely ornamental on the mantelpiece. 'I intend to turn that into a fish-bowl.' Sagoe puzzled how he would do this but refrained from asking.

'What will it be? Coffee or stronger?'

'I feel thirsty now. Have you beer?'

'You are frowning. What is the matter?'

'Was I?'

'Heavily.'

'I didn't know. I suppose I find it all very disquieting. Too quiet. Quite a disquieting quiet requite thee. How's that?'

Not even a smile acknowledged it. Instead he turned a hard face and said,

'How do you mean? You have something on your mind, what is it?'

'I don't know. Just give me a beer.' And Sagoe went and stood on the balcony.

Beyond reality lay the town, congealed sheets of rust and silver patches. A miniature forest lay below, life-size only in the fastness of its head of hair. The stream which they had crossed looked a discarded rope, the palm bases like big tubers. The block was that tall. A glow-worm alone shone equal, landing close by Sagoe's watch. Two in the morning.

'What are you thinking now?' His voice was quite harsh, resentful. 'You were thinking just now.'

'Was I?'

'You were frowning again. Why? Why do you keep frowning?'

Sagoe tried to co-operate, made a serious effort to discover why he frowned. But it had worse results. The quiet beat him and his effort at concentration was soon swallowed by lassitude. He promptly forgot Golder's existence.

'Well, if it takes you that long to remember what you are thinking . . .'

Sagoe woke up. 'I am sorry. I don't think I was working on it really.'

It happened four or five times; Golder was so persistent and Sagoe never recovered sufficiently to resent his needling intrusion. It was as if he continually fell asleep on an invited guest, and he remained conscious of ill manners.

'You are a very silent person, aren't you? You don't appear to talk much.'

Sagoe found this amusing. 'If only you knew.'

'So you do talk. Why aren't you talking then? You haven't said much since we met. You hardly open your mouth unless I prompt you.'

'Maybe I'm tired.'

'You are not tired. I know when a man is tired.'

'Well, lazy then. You know what I mean. Heights affect me this way and the quiet is doping.'

'But you are talking now. So tell me what you were thinking just then.'

'Do I have to think of something?'

'About yourself then. Go on. I want to know what kind of a person you are. Tell me what makes you tick. I know I am a misanthropist. I don't care for people and I don't want them to care for me. Most of them are phonies anyway. I've been to several European countries and human beings are all the same. Boring, insincere. I came here hoping Africans were different.'

And it went on like this. He sat on the railing poised like an inquisitor, but he only plunged deeper and deeper into his own case-history.

'I prefer my own company. Stay up here, and write. I am writing my second book, a historical novel set in Africa.' And then, with a mad edge to his voice, 'You are not listening. You keep thinking. What are you thinking about?'

This time, he came through and Sagoe sat up with a jerk. 'What is the matter? I said I wasn't thinking, and if I was and I don't want to tell you, that is my business.'

Joe Golder when he laughed sometimes, was frightening. He had big teeth and his lips slid apart in a near snarl. Sagoe was more alert now, and began to wonder if the man was playing a part. 'You like to act strange, perhaps?'

Joe Golder stopped laughing. 'Why do you think that?'

'Nothing. It occurred to me that I had better ask.'

'I am one of the most sincere people I know.'

'Even that can be a front. I mean, a deliberate attitude.'

'We will get stuck,' he said, going to a cupboard. 'These walks always make me hungry. Would you like something too?'

Sagoe apparently took too long considering the offer, and Golder jumped.

'Christ, you don't have to have it. I merely made the suggestion.'

'This is getting mad. Do you never ponder whether to eat or not?'

But he had gone into the room and he opened a cupboard. Sagoe followed him, making a distinct effort to be sociable.

'When I was in Paris,' said Joe, 'I knew a dancer from British Guiana, he was so goddamn proud it hurt him to say thank you, so he would avoid your doing anything for him. God! I hated his guts and he hated mine. He was starving in Paris, you know, and I had a good job in that library. And he would come to my flat after tramping to all the agents looking for work, he would flop in a chair and listen to records. His shoes were an eyesore and you could see he hadn't eaten for a week. But would he agree to eat? No thank you, in his best Oxford accent. No thank you! It made me so mad just seeing him seated there, pretending he had eaten when his guts were crying for a crumb. Oh he was so damn British. So bloody correct. He was a student in Oxford with me, you see, but he flunked his exams so we both came to Paris. It was dancing which interested him anyway.

'You know, I went to his room one day, a shabby rat-hole in an attic. I hadn't seen him for days so I went to look him up. Took me three hours to find the slum he was living in. He was in bed, weak, quite weak from hunger . . . I opened his cupboard and there wasn't even a garlic. But he forced himself up to open the window and tell me in that damn British manner that he'd eaten, oh God he was simply stupid with pride. I had to go out, buy him food and cook it for him, and you could see he was weeping inside to eat the food I had bought.'

Sagoe, fascinated by the man, watched him light the kerosene stove.

'I don't use the electric stove,' he said. 'Not since I got the first bill.'

He began to break eggs into a saucepan. He was breaking the third when Sagoe said, 'I hope none of that is for me.'

'You don't want any?'

'No, don't think so.'

'I see you are still thinking.'

'I don't want any.'

'Are you sure? Or is that the British in you?'

'The British in me of course. But I don't want any just the same, thank you that's very kind of you don't want to put you to any trouble absolutely sure so sweet of you.'

'At least you have a sense of humour.'

'I don't think I have, but it doesn't matter.'

'No? I must confess I derive a kind of pleasure from detecting hunger in people. It is another bad habit I picked up. I didn't tell you, before I took that library job I did a bit of starving myself. That put me off hunger for ever. The sort of people who claimed to be starving for art, starving for their freedom, starving for the day they would burst on the world their genius—all phut! They had nothing in them, the fools of the Latin Quarter. Oh I lived that life for some time. I was sent a little money from home, so I was lucky. Sickening, all those phonies. One thing they could all do well, sponge on you. They had a genius for that.'

'I saw some too in New York.'

'Oh yes. Greenwich Village.'

'And San Francisco. Your beatniks amazed me. Why do they congregate, why?'

'You mean you gave that serious thought? That dancer friend of mine, he starved, but he didn't parade it like those others. When he went broke he simply stayed in his flat and dreamt. We were great friends. I liked him a lot and I hated his guts. God I hated his guts I didn't know how much. You know how I found out? When he was ill, broke and in hospital. I hate hospitals, I never visit anyone in it. When my mother was ill once I thought up all sorts of subterfuge to avoid going to see her. But this boy, the moment I learnt he was really ill I went to hospital just to see him there, helpless, totally dependent. You know, he didn't possess a cent. I paid his bills, took him fruits and flowers. Oh he was really rotted with pride, you could see humiliation all over his face, never gratitude, I hoped it would slow his recovery. I paid his rent—he had been out of a job for some weeks before his illness, so he was in debt all over the place. I went and cleaned his house before he returned. Oh but he hated me, hated the sight of me like he'd never done before but he couldn't help himself. He had to accept my help and even ask for it. I did it, you know. He had to go for an audition and he needed new ballet shoes. I knew it but I said nothing. He had to ask. Ask! He asked me for money, damn him!'

Fresh air blew in from the balcony; reassuring. Sagoe felt plunged beyond his depth. What is the matter with him? What is the matter with him? In desperation his mind flew to Dehinwa and her gruff, exasperating affection, to Egbo, who could have matched Joe Golder for violence—of a more straightforward nature.

'Is it all right if I put this on?' He stood by the record-player.

'OK by me.' Sagoe did not add that his lethargic self-indulgence was already destroyed anyway, and that he still resented the fact. A soprano drowned the sound of spurting oil.

'Coloratura, Italian. Do you like it? I like the human voice. Next to a violin the human voice is the perfect instrument. I play my favourites only when I am alone. I am liable to cry, you see.'

'It is funny, but I am not surprised to hear that.'

'Do I look the kind who cries easily?'

'Let us just say that you are very vulnerable.'

Sagoe was standing by the only painting in the room. It showed white streaks on a fully black background. It could have been forked lightning on a black sky but he knew it wasn't. The tongues which darted from the main gash were wet, dripping. No power or violence but a deliberate viscosity, the trapped dreg of milk pushing through wrinkled film and trickling uncertainly.

'Do you like that?'

'I find it sickening.'

He stopped short. 'You are the first to say that. Others say they can't understand it.'

For a long time afterwards Sagoe would wonder why he asked the question. Unconscious that he had even framed it, unaware until it dropped, he heard himself ask, 'Did your dancer friend do it?'

'Yes.' And Joe Golder watched him for quite some time. 'How did you guess?'

'I have no idea.'

Instantly furious, 'You never like to say anything. So damn secretive . . .'

'Before you work yourself up over nothing, I tell you again, I have no idea.'

'I've noticed that. You Africans, once you've told a lie, you feel bound to stick by it. Even when you are confronted with the evidence which even a child must see, you must lie, lie . . .'

Sagoe was ready to strike him now. 'If I ever hear you talk that kind of shit again . . .'

'I can, you see, because I am not white. Take my first houseboy . . .'

'You affect much scorn for British attitudes and now you stand there calmly asserting one. You try that superior stuff on someone else.'

'So you can't even accept a simple truth. You Africans are so damned nationalistic.'

'Shut your blasted mouth!' He had got on his feet threatening.

Golder recoiled, visibly terrified. 'I hate violence.'

'Then don't open your big mouth again to draw profound conclusions from your houseboy! God, you Americans are so damned insufferable it's a wonder you get out of anywhere alive.'

The strain was worse when the record came to an end. Joe Golder pushed the food aside and went to the bottles. 'Now I cannot eat.' He was shaking slightly.

'What's stopping you?'

'I hate violence. Any form of violence upsets me.'

Sagoe did not relent. 'Then you should be more careful. There is violence in words too.'

'No, no, that is rationalising. Let me try and find you a photograph of this boy. I don't keep an album, but I keep all his cuttings. He is successful now; he's danced in Berlin and the States and in one of two other European capitals. I had a card from him recently—from Madrid.' He laughed. 'Yes, he began to get more regular work and he paid me every penny I'd spent on him. That's how he is. Paid it all back. But at least he took it, he had to accept my kindness. It was the only source of pride he had left—to pay back his debts. But I had broken him just the same. When he's broke now he doesn't hesitate to ask me for money.'

Joe Golder grew more and more distasteful every moment, but Sagoe felt he would wait. To keep himself there—and reasonably civil—he began to look for things in Joe to admire. There was his love of solitude, his deliberate self-isolation which was marked all over the room, and yet the room was repellent. It gave a crawling sensation down his back and he mouthed the American word—sick!

'You are not saying anything. I still do not know you, or isn't there anything to know? I mean, what makes you tick. Go on, what makes you tick?'

'Do you always make your friends—sorry, acquaintances if you prefer that word—do you always make them feel they are smuggled watches on sale outside Kingsway—ah oga, seventeen jewel, cheap-cheap automatic with calendar, try this one oga.'

'O-oh, I don't know how I make anybody feel. But I don't like mystery.'

'You like probing the works to see the tick mechanism.'

'I don't know what I like. But you haven't said anything at all. And I always want to know about people. I find that people exploit you. If you are kind to them they exploit you. I have tried to help people—lots of times, especially when I was in Paris where the world's bums are gathered. Not anybody, mind you. Only people of my colour. I like black people, I really do. Black people are exciting, their colour has such vitality, I mean it is something really beautiful, distinctive . . .'

Quite unfairly, because he knew it wasn't true, Sagoe said, 'You are mentally white, you know.'

'It sounds Rousseau but I have a right to feel the way I do. Black is something I like to be, that I have every right to be. There is no reason at all why I shouldn't have been born jet black.'

'You would have died of over-masturbation, I am sure.'

'You enjoy being vulgar?'

'A genteel British reproof. It is amazing how much English did get into you. Perhaps that's why you are constantly attacking. Look, the truth is that I get rather sick of self-love. Even nationalism is a kind of self-love but that can be defended.

It is this cult of black beauty which sickens me. Are albinos supposed to go and drown themselves, for instance?'

Until then, he had completely forgotten Lazarus. His mind went to him now and it made him suddenly restless. He stood up.

'Are you leaving?'

'Yes.'

'So you don't find your skin beautiful?'

'I have never given it any thought. I saw a white girl at a party the other night and I considered her beautiful. That is an aesthetic judgement. I cannot remember much about her colour. When you talk of this black vitality I can almost hear you salivating and since I happen to be black—neither fault nor credit to me—I find it all rather nauseating.'

'No, wait a minute . . .'

'I am astonished that black men can bear to be slobbered over, even by black men.'

Joe Golder rose. 'It is some distance. I'll drive you. Or stay if you like, it is quite late.'

'No, my friend would wonder what happened to me.'

'You seemed to be locked out when I saw you.'

'No it wasn't that. That Peter, the German boy with the smelly breath—he hasn't left. And I wasn't in any mood to face him.'

'You are staying together?'

'We are both guests of an old school friend.'

'Oh, I know Bandele very well.'

'And played him a mean trick. He got landed with Peter after you ditched him. One minute in the same house as Peter is a trial. Bandele is quite superhuman.'

'You can move in here if you like.'

Sagoe laughed. 'And your sudden moods? I hate to think of me relaxing here and you running all the way from the lecture room to throw me out. I don't quite fancy knocking my head on the stone steps.'

'No, no, I can always tell. There is no likelihood of my doing that.'

'No, I'm only here for a few days anyway and we'll only get on each others nerves. I am still rather startled, you know. I mean, look, you must admit you are a bit of a surprise. Much too much to absorb at once.'

'Stay tonight anyway. I'll drive you back first thing in the morning.'

Sagoe was tempted. 'I must admit I would sleep better knowing I wouldn't see Peter first thing in the morning.'

'Good. And there are no mosquitoes at all. Too high, I imagine. I'll sleep here and can use the bedroom.'

'No. I like this sofa. You stick to your bedroom.'

He had become very cheerful. 'No no, that is not my idea of hospitality.'

'You'll have to give in. I don't use a bed when there is a sofa. Even cushions on the floor will do me.'

'All right. Then we'll both sleep on cushions,' he said.

'Look, I don't . . .' But Golder had gone into the bedroom, and left by himself in the room the vague unease returned. Sagoe stood there, irresolute. When Joe Golder reappeared, he knew he was not going to stay.

'I've put out a new towel for you in the bathroom. It is right through the bedroom.' He put on another record. 'I hope you have made up your mind to use the bedroom.'

'No, I . . . don't think so.'

He spoke quite gaily, 'All right, we'll both use the cushions then.'

'No-no, I don't think I'll stay at all.'

Joe Golder retained the pick-up, incredulous. 'Why? Why have you changed your mind?'

'I never really did make up my mind.'

He turned in fierce accusation. 'You did, you had agreed to stay.'

'All right, let us say I did.' Sagoe was sure he was having more than his share of a night's annoyance. 'You haven't a monopoly of sudden moods, you know.'

'But why won't you stay?'

'I just do not feel like it.'

'No. That is not why. What is your real reason?'

'Are you seriously demanding a reason?'

'Yes yes. I want to know why.' His voice had turned shrill, all his poise, even at his most violently resentful had vanished. 'Just tell me the truth.'

'Well, for one thing, you have made it abundantly clear that you resent intrusion.'

'No, that was only to explain myself, which you, typically,

refused to do. It is true I am subject to moods, but I do want you to stay. You must realize that I want you to stay.'

'You'll get on my nerves.'

'For one night? What is the real reason?'

Suddenly Sagoe thought, we are both fencing, but why? What am I fencing about? What does he expect me to know for God's sake? In his mind, he sensed a blockage that prevented conscious admission of the issue, but tonight was one of his slow nights and he asked what, what, what? Joe Golder was taunting and Sagoe found that there was still another turn to his face; it was twisted and looked unripe, an abortion.

Finally Sagoe said, 'You have some suspicions on your mind. You can either say it out or keep it because I am going. And if my reason does not satisfy you, find your own.'

'You are the one beating about the bush; the English in you again . . .'

'For God's sake!'

'Yes, and you know it. . . . It is very kind of you really but I can't stay. Just like that dancing friend of mine who won't eat. I can't stand all the pretence. Say what is on your mind, I want to know.'

Sagoe looked at him with deliberate pity now and walked to the door. 'Since you are so obssessed with British this and British the rest I'll tell you one new reason why I won't stay. You will bore me to death. I hope that is good enough for you.'

'Wait.' He came closer, almost pleading. 'Tell me something, quite honestly. Are you afraid of me?'

Sagoe went past feeling; his mouth slacked open and remained there.

'You needn't look so astonished. I want an honest answer. Are you afraid of me?'

'Afraid of you?'

Again Sagoe was forced to give up; he had meant no contempt in his voice, no cause for Golder's subsequent rage. 'God, you are the strong confident type, aren't you? I knew it the moment I saw you. So cocksure, so damned sure of yourself. You are the strong black type, afraid of nothing. Where do you get your conceit from anyway? I asked what made you tick but you didn't say. The strong, silent type, so bloody sure of himself. Nothing makes you afraid.'

Deliberately Sagoe taunted him, 'I can take care of myself, yes. And what about it?'

And then he thought, he is mad. The man is mad. If he had a knife he would stab me. But why? What have I done?

The American was speaking again, much more slowly now. 'Do you think . . . are you afraid I might molest you? Is that it? Do you think I am a homo?'

'Good God, no.' The suggestion startled Sagoe and he did not even think before he rejected it. 'You have some rather effeminate mannerisms, but that is all.'

'Come come, be quite frank now.'

'I've answered you! Listen you, it is true I have spent some time in places where every possible perversion is practised, but I do not on that account jump to hasty conclusions. I happen to be born into a comparatively healthy society . . .'

He jumped on him. 'Don't give me that? Comparatively healthy society my foot. Do you think I know nothing of your Emirs and their little boys? You forget history is my subject. And what about those exclusive coteries in Lagos?'

Sagoe gestured defeat. 'You seem better informed than I am. But if you don't mind I'll persist in my delusion. I'm tired anyway. Look, I'm only trying to say that I suspect you of nothing. I have learnt not to jump to conclusions in so many things. Anyway, please, let's take this up some other time.'

He seemed somewhat mollified. 'I'll run you back.'

Up till that moment, Sagoe had kept nothing back, assumed no more than he admitted. He had erected the wall in societies where sex was the key to town planning, where designs for park railings were turned down because of unsuspected symbolisms. Unable, while in America to accept that three out of every five of his friends were perverts, active or latent, and that the fourth was in love with his mother, he simply pulled down a cast-iron shutter and developed a judo chop for those whose movements in a darkened cinema theatre left him in no doubt at all.

With men he learnt to ignore hints and searching questions for fear he had misunderstood. But where the language was plain, he calmly chopped the errant wrist and earned an insulating reputation.

'What are you thinking now?'

'Oh no, let's not start that again.'

He drove through the dirt track onto the rain-tree lined avenue. 'You see,' said Joe Golder, 'I like men.'

Sagoe was singularly stupid that night, or perhaps he never really listened. Joes Golder repeated it twice over, with more emphasis, before he finally admitted the meaning and began to curse his slowness.

'I mean . . . I really do. I like men like that, yes, like that. I thought you knew.'

'No. I'm afraid I didn't.'

'Well, I thought you did. I couldn't think of any reason why you wouldn't stay. But do you mean you didn't even suspect?'

'I am not usually this thick, it is very difficult to explain. But it must have crossed my mind a few times . . . I really can't think why it didn't fasten on. A reaction I have developed, I think. When I can't think what sickness belongs to a man, I don't go for fashion.'

'Well, I should have thought it was obvious.'

'No. I lived with this European conspiracy to de-sex men and it drove me mad. So I simply developed a most stubbornly rooted reaction. But even so . . . I surpassed myself . . . the drink must have congealed my lobes, I think.'

'Do you know, you haven't even told me your name.'

'Common with pick-up cases—don't you think?' Now that his mind was unblocked, Sagoe was not ready to be so nearly considerate.

He noticed then a book lying on the seat beside him and picked it up, holding the cover to the dashboard.

'It's *Another Country*, the latest Baldwin. Have you read it?'

'I spell it Another Cuntry, C-U-N-T.'

'You don't like it?'

'It reminded me somehow of another title, *Eric, or Little by Little*! Said with an anal gasp if you get my meaning.'

'You enjoy being vulgar,' he said again.

'And you? Why is this lying on the car seat? So when you give lifts to students you can find an easy opening for exploring?'

'You are trying to hurt me?'

They drove in silence the rest of the way. Golder pulled up outside the house and asked, still hopefully, 'Well?'

'Well what?'

'The invitation still stands. You can come and stay any time.'

'Thanks, but frankly, I don't think I will.'

'Because of what I said?'

'For the hundredth time, I can take care of myself.'

This always acted as a blow to his face. 'Oh yes yes, I forget' —and again the abortion sneer—'you are big and strong. Big silent African.'

Bandele opened the door for him. 'Wasn't that Joe Golder's car?'

'It was. And thank you for a most eventful stay. Thank you very much indeed.'

'What's the matter?'

'First Peter, then your native breed, now that Golder character. I just hope you haven't any more surprises in store for me.'

Bandele stared. 'Oh I see. Oh dear, I should have warned you.'

'Never mind. I suppose as a journalist I should take it all in my stride. Trouble is I don't see any of it that my editor can use.'

14

It was lunch-time again at the house of Faseyi. For Bandele, a pleasure of the gut which he never could resist, for it was an after-crisis lunch, and Faseyi's mother would be working miracles of the kitchen. As for the penalty, it was little to pay, he heard nothing that he did not wish to hear, made the appropriate sounds at the right time, and turned his nose towards the kitchen to catch the fore-whiffs of the feast.

Monica, accustomed to the drill, poured out the drinks and left. Faseyi hardly waited for the door to shut on her before he pressed Bandele against a wall. 'You saw it all, didn't you?'

You saw what happened. You saw how that woman disgraced me!'

The deprecating gesture from Bandele. 'It was nothing. No one really noticed.'

'How can you say that? Look, Bandele, you are always honest with me. Enh? What about Kola, was he there?' Looking directly at Kola but curiously addressing Bandele. 'Was he at the party?'

'I wasn't,' Kola said, very firmly.

'Wasn't he? I would have sworn it was he who went and danced with Monica afterwards.'

'No, no it wasn't me.' He turned to Egbo and began to talk to him.

'No, I don't remember seeing Kola,' Bandele said.

'You see how it is? I mean, I could understand if I was one of those who marry illiterate girls from London so that they can boast that they have a white wife. You tell me honestly, do I look that kind?'

Bandele said something about Monica being OK.

'So you see, for her to go and disgrace me like that! As if she does not know the simple rules of etiquette.'

'Look Fash . . .' But Faseyi interrupted. 'You are not looking at it from my point of view . . . wait, just a minute.' He went and listened at the door. 'Good. Mother is talking to her now. You know what the Prof's wife told her? She said she would never tolerate Monica's presence at her house again.'

Bandele murmured 'Terrible.'

'You begin to see my point don't you? To behave like that in decent society. Why? Sometimes I think that Monica just has no respect for Africans. That's all I can say. Would she do that in a white man's house? If the Professor had been a white man, would she have done that?'

'Have you seen the Prof?' Bandele next asked.

'Not yet. But I will have to go and apologise. Not that it can repair the damage. Do you know a Minister was present. Yes, and one or two other VIPs. Oguazor knows people, you know. I saw four corporation chairmen there, and some Permanent Secretaries. A thing like that, Kola, one is simply socially finished.'

'Yes, you, of course.'

'Look, let's face the facts. The university is just a stepping-stone. Politics, corporations—there is always something. Not to talk of these foreign firms, always looking for Nigerian Directors. I mean Kola, you are an artist, but I am sure it is all a means to an end, not so?'

Kola feigned deafness.

'I didn't sleep all night you know. In fact I am so glad you could come. Mummy is all very well—I went to fetch her first thing this morning—but one can really talk only with people of one's age. And Mummy is too fond of Monica. She really indulges her.'

'What did your mother say?'

'Nothing yet. She says she will hear her side of the story. As if there is anything left to be said.'

'Let's go to the balcony, Egbo.'

They left the sitting room to Faseyi and Bandele, Egbo murmuring, 'I will never figure out that Bandele. How does he stick him?'

'Don't ask me.'

'I had no idea what I was letting myself in for when I agreed to come.'

'I have—and that is my trouble.'

'How?'

'Monica.'

Egbo looked at him and shook his head, 'So. The pollen is blowing wild everywhere.'

'Have you found the girl yet?' Kola asked in turn.

'She has disappeared. I didn't know the vacation was so near.'

Kola laughed, 'I never thought to see you laid low.'

'Nor me,' Egbo admitted. 'I must be getting old.'

The face of the campus had changed, the sounds were different, the movement within it more ordered—almost in set sequences as one conference group filtered from one hall to the other and back to the gross dormitories, now sadly depopulated. Silenced now were the student rags, the vapid excrescences of national juvenalia which, appropriately named the 'Worm', or the 'Slime', outraged even the most liberal of the staff community and made them wonder if their efforts would not be better directed at the apes in the college zoo. But, always in the good cause, the Oguazors suffered a few nice boys to soil their cushion covers with their presence, hoping that tea and sandwiches might transfer some gentility to a redeemable few. But the guests returned to their mimeographs to throw one more muddied assault on staff inviolability, thriving on the apoplexies of turgid disciplinarians. Then they would eat their words with abject humility, carpeted before the Dean, but return to other students with loud boasts of their open defiance, not only of the Dean, but of the entire Senate. And the invitations would be tried out on safer selections, sons of Ministers and other famous nationals. But the tea would run cold and the sandwiches harden at the edges and the cushion covers lie unhonoured and Mr Oguazor would console his wife saying, 'What did I tell you? Those boys simply have no celture.' And the 'Slime' would slither again and the 'Worm' crawl, and the editors waited in vain for the logical repression, canonization and the inevitable rise in popularity in the name of 'free speech', with hope fixed on the coming Union Presidential elections. But by then the Chancellor was bored and the staff indifferent, and the students bemoaned a loss in 'academic dynamism'. And the blackboards too were clean now, and not of the mysteries of calculus alone but of the pornographic sketches and student half-witticisms. And the boards were free at last of the shrill retail of obscene gossip, with illustrations and unmistakable identities, figments of student imagination, vengeance for thwarted approaches, general frustration, anger at the existence of women in their midst who set up to be equal, who, outnumbered, must say a hundred nos for every yes and whose great privilege thus became, for the losers, an unforgivable arrogance, and so it was back to the boards and a hundred fictions and lurid diagrams and the wit of diarrhoeic brains . . .

'And yet from among them . . . sometimes it is incredible.'

'What is it?'

'I was just thinking that from among them—these students I mean—one finds the future genius.'

'Don't talk so conceitedly old.'

'Well, aren't I?'

'Thirty-one. Is that supposed to be old?'

'Thirty-two.'

'So? That is still the same generation as your students.'

'Generation isn't just according to age.'

'Anyway don't go sounding like an old boy addressing his alma mater.'

Kola stood up suddenly. 'That Bandele irritates me sometimes. How can he listen all that time!'

'Wait. Let them sort it out.'

But Kola had already opened the door, throwing aside the
last vestiges of compunction.

Faseyi was saying, 'It's no good, I tell you. The whole thing
has gone too far, my mind is already made up. I've only called
Mummy to let her know because she is so fond of Monica. I
didn't want to send her off without first telling Mummy.'

Kola felt himself sweat, and he refused to accept any of this.
Regretting now that he had left his own decision till too late,
for it seemed the path was being cleared for him anyway and
this was not what he desired. What he wanted at the least, as
some form of compensation, was for the man to be made to
lower himself altogether, to cheapen his rights to Monica.
Regretting, and he was full of regrets that moment, that
Faseyi could not show even a brief inclination towards manhood so that he could pull him down, ruthlessly, deliberately,
without seeking to excuse himself with the husband's weakness . . .

'Perhaps if you begged Oguazor, it might help.'

Faseyi turned to the voice, following Kola's approach like
the figure of hope.

'What do you mean if he begged him?' And Bandele's vehemence seemed unnecessary, filled with suspicion. Again,
Faseyi let him down.

'But Kola is right. I wanted to go this morning in fact but
Mummy said I should wait. It seems the only sensible thing
to do.'

'I would say just forget it, Fash.'

'Oguazor won't forget,' Kola warned, and he hammered it
further to leave no doubt. 'Oguazor is an elephant. I know
him. He won't forget a thing like that.'

'What do you mean?' Bandele snapped. 'You weren't even
there, according to you.'

'But I've heard all about it.'

'Then it's all hearsay—how can you judge anything?'

Faseyi looked from one to the other, gratified at the personal
tone of Kola's concern and its conviction. And in sheer gratitude he went and refilled the glasses. Bandele took the chance
to hiss 'Just what game do you think you are playing?'

'Let him grovel if he wants to.'

'Well let him make up his own mind.'

'What are you? His guardian uncle?'

Bandele looked long at him and coldly. But he would not say just what he was thinking.

Faseyi returned with the drinks. 'You see, everything really depends on Mummy. It's unfortunate really that Daddy is gone on one of his trips abroad. He might have been able to help. He knows all these people.'

Bandele walked away from them and joined Egbo on the balcony.

'I'll just tell Mummy . . .'

'Why tell her,' Kola said, 'she will only tell you to wait. Go at once and get it over with.'

'You are right of course. I'll . . . er . . . look, be a friend will you. If Mummy asks for me just tell her I had to go and do some urgent work in the lab.'

'Sure, sure.'

And Kola had the peculiar feeling that this was better, that it was necessary for him to take a hand in whatever would happen.

Monica came in some moments later. 'You always seem to get left alone in this house. I am sorry.'

'I don't mind at all.' And the awkward silence.

'Thank you for what you did at the party.'

'Please . . . not that British thank you business.'

'But I meant it.'

'I know. All I mean is there are things also for which one must never say thank you.'

'I don't know of any.'

'That's because you've been wrongly brought up.'

'Have you a drink?'

'No, I don't want one . . . My friend, the journalist sends his vow of devotion. He called you the Unknown Warrior of Oguazor's Cemetery.'

'Better not let Ayo hear you say that.'

'I will tell it to him directly if I like.'

'You must not.' She was silent for some time. 'How is the painting?'

'It will be finished soon. I may hang it up at Sekoni's exhibition—just the one painting by me.'

'Nothing else?'

'No, the show is really for Sekoni, only I can't think of a more appropriate occasion for trying out my biggest work yet.'

'I often see you coming to take Usaye, but you never think of coming up to see us.'

'Well it was she I wanted.'

'And you've no use for us—that's frank anyhow.'

'Her glasses should be ready next week.'

Thank you. It was very kind of you to have taken so much trouble.'

'There you go thanking me again. When all I've done is exploit the poor girl for my own work.'

'Of course, I remember now. You like to reject kindness and . . . what was it you called it again? . . . oh yes, fluffy emotions.'

'But I am telling the truth. She has sat for me hour after hour.'

'All right, I won't argue. Thanks for taking her to the optician, whatever the motive.'

Again they stood by the window, full of the awkward silence. There was Usaye playing beneath a line of white and lace and printed blouses, some distance from the tree stump.

'I don't know how it happens,' Monica said, 'but I always end up showing him up badly.'

'Is that what you honestly think?'

'I understand how he feels. I think perhaps I act silly sometimes.'

'Do you *believe* that?'

'Yes. Those were my husband's friends. And his society. I had no right to let him down in that manner.'

'That is a matter of opinion.'

'What is?'

'That that is your husband's society. That what you saw represents my society. That's all I mean. For your own conduct, that is for you and him to decide isn't it?'

'Yes. And my mother-in-law is very kind. I love her very much. I mean that. You cannot imagine how close we are. In fact she does not come here often enough. If Ayo didn't ask her she she wouldn't come at all.'

'What does she think?'

She was some time thinking about it and Kola said, 'Sorry, maybe I shouldn't have asked . . .'

'Yes. I was thinking whether I should be talking to you about this at all. But, I don't mind telling you. She thinks I ought to leave him.'

Kola turned away his face.

'You are shocked? It is not the first time she has said it. And when I consider it truthfully I think, well, why not? Isn't that the logical thing? After all this touches deep-seated attitudes and neither of us can change.'

She was worried now because Kola did not speak. 'You *are* shocked. Is that because it came from his own mother . . . ? I am sorry, this is really wrong. We shouldn't discuss it at all . . .'

Bandele and Egbo entered from the balcony. 'Well, I don't believe you,' Egbo was saying.

'I tell you, if I saw her face again I wouldn't even remember her. It was already dark when she brought the note.'

'But I've described her. You must remember which of your students it is.'

'I don't. Their faces all look the same I tell you. I can't tell them apart.'

Egbo appealed to Kola. 'Will you tell him I don't want to seduce her and even if I do want to it's none of his business. Why won't he tell me her name?'

'Does he know it?'

'That is what I keep telling him. I don't know the girl.'

'All right. Give me the names of all the girls who attend your lectures.'

Kola laughed 'You want him to do that right now?'

And Bandele, 'When we leave here we'll go to the office. Then I'll give you the list.'

'How many of them?'

'Altogether?'

'Among the second-years.'

'I don't know. Honestly I don't know.'

'Well maybe you have some essays you didn't return. I'll know her handwriting again.'

'Maybe. I will have to look through my office. Anyway it's your own fault. You should have asked her name.'

'I thought you could always tell me, so I didn't press for it.'

The kitchen door opened suddenly. Mrs Faseyi stood and looked swiftly through the room and into the balcony. 'Was that his car I heard just now?'

Monica also looked round her, aware for the first time that Faseyi was absent. 'I thought he was in the balcony with you,' looking at Bandele.

Bandele said 'No, I left him in here with Kola.'

And Kola, feeling Bandele challenge him said, 'Oh yes, he went to attend to some urgent work in the laboratory. He said he'd be back directly.'

Mrs Faseyi was a stallion, black, the solid black was like a separate dimension. She belonged to the race of handsome statues, defiant, carved proud like a halted thoroughbred in a Durbar charge. Now she sniffed her disbelief, and it included astonishment that such an easy lie should be employed to deceive her.

'Which of Ayo's friends are you?'

'Mother, this is Kola . . .'

She rode down on him, wrathful. 'So you are the criminal who wasted my cooking that other afternoon. And you are also a liar it seems. Gone to the lab, which lab? Oguazor's sitting-room laboratory?'

'I am sorry about that afternoon, Mrs Faseyi. I shall try to make up for it.'

'What makes you think I intend to offer you my food again after the way you last treated it?'

'I am really humble, madam . . .'

'My son told me you were already here. But when lunch was ready you had disappeared. What got into you?'

'It was er . . . I . . it is difficult to explain. I had a sudden idea for some work I was engaged on . . .'

'Yes, Monica has told me about your work. But what had that to do with wasting my food?'

Kola found himself beginning to feel truly guilty of a heinous crime. 'I am sorry, Mrs Faseyi, I only meant to run there and back, but the time passed . . .'

'The time passed! Ha? You artists seem to think you have a prerogative of bad manners. The time passed!'

Monica attempted rescue. 'Mother, you are embarassing the poor man.'

'As he damn well deserves. And ashamed too I hope.'

'Very much so, Mrs Faseyi. I assure you I . . .'

'I don't permit eccentricities to interfere with my cooking. If you want to do that sort of thing, go to Chelsea.'

Monica began to pull her. 'That's enough now, mother. I think he has learnt his lesson, haven't you Kola?'

Eagerly, 'Oh yes, I won't ever do it again, I promise.'

'Now come on Mother, let's see how the food is doing. Bandele, better reassure Kola it's all bluff so he won't run away again.'

'What do you mean it's all bluff?' But she had allowed herself to be pulled through the door by then.

Kola stood, dazed, and Bandele wrapped his hands around a glass. 'Drink that and relax. It's all over.'

'What did I do?'

'Ordeal by fire. It's a ritual with her.'

'But that woman was really raging.'

'She finds a *casus belli* with all first acquaintances. Especially those she thinks are Ayo's friends.'

'That's some irony.'

'Well you were lying for him weren't you? Or maybe you weren't. You made it such an obvious lie even a child would have seen through it.'

'What are you getting at now?'

'You tell me?'

'Look. Are you his godfather or what?'

'I'm sure you could have lied much better if you wished.'

'Shut up.'

'Why don't you just leave those two to sort out their own problem?'

Mrs Faseyi ignored them all when she returned with steaming platters, Monica protesting behind her, 'Let's wait a little for Ayo.'

'Nonsense. You!' Kola jumped. 'Did your friend ask us to wait for him?'

Kola blubbered a startled unmeaning.

'You see. I tell you he's probably lunching with his Professor now.'

'Kola said he went to the laboratory.'

She gave a loud laugh. 'Men have such a peculiar sense of honour.' She went in again and returned with more food. 'These loyal friends of his must think that I don't know Ayo at all. I only happen to be his mother. Come on, come on. Just seat yourselves as you wish.'

Monica said to Kola, 'You had better eat and eat hungrily.'

'My son gives me a bad name,' Mrs Faseyi continued. 'What for instance, am I doing here today? I can no longer meet any of his friends without thinking how they must be saying to themselves, That is the woman who runs Ayo's life. And it is a lie you know. It is all because he talks about me so much.'

'He must be fond of you,' Bandele said.

'Fond of me? Why? He would be an unnatural son if he did not feel something—but that we take for granted. As for being fond of me, that is another problem. I happen to be fond of Moni now, I don't have to be. But I am really fond of the silly girl—she is quite silly sometimes you know. But I care about her happiness.'

Monica was showing signs of distress, as if she knew what was coming. She muttered something about some food she'd kept for Usaye and left the table.

'If I didn't care, I would continue to patch up their quarrels. Instead of which I simply tell her, Go and find happiness elsewhere, you won't get it from this son of mine.'

Bandele, Egbo, and Kola most of all sat staring like gutted fish, wondering how seriously she spoke.

She broke into a loud laugh, and became hard, defiant. 'Well, well, don't you all look shocked? There is nothing mysterious in a broken home you know. I ought to know, so perhaps you will say that I am the wrong person to give advice. But I don't like unnecessary sentiment.'

Bandele said, 'Is it just sentiment, Mrs Faseyi?'

'What else is it? Young man, I've been separated from Ayo's father twelve years—no—fifteen. I know when a marriage is being propped up by sheer sentiment.' She was serving Kola, she hesitated a little. 'This is a hot number, but I cannot stand a Nigerian who does not eat pepper,' and with deliberate maliciousness, added more to it. She pushed the dish down in front of Bandele, then faced him, beating the point with movements of the serving spoon. 'You think I don't care enough don't you?'

'No-no. But I think if you told Ayo he must make a go of his marriage he'll do it.'

'No. What you mean is, if I told him he must not send Monica away he will obey me.'

'All right,' Bandele conceded. 'Same thing.'

'No, young man, not the same thing. Oh yes, if I wanted Monica to stay—which I do—she would stay, but what has that to do with their marriage? Better now for them to go their different ways before they have children to complicate their lives. So what I'll say to Ayo is what I have always said, You must make up your own mind. Do what you please. I said the same thing when he wrote to me he wanted to marry a white girl. And I know what his mind will be about this, so I've warned Moni to prepare herself.'

Once Kola would not have dared look up. Now he examined their home, puzzling why he felt no elation. It was hardly the plea he had expected. When Monica first told him what the mother said, he obtained only a picture of an embittered woman. Listening directly to her now he was forced into a re-assessment.

'Is your friend married? I know you are not.' She spoke to Bandele.

Suspiciously Kola scanned her face, but it was a genuine question. 'Are you married?' she repeated, facing him now.

'No.'

'But you have children perhaps?'

'None.'

'Well you needn't look so virtuous. You probably knew what to do. Too many young men don't or they simply don't care.'

Monica came in again. 'Has Usaye been here?'

'Come on here, girl, come and sit down. You and your husband leave your guests alone and expect me to take care of them. What do you think I am? Your footman?'

Monica relaxed into her chair, asking, 'Is Mother still playing tough?'

'Well you better start learning to play tough. You know this silly girl nearly ran home a week after she arrived? I went to meet them on the boat and I saw her, you see, leaning on Ayo's arm, a bit scared by the whole strangeness. Oh I am very silly too sometimes, you know what I did? Burst into tears. But Moni didn't understand, she thought I was disappointed or

212

something. She thought I didn't like her. No, you cannot beat a white girl for silliness.'

Kola asked, looking directly at Monica, reckless of what confirmation Bandele drew from it, 'You call her Moni, was that your idea?'

'And whose idea would it have been otherwise—my son's? He has as much imagination as his father. You would have thought it was obvious, that he would be calling her Moni already—we haven't a more beautiful name I can think of. But oh no, he calls her darling. And he calls me Mummy.'

Bandele said, 'Well you can't blame him for a childhood habit.'

'Childhood? But he didn't as a child. No, that Mummy habit he picked up in England, And what annoys me is that he does it only in front of people. Why? You tell me why?'

Kola found he was not looking for justification, all he wanted was enforced abdiction, a transferred deed of possession. He was not even looking for his own exoneration, for this implied acknowledgement of a trial for guilt, and the acquittal. He wished suddenly that he had been left to follow a course blindly, thrown against an equal, pitted against a reluctant loser. In his mouth, a slow sick taste which soon involved Monica, until he found he was despising her, her crime of nearness, of a lack of discrimination, her plain crime of poor judgement becoming slowly worse that Faseyi's self-cancellation. What had she seen anyway, truly? Realising that there must have been talk of love, and oaths . . . and what of the love-making . . . ?

'What is the matter?' Monica's voice directly before him.

'The chicken is already dead, I assure you. No need to stab it like that.'

How much was he showing? If Bandele saw, he would misunderstand. But if he only knew the truth, if he knew his present state of mind . . .

Mrs Faseyi was still talking. 'He will return home and expect this poor child to understand. Darling, they asked me to lunch, it would have been ill-mannered for me not to accept . . . oh I only thought I would look in on my way from the lab.'

The reversal of feeling neared completion, and Kola wondered if Mrs Faseyi would ever know what unwitting purge she achieved by weighting the scales so heavily, against which Faseyi's values took sweeping vengeance, turning all that touched him to equal ineffectuality. For Kola was looking at Monica again . . . was it just the desire to see Africa? When she loved him, was it the dreams she loved, and the sun and the fabled laughter and vitality that never ceased, so they said? . . . for the husband, Kola had no generosity and gave Faseyi no benefit, the prestige of a white wife, above all the prestige of a white wife but why, why, for they said Faseyi was a brilliant man, his colleagues at the hospital respected his knowledge, then why . . . ?

And his mind jumped to the beginning of the meal, Monica sitting with her head inclined, her hands folded across her breast, and Mrs Faseyi's voice cutting across Kola's admiration, 'Please, please spare us the Grace, save that for when you and your husband are alone together.'

He left the house that afternoon defeated, and he could not say with any clarity what he truly demanded, only that, with logic, he resented this contamination of Monica. Returning to the studio he perched Usaye on her stool and took out his brushes. It was this new feeling, he felt, that was the betrayal. Although not a word had passed between them he felt now that he had betrayed Monica.

'Usaye please, please sit still.'

But Usaye was restless that afternoon, lowering her head to scrutinse the silk tassels of the special smock created for Obaluwaiye's handmaiden. 'Usaye, please please . . .' But he found he had little enthusiasm anyway, and he let her go. She did not leave the studio immediately but continued to move among the easels, her eyes stuck to every object as if she inspected them minutely. The door opened slowly and Joe Golder entered.

'I saw your car outside.'

'Come in.'

'Aren't you working? I am dead beat rehearsing for the Vacation Concert. You will still be around won't you?'

'I'm not going anywhere.'

'Isn't this compound nearly healthy again? The students are all gone. Every building is blissfully empty.'

'It is a little more peaceful.'

'When the staff go the cure will be complete.'

'I suppose so.'

'Is something wrong? You are not really attentive.'

'I am, go on.'

'I think residential universities like this exist for the few months of the year when they are wholly empty. That is when they are really worth living in. Now that's a nice academic paradox for you.'

'Yes.'

He lowered his voice. 'It is good for me. When the campus is emptied, there is less temptation. God God, term time is hell for me, hell, hell!'

Kola was apprehensive. He was in no mood to deal with Golder's periodic fits of depression, self-hatred and physical abasement. For he knew the various phases of his disease. Joe Golder, sitting for his portrait, breaking down all at once and beginning to weep, shamelessly, without restraint. He had said once, You should paint me as one of those Indian gods, hermaphrodite. Kola laughed and said, You'd be surprised, we have a few gods like that. In one area they are male, in another female. But he shook his head—No, there is more precision in your gods, as if they made up their minds from the beginning; the remaining confusion is only in the minds of chroniclers. And your carvings of them are strong, masculine. Even in the female deities. Organically Indian gods are hermaphrodite, neither, nor. And with a face fiercely distorted, with an anguish which Kola foolishly, vainly tried to place on canvas, with anger and deep self-hatred, Joe Golder would bellow suddenly, God! They disgust me.

Hunched on a stool like a soul deformed, Joe Golder began to weep out his life.

Joe knew the torment of edging conversation in tutorial classes towards his craving, trying to find cult members, casually discussing the Wolfenden report and watching hawk-like for a reaction. And he had a book of Indian paintings. When he invited students for tea he would show this to them, and watch their faces when puzzled they asked, Is this meant to be man or woman? He lent them his *Life of Nijinsky*. And there was a spate of Indian films in all the theatres and Joe Golder who loathed the tawdry, cheap imitations of Hollywood banalities, would offer to take students to the picture.

'They have such handsome heroes,' some student always said.

'You think so?' Joe Golder would ask. 'You like that sort of beauty?'

'Oh yes, I would give a lot to be as handsome as that.'

'But don't you think he is too effeminate, rather like a woman.'

'Of course, he is almost too handsome.'

'But you wouldn't mind being like that?'

'What is wrong with being handsome?'

'Sometimes,' Joe would say, 'I wonder if their men take after their gods or the gods after their men. Anyway, it's all very well for their gods but you could get assaulted if you looked like that—by men, I mean.'

'You mean I'd be mistaken for a woman?'

'Yes and no. With some people it makes no difference.'

'What sort of lunatics are those?'

Chagrined always to discover that the craving for beauty or 'handsomeness' was only one more student aesthetic malformation, Joe Golder roamed the college at night, roamed the night-clubs where he misjudged the swaggering hips of a tight-jeaned thug, the cultivated indolence of his eyelids, the pomade of his hair; and took a savage beating in his flat from the incredulous mortally insulted thug and dared not call the police.

And his houseboy blackmailed him once, so that in desperation he ran to a lawyer who told him to ignore the threats, and efficiently had the blackmailer fleeing to the safety of his home town.

Joe Golder asking them to sherry and recitals, accidental brushes with the knee, begging reciprocation.

And Joe Golder fleeing to the reference hall of the library when the craving took him and he feared the consequences of probes that did not succeed. Here he would watch them and despise them. Grubs, he said, mere maggots. They fill their heads with knowledge and churn it out but they are not changed in the process, they are like the single straight gut of the cockroach, mixing knowledge with saliva and spitting it back at the examiner. He despised them but not their bodies, so he stood in the reference room and watched them come in, watched their reflections on the shiny floor and marvelled at their beauty, letting it overpower him, and in satiety alone did Joe know safety, and something approximate to cure. From that floor rose their sensuousness and their mockery, his fantasies, and once he said, as in a crystal glass, his fate. In huge numbers he was safe, his senses confounded him and he knew not where to turn and desire died. Joe Golder stood in the library staring at huge tomes of encyclopaedia, watching legs in shorts, slavering over blackness until he felt sick and giddy and was gradually restored.

Joe Golder, ugly on a stool, confessing, 'Do you remember that first time I asked you for drinks? That afternoon when . . .'

How could he forget? Entering the flat, he was astonished to see Joe lying on the sofa, naked, with a scant towel on the small of his back and pretending to read *Giovanni's Room*.

'It is so terribly hot, isn't it? What time is it? I was just going to have a bath.'

But Kola had seen Joe as he came past the block, and Joe was then fully dressed, standing in the balcony. When Kola entered he rose, he let the towel fall completely and stood up in uncircumcised nakedness. Kola went to the fireplace and said, 'Didn't know these flats had fireplaces.' Joe Golder tried a few more experiments, giving up eventually, and they could then become friends. And of all his models, only he would pose fully in the nude. He had a hard-sprung body, truly beautiful. 'You see,' he said, 'my body is fully negro; it is simply an act of perverseness that I turn out mostly white.' And then he leapt up suddenly ran round to look at the first brush strokes. 'For God's sake, blacken me. Make me the blackest black blackness in your pantheon.'

'What I really came to ask,' Joe Golder was saying, 'was about Sekoni's work. You know I want the Wrestler.'

'I am holding an exhibition of his works soon. Someone is coming from Lagos to help me assess them—all the money will go to his wife.'

'He was married?'

'Yes. A long time ago in fact.'

'Children?'

'One.'

'I never guessed it.'

'If possible I will time the exhibition for your concert. We could even hold it in the theatre foyer.'

Joe Golder was overjoyed with the idea.

'I will mark the Wrestler sold then, but you won't get it till after the exhibition.'

'Suits me. Thanks, Kola. And that idea of yours for using the theatre is great—simply great.'

The door opened again and Bandele entered, throwing Kola instantly on his guard, almost belligerent, 'If you have come to start . . .'

Bandele raised his book. 'I only came for some peace. Simi's found out Egbo is in town. She was waiting in my flat when we got back.'

Kola gave a long thin whistle. 'Does she know about the other girl?'

'I didn't wait to find out.'

15

Power . . . and Kola found he was thinking about what Egbo had said. For Egbo, saying it, made it sound almost like experience, and Kola had often felt from this point alone if for no other, that his role and Egbo's should be reversed. Fitfully, far too fitfully for definite realisation of the meaning, he had felt this sense of power, the knowledge of power within his hands, of the will to transform; and he understood then that medium was of little importance, that the act, on canvas or on human material was the process of living and brought him the intense fear of fulfilment. And this was another paradox, that he dared not, truly, be fulfilled. At his elbow was the invisible brake which drew him back from final transportation in the act. It was typical that Egbo would volunteer to return with him to Noah, for Egbo did not hesitate to pursue the elusive, never sought to define even in their frequent futile arguments. In fact it was the point of Egbo battling with the world that experience led him to his spoken acceptances, and he formulated nothing before. And Sekoni, there was also Sekoni, and he had exploded suddenly with this fact of power, but Kola cast back his mind and knew it was not so sudden. For how could the actual artifact be more important than the revelation in the man's living power? The Wrestler he recognised belatedly, knowing its physical identity came from a long forgotten fight in the Mayomi club, begun inevitably by Egbo. Egbo had been truly brittle that night. Some thoughts evoked the darker passes of his mood, and then of course he would turn fox in the fable—you spoiled my water—no?— well if it wasn't you it was your father—any slight served him then, swatting nagging thoughts with sudden violence. A waiter provided the excuse, passing undisguised comments because the chairs were stacked and the other customers departed, and only their table was left occupied and silent and the waiters were eager to be home and sleeping. But they sat on and on not drinking or moving, not even talking. No one knew how it began but the insolent one passed close to Egbo and Egbo tripped him. In a moment the night was chaos. Bandele sat unconcerned until the door-keeper, a heavy tightly jeaned chucker-out fell against him as if by accident, and Bandele was catapulted backwards into a stack of chairs which fell over him completely and buried him from sight. The thug —he was called Okonje—swaggered round while Kola kept him at bay with a bottle, longing for the police to arrive and take the burden of self-protection from their hands. But suddenly, Okonje was down. Without warning, for no immediate cause, Okonje was down. And then they saw it was a twin object, a pair of hempen loops frayed, it seemed, at both ends, which groped silently through the debris of chair legs and jerked Okonje by the legs. And just as efficiently, they began to truss him, working swiftly. One end passed beneath the thug's arm and round his throat, across his back. A piece seized the man in the knee and thigh joint, forcing his thigh across his chest. Grotesque he was, like a folded dessicated corpse of the Maori, emitting squeaks like a pig thigh-bound for slaughter. Even Egbo was stopped in his next propulsion by the sight. Of the rest of what belonged to Bandele there was little sign, so the man seemed to be tied up on his own. Swiftly Okonje was dragged towards the pile on his buttocks and he slid like a dog's dirty habit, backwards until he came against the edge of the mound. Gradually the sinews vanished behind a more complacent skin, relieved of tension . . . and Sekoni moved round the captive thug, stricken by the result. His eyes followed the arms observing the patterns of twine and stress while Kola and Egbo carefully unpiled the wrought-iron catafalque. Sekoni, in tumbling degrees of disbelief, thrill, admiration and anticipation, worked himself into a state of soothing dumbness. The fight was several years before the Wrestler, before they all left the country and scattered over the face of the Western World, and Kola was remembering now how the tension of the sculpture had been at once familiar and estranged . . . but Sekoni had kept this knowledge within him until its power burst out of itself, in a work seemingly divorced, of much pain and piety. Obscuring his own identity.

So perhaps, for himself and, if this final intuition did not betray him and the canvas was ready, Kola would hang it up at Sekoni's exhibition . . . 'if we ever get back alive,' speaking aloud the same thought as beat in Egbo's head.

For they were lost. The rain had begun early in the afternoon, washing out every landmark and submerging huts and the smaller market stalls. In settlements around the lagoon, the water rises quickly, blotting vegetation from sight and fouling raised stores of clean water, even on high shelves among the rafters.

Bobbing potsherds, soot-glazed without and fouled within by congealed messes of oil and coins and the sacrificed fowl—it was as if the jealous sea had burst from underbowels of earth, sweeping off the offerings for lesser gods and clean-picked reeds of sleeping mats . . . they deserted the car at a bridge of squelching planks—all the bridges looked the same—makeshift and unsafe, four planks laid across sluggish semi-canals of lagoon seepage. A dead goat, enormously distended, was wedged against a corner of the planks and two dogs tried to pull it out without wetting their muzzles. They held their noses against its stink and went forward.

'So ends the reign of Noah as the sunshine saint.' Kola grumbled.

'We didn't pass through so much water, Kola. We cannot be anywhere near the place.'

'No, we are right so far.'

'Let's go back. I am not for this aquatic treasure hunt.'

'No, what we ought to do is split. You take that direction and I'll take this. If either of us finds the way, we come back here and wait.'

'Not just wait, shout. The sound will carry well on the water.'

'All right. Let's say we search initially for thirty minutes.'

'Initially my foot. After thirty minutes we go back home.'

A heavy course of submerged objects, late corn stalks dragging their heads on the copper lap of floods. The ground below was treacherous, Egbo pulled out a stake and began to test the water as he went along, pulling out each foot with increasing boredom from the suck of earth under shallow but dangerous puddles. It was impossible to skirt them all and even the bared earth was clogging all the way. 'I can't believe our cars passed this way ever,' Egbo insisted. Now it seemed possible to miss a foothold, to misjudge the ground and disappear forever in some hidden bog.

Under the heavy brood of grey, Egbo began to wonder how high the water had risen in the church of Lazarus. He remembered now that it was built on a slight rise of land, but the floods seemed ambitious enough for the main church, even for the altar several steps above the nave. A rotted half of a canoe shifting silt and slopping water reminded him of the telephone operator's voice in Sagoe's office which drove him mad and he was wondering what he had known, what he had seen, for he knew humanity welled in his throat like bilge-water in a black, decayed dug-out. Often he had watched Sagoe heave from heel tendons nostalgic for the company of alienates where he could sniff and unsniff emotions like a stranger . . . Sagoe, Sagoe . . . but then, weren't they all caught in a common centrifuge through the hurt of gilded abstractions, full of flies, reaching for a long time-whisk to brush away thought-smarts embedded in each sting. . . .

It was not possible that this grey dragging silence could be part of the morning's sea of brown shingle and gentle laps against the beach, for now Egbo saw the cross. As if it hooked a branch within its armpit, the cross, its base stuck in the mud below, raised a short length of the head above the water,

221

pointing at Egbo. Egbo looked around, but the church was nowhere near. It was already dark but he realised now that he could not be far from the church and he balanced dangerously on the tree and squinted into the distance. He could not be certain, but it seemed he could discern the outlines of the church against the even grey. Egbo went forward, darkness overtaking him completely.

Egbo-o-o-o-o-o Egbo-o-o-o-o-o Egbo-o-o-o-o-o. The voice was so distant, leaping, a reed-fly of sound, from surface to surface of the water, hardly disturbing it with a ripple. It sounded so distant and remote, like his aunt calling from nearly the length of the beach against the sea of recurrent surfs which beat about his ears and deafened him. Egbo-o-o-o-o-o Egbo-o-o-o-o-o . . . for it was his first glimpse as a child, there was his excited rush to bathe his feet in sea water, succeeding against the frantic caution of his aunt who lay tired under the moon and shut her eyes for too long a brief moment. And he had thought it strange that she who took to air so freely should live in such terror of the sea. 'Just stay near me and let the white fringe come and lick your feet. Wait right here and the water will come to you.' But he ran far far away from the sleeping figure . . . 'Help, help! Egbo, come back, Egbo-o-o-o-o-o.' But he meant to catch two full pulses of the sea and he wanted the water up to his knees, not merely on his toes. As the water retreated the aunt caught up and her blow catapulted him into the very danger from which she sought to protect him.

As they returned to where her wrapper was spread, 'Is it now the Mammy-water will come out?'

'Just shut your mouth and come along.'

Egbo-o-o-o-o-o Egbo-o-o-o-o-o. . . . Leaping on the glaze of water where he stood.

Kola! It was long past the agreed half hour and Kola would be anxious for him. He stopped. He was fed up with the abortive search anyway . . .

And then he saw flames. From what had been until a moment before total darkness, a sudden leap of flames throwing flickering reflections on the corn-mill presence of the church. In an arc, framing a canoe which sat between two lines of flames, on water which danced madly with fires within but only pulsed gently on the surface. The flames—and frantic with the mystery, Egbo was seeking solutions—were no higher than the ribs and they ran nearly a hundred yards along the shore. In the glow Egbo now saw clearly fishermen's stakes driven into sea-bed, a narrow fish-trap blocked from the body of the sea by a siltbank. Within this long inlet, on a mere finger of water, rose the flames, for there was no doubt about it, they burnt from the surface of the pool.

A change in the wind, bringing the acrid smell of petrol and the sight of a barrel on its side told the rest. There was no other human within sight, and now he made out the two figures who waited at the other end of the trap, Lazarus and Noah.

The flames had hardly risen when the canoe moved forward, cutting cleanly through the passage. It took no time at all before swift strokes took the rowers to the end where Lazarus and Noah waited. Lazarus stepped in the canoe, balanced himself, then stretched his hand to Noah. Egbo strained hard for details and it seemed that the white sleeves of the rowers had been scorched black on the inward journey. Sweat had broken free on their faces, and they kept, in that wait which surely lengthened, to the centre of the cross-benches. And their discomfort grew in the heat, because Noah did not move. Lazarus stretched his hand and withdrew it instantly as flames licked hungrily at his sleeves. But Noah stood transfixed unable to withdraw his eyes from the fire. Lazarus waited and the two rowers dared not look on the shore but waited for Lazarus to act. There was no word spoken, only waiting, until Noah the apostate should find his courage, or the pale reed, erect in the fire-framed canoe should yield and journey alone through the passage of fire.

Noah did not look Lazarus in the eye, and this much was plain, that Lazarus waited for the moment when he would do this. The wait had been too long already, and tar began to glisten with a dangerous wetness on the canoe sides. Behind Lazarus, the unmasked sea dissolving into darkness, dark pools in the vastness, feeler eyes of Olokun; would the canoe remain beyond endurance, burnt offering at midnight for the god?

And still Noah would not take his eyes from the flames. There was a crack from the wood and the rowers looked, not pleading, but they looked at Lazarus as if to say, surely now they should wait no longer. There came another crack and something snapped in Noah. He turned and began to run. In Egbo's direction he ran, even as the flames began to die and the canoe, wholly frizzled at the sides, emitted weaker sounds and the line of watchers rushed forward, using a pole and pulling Lazarus shorewards. Noah ran blindly on while Lazarus stood, heedless of the mooring of the boat, and the apostles watched the receding figure of Noah, stumbling in thick mud, entangling himself in hidden nets. Egbo heard the repulsive squash of night crabs, squashed under Noah's bare feet as he looked back in fear of pursuit. And the flames went slowly down, throwing a long shadow of Lazarus against his church. He stood a long time while the Apostles waited. And then he moved inland and the church swallowed him, alone with the enormous burden of his defeat.

Egbo wondered why he felt no pity for Lazarus, but he was glad that his presence was unknown to the albino. And as he walked back in the direction Noah had taken, it seemed to him that he must keep the secret of this man's defeat.

16

And of these floods of the beginning, of the fevered fogs of the beginning, of the first messenger, the thimble of earth, a fowl and an ear of corn, seeking the spot where a scratch would become a peopled island; of the first apostate rolling the boulder down the back of the unsuspecting deity—for they must learn the first stab in the back and keep inferiors harmless within sight—and shattering him in fragments, which were picked up and pieced together with devotion; shell of the tortoise around divine breath; of the endless chain for the summons of the god and the phallus of unorigin pointed at the sky-hole past divination; of the lover of purity, the unblemished one whose large compassion embraced the cripples and the dumb, the dwarf, the epileptic—and why not, indeed, for they were creations of his drunken hand and what does it avail, the eternal penance of favouritism and abstinence? Of the lover of gore, invincible in battle, insatiable in love and carnage, the explorer, path-finder, protector of the forge and the creative hands, companion of the gourd whose crimson-misted sight of debauchery set him upon his own and he butchered them until the bitter cry pierced his fog of wine, stayed his hand and hung the sword, foolish like his dropped jaw; of the one who hanged and did not hang, who ascended on the llana to sky vaults and mastered the snake-tongued lightning and the stone of incandescence, long arms of the divine sling playing the random game of children, plucking houses trees and children like the unripe mango; of the bi-sexed one that split himself into the river; of the parting of the fog and the retreat of the beginning, and the eternal war of the divining eyes, of the hundred and one eyes of lore, fore-and after-vision, of the eternal war of the first procedure with the long sickle head of chance, eternally mocking the pretensions of the bowl of plan, mocking lines of order in the ring of chaos; of the repulsive Scourge riding purulent on noontides of silent heat selective of victims, the avaricious one; of the one who stayed to tend the first fruits of the ginger of earth with passages of the wind around him and of the heat and the rain, and the marks of the moulting seasons . . .

Kola said, 'It requires only the bridge, or the ladder between heaven and earth. A rope or a chain. The link, that is all. After fifteen months, all that is left is the link . . .'

Egbo interrupted, 'The moment that you say *to*, my knife will go in the neck of this ram. *To*, and a fountain of blood will strike the ceiling of this studio.'

'I hope you like it,' Simi said.

'You know what she first bought?' Egbo asked. 'A white ram. A white ram, if you please.'

'Well, you said a spotless ram.'

'The more reason why it should have been a black ram. A white ram cannot be spotless, it cannot really be spotless, can it?'

'Joe Golder would have given you a lecture if the ram had been white. Inferiority colour complex, he'd have called it.'

'Who is Joe Golder?'

'You've never met him? Come to think of it, you didn't attend his concert the other time.'

'No, I didn't, that was the time she didn't turn up, the faithless bitch.'

'That was your fault. The message you sent was that you would come to my house.'

'No, I said you were to meet me at Bandele's.'

'I've told you, the boy said . . .'

'Are you two going to start that all over again? And I haven't thanked you for the ram, Simi.'

'You should thank me, not her. I asked her to buy it.'

'Who paid for it?'

'That is not the point.'

'It is as far as I am concerned.'

Monica came in, stopped short on seeing Simi. Egbo introduced them and Monica was full of admiration. 'Of course. You are the beautiful lady, but . . . it is incredible.'

Kola explained, 'She was convinced I had idealised her in the painting.'

'Yes I thought he . . . oh how rude of me to keep staring, but she really is beautiful. I don't think your goddess in the flesh could be any more beautiful. Honestly, Kola, now I've seen her, your painting doesn't do her justice.'

'Just one moment,' Egbo stood up. 'I thought none of us was supposed to see that thing until the full completion.'

Monica's hand flew to her mouth and she gave a little squeak, flushing furiously.

Kola waved his hands blandly, 'It was an accident . . .'

'I'm sure it was an accident, go on.'

'Well it doesn't matter because she hasn't sat for me. I couldn't have you . . . well, you heard the kind of thing she's been shouting since she came in, as if I asked Simi to come here and pose for herself. Suppose you all took to complaining that I've made something of you which you aren't . . . I mean, the whole point is that you are substituting . . .'

'Sure, sure, we understand, don't we Simi?'

'Well, it was an accident as she said, only it doesn't really matter with her, you see.'

'Oh please, don't explain, we understand.' Egbo quickly dodged a paint tube while Simi smiled within the placid framework of her enigma.

'Come on, Simi, some wait for fifteen months to see a masterpiece, others storm it in a week.'

'Tether the ram outside on your way out.'

'Sure, sure, we know we are not needed.'

'You are not working,' Monica said; they had been alone for some time.

'No. I am still waiting for Lazarus.'

'Lazarus? I thought it was Noah you called him.'

'I have done with Noah. This faceless creature here is Noah . . . come over . . . he is the treacherous servant rolling the stone that would crush his master.'

'But you said . . .'

'That was an error of judgement. Noah as the link? I ought to drown myself for my stupidity. I had him here, sitting here, while I tried to formulate Esumare around his neutrality. I was wrong, woefully, amateurishly wrong. When I had fought him four hours without the trace of a beginning, I had to stop and for the first time I truly looked at Noah. If I hadn't been suffering from an overdose of cynicism I would have seen it that first time. Noah was simply negative. The innocence of his face was unrelieved vacuity—he had nothing, absolutely nothing. I despised my lack of perception.'

'So who is Lazarus?'

'Noah's master. Some religion-peddling albino whom Sagoe picked up. He is bringing him up this afternoon, it's he I am waiting for.'

'And then?'

'Then, it is finally finished. I will work all night if necessary. You know, Monica, I have become so desperately eager to be done with it. Apart from the exhibition tomorrow I am fed up, simply sick and fed up with the sight of this canvas. And then . . . never mind, that can keep.'

'Why? Tell me.'

'No, it is not important, believe me. You must know by now that I am not really an artist. I never set out to be one. But I understand the nature of art and so I make an excellent teacher of art. That is all. This canvas, for instance. Egbo started me on it, unwittingly of course, and in fact he should be labouring it out, not me. For one thing he is closer to the subject, really close you know, and he is sufficiently ruthless.

But at least I can record, my intimations of all these presences have been too momentary and they come in disjointed fragments, that is why I have taken so long . . .'

'Fifteen months is not a long time, and you have done a number of other things in between.'

'Nothing that I am particularly proud of. Nothing I would place beside Sekoni's works, even leaving out the Wrestler.'

'And the Pantheon?'

'The Pantheon is weight. It will confound the senses, browbeat objective responses. But I talk of myself now, and the process of living. Even Sagoe has a sort of seventh sense, a kind of creative antenna with which he pursues his vocation. But I . . . you tell me, would Egbo ever have mistaken Noah for Esumare, would he? It is accidents like that which kill spontaneity and make a fumbler of the artist. And I mistook the nature of his apostasy. . . .'

Monica stood close before him and, doubtfully, taking the initial step at last that would commit them both, she nuzzled her long blonde hair against his neck. 'Isn't it simply that the work is nearly finished and you are filled with doubts? Kola, but it is a normal thing, the desire not to believe in yourself because you fear others might not.'

'No it isn't . . .'

'And you are so afraid of compassion, even of tenderness as if this might weaken you. But your nature is a tender one, so why look at Egbo especially as you misunderstand him anyway.'

'Misunderstand?'

'You are not the only one. Bandele also thinks you all lead callous, indifferent lives.'

There was a sound of a car and Monica sprang away.

'I hope it's Sagoe at last,' Kola said.

'It's him,' the voice announced from the door. 'Lazarus is outside. Shall I bring him in?'

'Of course.'

'Your last figure is here, I won't disturb you.' And she made for the door. 'What did you call him?'

'Esumare. The vomit streak of the heavenly serpent.'

And Kola began work like a man demented while Lazarus sat with monumental stillness, easily the best sitter he had ever used. That he had something on his mind was obvious. He looked round the studio with a question in his eye, but it was one which Kola chose to postpone until he had the man imprisoned in the existence he had formulated and daily re-shaped. Lazarus was obediently still and Kola worked in a ferment, as if the world would wait no longer for a drawn-out pledge.

Two hours passed before he began to ease, and Lazarus shifted also on the stool. 'Where is Noah?'

'Roaming the college, I expect. He comes to eat when he is hungry. The houseboy looks after him.'

He appeared to collect his thoughts again. 'At the very least, I thought, a successor. I needed one from outside the church. The Apostles are only human, they are jealous of one another. I was looking for a youth, reckless, a youth with an inner fire.'

'Like the other Apostles?'

'Yes,' he admitted. 'Like the others. There must be something to convert. A peaceable man makes a good church-goer but he is not a reliable christian, full of fire and dedication. The more evil a man has known in fact, the more strength I have got from him. I know these things. I taught them to myself by trial and discovery. The church is my dedication and I am a self-taught man in everything. I can read the Bible in Greek, did you know that? In Greek. Because I found an old Bible in Greek and I was seized by a desire to learn the language of the Greeks, thinking this was the same as Hebrew. It wasn't, but at least I gained a knowledge of Greek.'

'Few people can boast of that.'

'What is truly important to me is that I know the arithmetic of religion. The murderer is your future martyr, he is your most willing martyr. Few fools know that.'

'Tell me, how did you convert Noah?' Kola was only half-attentive, and the albino's reaction shattered his concentration.

He was nearly shouting. 'Convert! I converted nothing. What you wrestle with, what you fight and defeat, that is true conversion. To change the nature of a real thief in a week, did you ever hear of that! I persisted only because it was the time of floods and this is the time for our Revivalist Services. We needed Noah. My true disciples are the thieves, the rejected of society. One of the apostles is a forger who has spent five years in prison. Another was the only member who escaped arrest when his gang was caught after a bank robbery. Urgent though my need was I could not break this rule. I had to find a sinner.'

'Any murderers?' Kola asked.

'One. He matcheted his wife in a village near Ughelli.'

Some minutes later, recovering his calm, he said, 'I must try and see that Noah does not return to the gutter.'

'You have plans for him?'

'None. He is free to go where he pleases—outside Lagos.' And he grew vehement again, 'I do not want him in Lagos. It is not right that any of my church should meet him picking pockets or loitering in the markets.'

And as the thought took possession of him, Lazarus rose suddenly. 'You say you do not know where he is? You have left him to go as he pleases?'

'He can't be far, please sit down.'

'Let's go and find him.'

'Just a few more minutes.'

'We will come back, Mr Kola, you should not hurry so much, and after all I have submitted to your law of stillness since I came.'

'Noah is all right. He only plays around.'

'You should have more patience. Even the man who holds the gift of creation is full of patience.'

'Is he? If we are thinking of the same person didn't he fix the world in six days?'

'Please, let us go and find him now. I have this feeling of danger to myself when I think of the path that lies before him from now.'

'All right, if you feel you would like a break . . .'

'No, Mr Kola, it is not a matter of resting. If a man meets Noah now and he says come, let us go and steal a fowl, he will follow him.'

'Why should that worry you? If he lands in gaol you will only sleep more peacefully.'

Egbo, driving Simi back to Bandele's house, saw Noah beneath a mango tree and stopped the car. He stood among the other fruit-raiders hurling sticks at the lone ripe mango on a branch of hard green clusters. Egbo called him, Noah made no response and he began to wonder if this was the same Noah.

Of his experience of a few days before there was no trace; something, he did not know what, should be there to remind him of the fire scene, but Egbo found no hint, no evidence of his terror and his flight. Nothing of the whipped gratitude with which he accepted the offer of a lift, his pathetic eagerness when Kola asked, would you like to come with me to Ibadan? and the way he cowered in a corner at the back making no sound until Egbo dropped off at his flat and Kola returned to Ibadan with his prize.

'Who is he?' Simi asked him.

'One minute, I won't be long.' And over the rotten fruits he went, with the rise of fat, bluebottle swarms and he tapped Noah on the shoulder. Noah started, looked blankly at him. Scanning him closer, Egbo found that the result was the same; the experience of the passage of fire had been washed off or had simply never been. Noah was cleansed of every moment of his past except this new instant of mango raiding.

'You are a phenomenon,' Egbo said.

'Sah?'

'Come with me.'

It was a sudden moment of curiosity. What would the confrontation of Noah and Lazarus after that night be like? He found he wanted to be present at the meeting. Noah came happily with him, although—Egbo was sure—he did not remember him at all. To cleanse, Egbo was thinking, to really cleanse a human being, you must leave him like Noah, dead, devitalised, with no character of any sort, a blank white sheet for accidental scribbles.

'Were you always like this, Noah, or is this the work of Lazarus?'

'Sah?'

Simi hit him playfully. 'Why do you talk like that to him when he doesn't understand?'

'I am talking to myself, really, I am bouncing back my voice on the smooth brass reflector of that . . . ah, I cannot even call him an apostate now. We were all wrong, all disgracefully wrong. Kola left the heavenly bodies out of his Pantheon or he would have known Noah for what he is. Noah's apostasy is not the wilful kind, it is simply the refusal to be, the refusal to be a living being, like a moon.'

'What are you talking about?'

'Never mind. If you weren't a cannibal you would probably have gone the same way. . . .' He leapt out of the car before Simi could touch him. And his face turned grave almost at once, and he entered dragging his feet, waves of shame over him, recalling how once he had called his grandfather an apostate.

Egbo saw a secretive movement in the corner just behind the canvas, and he stood, watching. At last a white face peeked out from behind the easel and a man came out, grinning sheepishly,

'Hallo.'

'Who are you?'

'Sorry to look so guilty but I sneaked in here to take a look at the canvas. I couldn't wait to see the latest addition.'

Egbo walked slowly towards the man, still eyeing him with suspicion.

'You must be one of Kola's friends. I am Joe Golder.'

'Oh, the singer.'

'Yes. Were you looking for Kola?'

'Where is he?'

'I saw him go out with the man from Lagos. I can see this place from my flat you see, so when they left I thought I would sneak in here and have a look. To tell you the truth I do that all the time, but please don't tell Kola!'

'I think I'll borrow a leaf from you. I seem to be the only one with too strong a sense of respect for this artist.'

Joe Golder laughed, he was almost childlike in his delight at a fellow conspirator. 'I think I know which of the figures you are. In fact I recognised you at once. What do you think of the latest bit?'

Egbo took his eyes away from what he really wanted to see, his own presence in the overpowering canvas. The unfinished part was an arched figure rising not from a dry grave, but from a primordial chaos of gaseous whorls and flood-waters. He is wreathed in nothing but light, a pure rainbow translucence. It was Lazarus, Kola's new dimension to the covenant.

Egbo moved his head gently from side to side, as if he meant to clear it.

'I am confused,' he admitted.

'Why?'

'I cannot accept this view of life. He has made the beginning itself a resurrection. This is an optimist's delusion of continuity.'

'I think it is very clever.'

'I said nothing about that.'

'It works. What more does one demand?'

'My friend has very uneven talents. Look at that thing he has made of me for instance, a damned bloodthirsty maniac from some maximum security zoo. Is that supposed to be me? Or even Ogun, which I presume it represents?'

'What is wrong with it?'

'It is an uninspired distortion, that is what is wrong with it. He has taken one single myth, Ogun at his drunkennest, losing his sense of recognition and slaughtering his own men in battle; and he has frozen him at the height of carnage.'

'Well, surely you must concede him the right to select.'

'It is his selectiveness I quarrel with. Even the moment of Ogun's belated awareness would have been . . . at least that does contain poetic possibilities. This blood-spattered fiend is merely melodramatic. And then there is Ogun of the forge, Ogun as the primal artisan . . . but he leaves all that to record me as this bestial gore-blinded thug!'

'You see, he was right. He always said it would be like that if he let you near the canvas.'

'It's all very well for you. Isn't this your steel-plated head doing office here for Erinle?'

'I find it most unflattering. But perhaps the god is even worse off—I take consolation from that, you see.'

'I am leaving,' Egbo announced. 'And I'm taking my ram with me.'

'Oh, is that beautiful ram yours?'

'Yes, I had it bought to mark the finish of the painting, and Sekoni's exhibition—oh, I forgot it isn't just for that palette clown alone.'

'You mean, to . . . kill it?'

'What else do you do with rams? Milk them?'

Joe Golder reacted with a nervous expression which Egbo caught but misunderstood.

'Don't you like goat meat?'

'No, it isn't that. It's the killing. The thought of blood makes me feel funny inside.'

Egbo looked at his hard-knit head, his strong, compact, muscle-tense body, and could not believe it.

'It's true. I really cannot stand the sight of blood.'

Egbo went out shaking his head. 'Where is Noah?' he asked Simi.

'He came out after you. I thought he followed you into the studio.'

'Oh to hell with Noah anyway. Let's go.'

Her favourite movement when Egbo was angry, she began to caress the nape of his neck. 'What annoyed you in there?'

'It's that irreligious dauber. You should have seen the monster he made of me.'

'Oh, you saw it? What about me?'

'You? Oh, you. I had forgotten you were even on the damned thing.'

He started the car and drove off furiously, leaving Noah in the studio with Joe Golder.

17

The chilly arms of darkness and the lights of the Eucharist—Egbo contained the liturgy in drum resonances of his head, not out aloud, as on his first night with Simi—and I do not fear to wake into the fear of closure for there are lights in Simi's thighs. I shall flood the Grail from you woman, immolate me on your wantonness and I will argue it till judgement day, if this be sin—come . . . No other woman had this power, to plunge him through infinite sounds and acute timbres of the skin.

'You are not with me tonight, Egbo.'

'I am not?'

'Who are you thinking of?'

For he was truly trying to discover why he had sought the

power of that stranger girl to erode the week-end hold of Simi's love, and her mystery was strong with him again, so that he longed almost to leap up as soon as the love-making was over, to leap up and run to seek her wherever she was hidden. And he could not understand, because she had sent the note to console him when Sekoni died, and she had given before as she now gave by that act of kindness he could not say which humanity touched him more, the afternoon of the river or the ugly scribble on the paper which truly worked a measure of consolation. She guarded her thoughts, gave no more than he found willing, and he had gazed on her, loving her, adoring her, saying, this is the new woman of my generation, proud of the gift of mind and guarding her person from violation. But the rememberance was bitter because he had not fully taken from her or given in turn, for she held herself like a goddess so that they fell apart, strangers. And so was Simi, but in such a different sense that his head spun in confusion and he lay back, bitterly frustrated.

Simi also had her ritual. Solemnly she would first lock up his trousers in the wardrobe and hang the key from a long thread nearly dangling to the ground.

At two o'clock she heard the sound of stones against the window and woke him. He went to the window. Standing in the yellow light of a street lamp was Bandele.

'What is it?'

'Come down. Put on your clothes and come down.'

Egbo's mind was a blank and he declined to strain it. Simi had sat up and was looking at him.

'Who is it?'

'Bandele.'

'At this time of night?' Egbo pulled up the key by the string. 'What does he want?'

'I didn't ask. You were listening.'

'You've arranged this with him.'

'Yes.'

'Oh, I don't mind.'

Egbo dressed swiftly. 'When are you coming back?'

'How do I know!'

He ran down the stairs and joined Bandele in the car. Sitting in the rear was a man he did not know. He was a drivelling, sagging ape, he looked as if he had been bulky but was now depleted and he moaned streams of raucous jargon to which the constant intelligible refrain was, 'I don't want to have to leave the country . . . I don't want to have to leave the country . . .' It was only the ability to speak at all which separated this figure from the wreck that was Noah on the night of the trial by fire.

Bandele starting the car said, 'Noah is dead.'

He stopped the car at the home of a doctor friend, and Joe Golder was given a sedative. Only then did Egbo perceive a remote resemblance between the man in the back of the car and the Joe Golder he had encountered that afternoon.

There was a light in the studio and Kola was up working late on final touches while Lazarus stretched out on a camp-bed although he was not asleep. Bandele stopped the car a little down the road and said to Egbo, 'Better call him out, Lazarus may be in there.'

Kola came out and Bandele said, 'Noah is dead. Joe says he fell off the balcony.'

On Joe Golder, the sedative was beginning to take effect and he whined in a drowsy monotone, 'I told him to stop . . . I shouted stop! stop! I swore I wouldn't touch him . . . I pleaded, I swore I wouldn't touch him . . .'

Bandele said, 'Egbo, just quieten him, will you?'

Egbo leaned over the seat and patted him on the knee.

'Was he up to his stuff?' Kola asked.

Bandele nodded. 'I was asleep and I heard him knocking on the door, wildly. He came in already hysterical, babbling, incoherent. Anyway I managed to gather that Noah took fright when he began the usual stuff.'

'What's all this? What's this stuff business?'

'Didn't you know?' Bandele asked.

'What am I supposed to know?'

'About Joe Golder, he's queer.'

As from vileness below human imagining Egbo snatched his hand away, his face distorted with revulsion and a sense of the degrading contamination. He threw himself forward, away even from the back seat, staring into the sagging figure at the back as at some noxious insect, and he felt his entire body crawl in disgust. His hand which had touched Joe Golder suddenly felt foreign to his body and he got out of the car and wiped it on grass dew. Bandele and Kola stared at him, isolated from this hatred they had not known in Egbo, and the sudden angry spasms that seemed to overtake each motion of his body.

Kola asked at last, 'What do we do now?'

Bandele shrugged. 'Tell Lazarus.'

'Have you seen the body?'

'Yes.'

'You are sure he is dead? Have you called a doctor?'

'He is dead.'

'Well, let's tell Lazarus.'

Bandele came out of the car, and Egbo leapt out suddenly away from the physical intimacy of him alone in a car with Joe Golder, and followed them.

Lazarus, the bridge of moon-beam piercing sky and earth, slight as a ghost and weary as the resurrection, sat arched on the camp-bed as if he waited for them. His body was expectant and he watched them approach.

Bandele said it simply, standing over him. And Lazarus did not stir, his face bore no change of feeling. At last he said,

'Did they catch him stealing and beat him to death?'

Kola looked up slowly at Bandele but Bandele said nothing more. Egbo kept away from it all, sitting on a stool and glaring at Kola's canvas. And the feeling grew in him that he was trapped on it, for ever, with the primal slime of all creation.

'He escaped once before,' Lazarus was saying. 'Perhaps he thought I would always be around to rescue him.'

'He wasn't beaten to death,' Bandele said. 'He fell from the top-floor of a building.'

'He couldn't even scale a window like a decent thief,' said Lazarus.

Bandele turned round then, and looked at Egbo sitting away from them. And he appeared to make up his mind. 'Yes, the flat-owner surprised him and he fell trying to escape.'

Bandele said it with obvious loudness. Egbo was only briefly startled and he looked back scornfully at both him and Kola. Lazarus turned over on his side and they all went out from the studio.

'You must get him somewhere where he'll be safe and quiet. If he gets talking he will endanger himself.'

'We will have to tell the police and that is where there'll be trouble.'

237

'I will speak to a doctor. If Joe is ill from shock then he can't make statements.'

Egbo refused to enter the car. He said he would walk the four miles to town and Simi's house.

18

'There would have been little wrong,' Sagoe said, 'if the man had stated it starkly. But he sent his imagination on a wild horseman riot.' And Sagoe read aloud the editorial again . . . 'In conclusion we would just like to say of this brain-child of the Honourable Member for Leko Division, spattered on the hallowed walls of an astounded House of Parliament, that it had all the discharge of spontaneity, without the freshness.'

They seized upon it gratefully, for Noah was a subject to be pushed from thought, to be wholly effaced from conscious recognition.

'You wrote that, I suppose?'

'Of course. You can recognise my style.'

'You led him astray in the first place.'

'Not with intention. Listen, and Bandele, I want you to give your opinion on this . . .'

'Please . . .'

'All right, all right. Now, Kola, this is what happened. I meet this man at one of these politician parties, thrown to keep newsmen in a good humour. And the man says to me, you young men are always criticising. You only criticise destructively, why don't you put up some concrete proposal, some scheme for improving the country in any way, and then you will see whether we take it up or not.'

'So you jumped at it.'

'Only to get rid of him. I told Honourable the Chief Koyomi —he is the one by the way who kneels and kisses the hand of every Minister—I told him, you should do something about the sewage system, it is disgraceful that at this stage, night-soil men are still lugging shitpails around the capital. And in any case, why shouldn't the stuff be utilised? Look at the arid wastes of the North, I said. You should rail the stuff to the North and fertilise the Sardauna's territory. More land under cultivation, less unemployment.'

'Sounds economically sound,' Egbo conceded. 'Bandele, you are the economics man, what do you . . . oh, I forget, he isn't talking.'

'Wait, I haven't finished. In return I proposed the North should send its donkeys down so that we use them for the conveyance of the stuff within the town. That releases more men for the new industries springing up from the new land programme.'

'One practical difficulty,' Egbo objected, 'the night-soil tribe won't stand for it. It seems they consider it their vocation.'

'Well if they are so in love with the stuff they can go on the farm and turn it with the sod. I told Chief Koyomi special night trains would be run, coupling sealed wagons of local contribution at every station, night collection rail-rolling to the North, fertilising less productive land. In a year, I told him, the country's farm products would be doubled.'

'Wait a minute, wait a minute,' and Egbo grabbed the newspapers, looking for the report. 'Aha, I thought so, that's almost the man's speech word for word.'

'I must concede it to him, he has a fantastic memory, unless he knew shorthand of course and took it down behind his back. Mind you, I had had a few and that is when my air of conviction is truly irresistible. I think I pointed out the metaphysics of the plan to him too—bringing the wheel full circle.'

'I have it,' Egbo exclaimed, 'that must be what he called mental physics and chemistry.'

'You see. I told you the man went loose on imagination.'

'Listen to this—another piece of your reportage I bet . . . "the collection of sewage pails, declared Honourable Koyomi, was inhumane, and as the honourable member spoke, his long repressed brain grew fertile and the scheme became grandiose and sprouted the most unexpected off-shoots of various colours and odours . . ." that's you, isn't it?'

'Couldn't possibly mistake the style. You know, that Mathias

239

is a traitor. The editor called me and said, "Mathias tells me you are interested in this sort of thing, how would you like to take it up"?'

'I confess I like the donkey idea,' Kola said, 'except that they may be allergic to the smell.'

'Gas masks. The police can supply all they need.'

'That could be a security risk, to leave gas masks at the mercy of donkeys. Suppose they stage demonstrations? Teargas would be ineffective against them.'

'I still go for donkeys, and not merely within town. Why not all the way to the North?'

'You find trains too, too, prosaic?'

'That's it.'

'Hm. You may have something there. Just think of the nomadic sight—cattle tracks coming South and strings of laden asses trekking North in shit caravans.'

Bandele got up and left.

They stared at the slammed door some moments. 'What,' Egbo asked finally, 'is eating that man?' He looked at Simi, then at Dehinwa, 'What do the women say? Is there anything your intuition may have told you which we have missed?'

Simi played with the back of his neck and Dehinwa said, 'Your talk is enough to drive a man up the wall.'

Sagoe laughed. 'You won't believe this, Kola, and you too Egbo, but one drunken day I foolishly promised that woman that when we get married I will burn my Book of Enlightenment.'

'You swore it.' she reminded him.

'And unfairly though it was extracted, I will redeem my oath.'

'How on earth did she do it?'

Sagoe looked vengefully at her, 'Shall I tell them?'

'If you dare . . .'

'I do.'

'You won't dare . . .'

'It was, shall we say, in a moment of extreme . . .' Dehinwa rose and fled upstairs and Sagoe's laughter rang out after her, 'what a price to pay, Delilah! What a price to pay for Delilah's maidenhead!'

Simi asked, 'Are you really getting married?'

'I am trapped,' Sagoe sighed. 'Trapped and I love it.'

'Let me know when,' Kola said, 'and I will present her with a pair of handcuffs.'

'And you can have chamber-pot from me.' Egbo promised.

Bandele came in again, a palace housepost carved of iron-wood. 'Is Joe Golder really going through with this thing?'

Kola smiled, 'Bandele, you fail to understand. What is the man to do? The alternative is for him to sit and brood and fall to pieces.'

'You act sometimes,' Egbo began, 'as if you do not feel . . .'

'I didn't ask you, Egbo.'

Egbo stood up. 'If you are going to continue acting in this childish manner I'll get out of your house!'

Bandele's voice grew quiet. 'The door is open. I can't forget that I came to you this morning for help and you failed me.'

'I did not refuse you anything.'

'*I* asked *you*, didn't I? Kola's house was nearer but I came and asked you!'

'But not for yourself. You asked help for that disgusting cessation of nature, and I didn't even want to know him. Come on, Simi, let's get out.'

'Before you go,' Bandele said, 'I have an important message for you . . .'

'It can keep.'

'. . . from a student of mine.'

Egbo stiffened, his whole manner had changed. 'From . . . her . . .?'

'Yes.'

'How long have you had it?'

'Better come out.'

Forgetting Simi's presence, Egbo half-ran from the room. Dehinwa gave Simi a quick look of woman-sympathy and took Egbo's place beside her. Sagoe tried a hearty remark but soon gave up, shrugging.

Outside, Bandele said, ' I know where she is.'

'Look, just fill up one gap before anything else. What the bloody hell is her name?'

'You listen to me, Egbo. I will only give you her message as she gave it to me, and as she begged me to deliver it. I think of course that she is cracked in the head, but you probably know that yourself.'

'For God's sake what is it? Is she pregnant?'

'Yes.'

'I see.'

'And she knows you and Simi are still . . . she saw you at some party or the other.'

'She hasn't done anything stupid has she?'

'She wanted to. She went to a doctor at the hospital, that buffoon Dr Lumoye, and he was his normal stupid self. I think he even wanted to sleep with her and when she wouldn't he said no help. So Lumoye has been spreading the gossip all over the place and since she is quite lunatic she's gone right to the other extreme. Now she's going to keep the baby she said, and continue here as a student.'

'Where do I find this doctor?'

'I said I have a message for you.'

'And I said where do I find this fuckin' quack?'

'You're shouting, Egbo.'

'Tell me where he lives or keep your blasted message!'

'As you wish.'

'Wait.' Egbo held him, swallowing bile, feeling its poison froth inside him. 'Bandele, Bandele, this torturer role does not become you, tell me where to find the man.'

'I only called you to give you a message.'

'All right, all right, go on. Where is she? Does she really mean that—about returning here?'

'The Registrar told me himself. She's sent him a letter.'

'Where is she?'

I don't know.'

'You are lying, Bandele.'

'I don't know or I won't tell—believe what you wish.'

'All right, get it over with. Give me your message.'

'When you are sure what you want to do you are to tell me and I will pass it on. And I am supposed to make you understand that you are under no obligation. I hope I have succeeded—that's all the message.' And Bandele turned to go in.

'No wait.' Egbo held him back, looking into his face. 'This explains a lot of course. I suppose this has been at the bottom of your peculiar . . .'

'Don't be so conceited. You think it is just this?'

'All right, let's leave you out then. Now for God's sake talk

242

to me about the girl . . . I mean, she is such a peculiar creature, in a manner even wild. I don't think . . .'

'I wish to keep my involvement to the minimum. So please, only your reply whenever you choose, nothing more.'

This time, Egbo made no move to stop him. He stood a long time at the steps, then he turned from the house and walked into the darkness.

Bandele went straight up the stairs and they heard him splashing about in the bathroom. 'That man,' Kola said, 'is killing himself inside, but why?'

'What he needs,' Sagoe remarked, 'is a long session of Voidancy.'

Simi had grown sad, and Dehinwa chatted with her with unceasing gaiety.

They were getting late for the recital and they knew it, but none of them rose to suggest that they leave. Sekoni's exhibition had been opened in the afternoon to palm wine and roast meat from the black ram, and its congealing blood still stuck to Kola's studio floor. Bandele had said, 'What do you need the ram for? Haven't you had your sacrifice?' And for a long moment, it seemed that Egbo would plunge the knife into his throat and they all stood, horrified, round the reek of blood and the convulsive vessel of the severed throat. But Egbo gave the knife a playful flick in his direction and a thin streak of blood marked Bandele across the shirt. Immediately the tension was loosened and laughter replaced the unmeaning moment of antagonism; even Bandele smiled, remembering that this, after all, was also for Sekoni. On Kola's canvas the paint was hardly dry on Esumare, but they carried it and hung it in the foyer of the theatre where Joe Golder would sing later at night. And all the patrons came, including the Oguazors, but they left quickly as a housefly or two were seen arriving on the heady trail of palm wine. The act of the slaughter, and the taste of wine on the pungent smell of roast flesh reached backwards again for Egbo and plucked forth the single, isolated act, the first companion to his sanctuary by the river, and Egbo knew he could not hold her merely as an idyllic fantasy, for the day rose large enough and he was again overwhelmed by her power of will . . .

And now Egbo walked and walked. And in Bandele's sitting-room they all sat, dreading the moment when they must go and face Joe Golder across the lights. Bandele came down the stairs.

'Is it not time for the freak-show?'

'You want us out of your house?'

'No. In fact I am coming with you. But tell me, you who understand, I notice on the programme that Joe Golder will sing a Requiem in the second half. Is that his idea of expiation?'

'The programme was arranged months ago,' Kola spoke quietly.

'Ah, then the other act was the inspiration.' Bandele's tone was dry brittle grass as when he once said, 'If you drive the bigger cars, they lie on the road and let you kill them.'

'You will snap,' again very quietly from Kola.

'No. It seems we are all going for a needless self-flagellation and I expect Joe Golder has put years on me. But I will not snap.'

Bandele was a total stranger, and becoming increasingly inscrutable.

It was as if he had neither pity nor indulgence, and yet the opposite was true. At the theatre he sat apart from the others; after he followed them into the same row, but put some seats between them. He sat with Simi; Kola, Sagoe and Dehinwa sat some seats away, and Kola had selected those seats, seeing where Mrs Faseyi and her daughter-in-law were and choosing for himself the seat directly behind Monica. In the front row sat the Oguazors, and with them was Ayo Faseyi.

And Bandele held himself unyielding, like the staff of Ogboni, rigid in single casting. And it seemed he was asking of the outwardly composed figure on the stage, what have you brought us to witness? Some deceit of expurgation? Bandele sat like a timeless image brooding over lesser beings. And Kola, who tried to see it all, who tried to clarify the pieces within the accommodating habit of time, felt, much later, in a well-ordered and tranquil moment, that it was a moment of frustration, that what was lacking that night was the power to shake out events one by one, to space them in intervening standstills of the period of creation.

Sometimes I feel like a motherless child . . .

And so Kola looked at Bandele and he thought, if only we were, if only we were and we felt nothing of the enslaving cords, to drop from impersonal holes in the void and owe neither dead nor living nothing of our selves, and we should grow towards this, neither acknowledging nor weakening our will by understanding, so that when the present breaks over our heads we quickly find a new law for living. Like Egbo always and now, Bandele.

Sometimes I feel like a motherless child . . .

Some bones on that stage were bared, sandbags and trans-verses, collapsible platforms billowing black drapes on the two sides, two naked spots converging and Joe Golder. Beyond him, deep void and total dark, and Joe Golder. And outwards from the black edges of the moveable proscenium which framed him, an archaic figure disowned from a family album, Joe Golder sought the world in hope, the faceless, unfathomed world, a total blank for the man whose every note tore him outward. Joe Golder bared his soul, mangled, spun in murky fountains of grief which cradled him, the long-lost child, but would not fling him clear . . .

a long way from ho-o-ome, a long wa-ay from home.

And he knew it was not a mere question of geography, Kola, a hard band around his leg, as he looked down and saw Monica's arm trembling in its harsh grip. Kola held her hand, admitting, it is a night of severance, every man is going his way.

Overcome by a feeling he could not explain, Kola turned towards the exit. By the door stood Egbo and even in the faint spill of light from the foyer, he looked strained and star-crossed, like a man who had suddenly lost his youth.

Egbo had walked nearly the length of the college, indifferent to the gathering of the mercury pall above him, the sudden dry crackles which electrified his skin as when his hair would rise along the arm in waves to a passing comb. They reminded him of the quality of Bandele's anger, a static current break-ing clean harmattan air, a quiet rustle of antagonism. But the clouds held the water, though he longed for the rain to fall, to break, even if the sky held firm, to break at least the earth beneath his feet into loose sands, liberate his skin from the fevered tingling into the running freedom of skin clarity, bared quartz in quick runnels, hearing his racing heart pound now slow but strong against staggered flagstones of threaded granite . . . but the rain stayed dry above him and the earth was mere wet clods against his futile kicks...unconsciously he was drawn to the sound which filled the night through aluminium louvres, a thin cracked cry of a castrated bull, and Egbo moved towards the door asking, who is this man to bellow his cleavage from the world of understanding!

The double spot bore a hole in the ground and Joe Golder stood with his feet in this circle of emptiness, Egbo thinking how they would take possession of the dyers' compound when the women were gone, standing on the rims of the enormous pots of the dyers, buried deep in black drenched sands. When the women were gone they would jump up and clutch the cross-bamboos and be suspended for a while. But at times the bamboo broke and a child fell into the dye-pot and a huge outsplash of dye flew out above the rims, and the child emerged shedding indigo tears, blackened to the eyeballs. The blackness swallowed Joe Golder now before his eyes, and Egbo heard the shriek of the child's terror once again and the blackened hands that flailed desperately for hands to touch his and lips to meet his and clean waters to lave him and the waters did. Indigo fountains rose and swirled his feet. Joe Golder seeking blackness ever, walked in the backyards of old women through criss-crosses of bamboos so low it seemed a place for hanging dwarfs, and he went crouched and hump-backed through crossing jet-stained bamboos chipped and knotted, hung on wooden crocks, and the dye-cloths dripped unwrung. There were black rains from dwarf skies, and clean quicksands beneath his feet were drenched in this one dye of his choice. Joe Golder pressed his foot anywhere and springs uprushed of dye and old women's long straddled piss, straddled across the rims of their own dye-pots, and black pap frothing through black bubbles from cornices from black lava deep in the bowels of seasoned pots deep in rim levels with the ground, oh I've played among them Egbo said where old women dye their shrouds, and grief is such women, old as the curse from snuff-lined throats. Joe Golder uprushing dye from quick-sands stepped through the torn mouth of sunken cauldrons and wet shrouds swirling heavy in the wind, frothing indigo lather. They wrapped his feet and bore him round and round and down and down and the black bubbles were huge as Olokun's angered eyes bubbling, Egbo-lo, e-pulu-pulu, E-gbo-lo, e-pulu-pulu, E-gbo-lo . . .

Till the houselights flooded him suddenly and he heard the sound of clapping, and the house rose for the interval.

'Frightened! I tell you these English girls are so silly. What was frightening her now? I was crying.' And Mrs Faseyi still was, an awkward mixture of sniffles and the baritone laughter.

She caught Bandele's eyes where he stood apart with Simi, and Bandele bowed to her with a quaint formality which astonished her, and she looked away, hurt and incredulous. Sagoe was battling with society to get at the drinks table, and he came face to face with Oguazor and they both, for an instant, admitted recognition. Faseyi dashed to them just then saying, 'Oh, I'll get them, Prof, just tell me what you want.' Sagoe beamed and said, 'Please let me, I owe the professor some drinks' and Oguazor turned his back on him and spoke to Faseyi. And the Professor departed to join his Ceroline who stood before the Pantheon testing the paint to see if it came off. A moment later, Sagoe caught her looking back.

Sagoe took a glass to Simi and offered another to Bandele, who continued to stare fixedly at Sekoni's carving. Simi, afraid and unhappy, took the drink from Sagoe and tried to press it in his hand.

Monica, watching, said, 'Bandele seems angry about something.'

'You've noticed it?' boomed her mother-in-law. 'He nodded to me just now in the most peculiar manner, what is wrong with him?'

'Oh, well you see . . . er,' Kola stopped, but Sagoe came to the rescue. 'A friend has gone and left his woman on his hands, and Bandele is not enjoying the situation.'

'Men,' Mrs Faseyi pronounced, 'Beasts!'

'But why won't he join us?' Moni asked.

Kola grew increasingly distressed. There was no one present who did not know Simi, notorious, international courtesan. And Bandele stood so forbidding, hardly aware that she stood beside him. She was out of place in that gathering and she needed much attention. The pasty patches of disapprobation had already begun to whisper and to nudge one another, comments floating delicately on babycham bubbles.

'I think I ought to bring Simi to join us,' Kola said. 'If you have no objection Mrs Faseyi . . .'

'Objection! What for? Or isn't it that lovely woman with Bandele?'

'Yes, I thought . . .'

'Young man, that woman over there is Simi, and her little finger is worth ten men put together outside this place and all the men in here at the moment. Bring her to join us.'

'Look. Isn't that one of Ayo's friends over there?' Mrs Faseyi next asked.

'It's Egbo. Egbo, over here.'

'He isn't Ayo's friend, Mother,' Monica corrected her. 'Bandele brought him for lunch. Stop calling everybody Ayo's friend.'

'Egbo! Over here.'

Kola, on his way to fetch Simi heard and stopped, wondering if the move was now wise, now that Egbo would soon join them. He walked instead to Egbo but stopped short, attacked, it seemed, by the glare of a savage dog. And he followed Egbo's kernel-hard eyes into the group that conversed a mere pace from him, so near, so heedlessly near that the lewd gusts of Dr Lumoye's laughter blew the man back again and again into Egbo, mumbling a quick beg-pardon and returning to the circle of rapid wit.

'You mean she wrote, she actually wrote and said she wanted to return?'

'In her condition?' said Caroline.

'Wit in full belly?' Lumoye, still open-mouthed.

'But why are you surprised? Merals mean nothing to these modern girls.'

'And she looked ever such a nice, quiet girl,' Caroline added.

'Ha ha' warned Dr Lumoye, 'the quiet ones are generally the fastest. As soon as she came to the clinic I knew it. One of the quiet ones I said, I bet her trouble is the old penalty kick into the net ha ha ha ha ha . . . oops beg-pardon.'

Faseyi looked somewhat dubious. 'I don't know, some of these girls are very highly strung. You have to be careful or they try all sorts of desperate measures . . .'

'Oh, they know their way about,' Lumoye assured him. 'You mark my words, when the college resumes my little patient will be as slim around the navel as my little daughter ha ha ha ha.'

'Just the same,' Faseyi said timidly, 'one feels rather sorry for them.'

'Don't waste your pity on sech girls. They must learn to pay for their pleasure.'

Egbo's eyes were outheld on black cuspids, embers on the end of a blacksmith's tongs.

'The standard of morals has really gone down,' Caroline commented.

'The whole centry is senk in meral terpitude. We are jest wetting to discover the responsible student, then we will know what to do with him.'

'Oh you won't get him. I bet, prof because I bet you that net will be empty next term ha ha—oops 'scuse me . . .' Over his shoulder he said it, his face lifted in a wide grin transmitting a little of the pleasure of his mirth to the stranger behind him. It was a cheery face he raised to Egbo, twisting his neck to achieve the look without recognition and Egbo, whose mouth did not seem at all to move, spat on it. Lumoye staggered forward blinded and shocked, his arm drawn instinctively across the thin squirt, thin because Egbo's lips and throat had long dried and his tongue was freshly soldered at the root. But he spat even without knowing and Faseyi into whom Lumoye staggered was asking,

'What is it? Have you something in your eye?'

But Egbo was inside the group, now waiting only for Lumoye to open his eye and see him. Lumoye, sensing mortal danger, realising after Faseyi spoke that no one had seen the attack, chose to remain under protection of his blindness. His instinct served him right because Egbo waited, and Caroline, baffled like the others fussed to help the assaulted man.

Dr Lumoye was no fool; as he strove to diagnose the event he hoped that a scandal could still be avoided. That, above all; wishing hard that his 'beg-pardons' had been more personal, because he could not recall the face of the man who had so baselessly abused him.

A mild voice came from his elbow, recalling Oguazor from the bewildered look he cast from Dr Lumoye to the silent man in whom he sensed a tenuous link; and Egbo's vague menace rendered Oguazor obtuse to the quality of Bandele's presence, which demanded, 'And what would you have done, professor?'

Faseyi, uncertainly, 'Hallo, Bandele. Didn't know you were here.'

And Oguazor, yielding some paternal room for him in the crowded circle, said, 'Oh do cem and jein us. We were just discersing wen of your students.'

'Oh, is she yours?' Caroline asked of the intrusion, but Bandele hardly heard her.

'I was asking, professor, what would you do exactly if you knew the father?' Leaving no room at all for mistake.

Egbo had caught it from the start and his whole manner resented Bandele's interference. Quickly he looked again at Lumoye hoping that the man would open his eyes once quickly so that he might seal them in raw swellings before the new danger robbed him of his right to anger. The tone of voice reached Dr Lumoye and he knew he had been saved.

'If you mean the boy responsible for that girl's condition . . .'

'I do.'

'Well, see that he is expelled of course. He deserves nothing less.'

'I see.'

Angrily, feeling somehow challenged and his challenger impertinent, Oguazor was near shouting, 'The college cannot afford to herve its name dragged down by the meral terpitude of irresponsible young men. The younger generation is too merally corrupt.'

Lumoye jerked up his head, recovered, and bolder for being well away from Egbo. 'Yes, I agree. They dishonour their family name for nothing, that is the saddest part of it.'

'As a doctor of course,' Bandele said, 'you would prescribe death before dishonour.'

'Look here . . .' Oguazor began.

'I was asking the doctor. Death before dishonour, isn't that the idea? Quack abortionists because they—know their way about?'

'I don't know what you are talking about.'

'Don't you? But you are familiar with these problems. Even among those who first come to you for help.'

'I hope Bandele doesn't think that a university is a social welfare centre.'

Bandele looked at him then thoughtful, and he looked round the circle, calm, his body lax again. He was looking at them with pity, only his pity was more terrible than his hardness, inexorable. Bandele, old and immutable as the royal

250

mothers of Benin throne, old and cruel as the *ogboni* in conclave pronouncing the Word.

'I hope you all live to bury your daughters.'

End of interval; and the bell recalled them, distant and shrill like a leper's peal. But they stood unbelieving. By Sekoni's Wrestler Simi waited, Kola poised near her in confusion. Egbo watched her while she walked towards him, eyes ocean-clams with her peculiar sadness . . . like a choice of a man drowning he was saying . . . only like a choice of drowning.

NOTES

p. 7 drink lobes: A poetic rather than a physiological organ. It seems to be the seat of all Sagoe's sensibilities. Sagoe's own explanation of this elusive organ is given on p. 35.

p. 8 'Two puddles ....' – A flashback to an earlier episode when Egbo tried to decide whether to take his grandfather's chieftaincy or to continue to work in the foreign office.

p. 8 'Your Chinese sages ...' – A favourite thought of poets not only Chinese. See for example John Donne:

Nor are (although the river keeps the name)
Yesterday's waters and today's the same.
('Of the Progresse of the Soule – Second Anniversary')

p. 8 *Oshun* One of the principal Yoruba river deities from whom the river takes its name. There is a famous Oshun Shrine at Oshogbo.

p. 9 Sekoni the stutterer is a deep thinker. His deep religious attitude contrasts with Egbo's flippant atheism. Soyinka distinguishes his 'interpreters' very well by their personal characteristics.

p. 10 A good incidental glimpse at the futility of war – 'fishes over whom the hunting rights were fought fed on the disputants'. *Osa* the name of Egbo's grandfather's Kingdom.

p. 12 Egbo's choice well expressed 'the warlord of the creeks against the dull grey filing cabinets of the foreign office.' His decision on this occasion is expressed in words which imply a mild condemnation; he decides to go 'with the tide'.

p. 17 Egbo's adventures with his guardian – an example of Soyinka's neat economical narrative and descriptive technique.

pp. 20–21 The *apala* band's another good economical description in depth.

253

p. 22 Sekoni has been making a drawing of the dancing woman and distorting her features in the process, giving her a goitre among other things. This arouses Sekoni's 'cobbles'.

p. 27 The sudden translation from the excitement of Sekoni's imagination to his boring desk job makes his frustration plain without need for excessive comment.

p. 27 A good example of Soyinka's satirical portraiture is the Chairman of Sekoni's board.

p. 36 The contrast between Dehinwa, now a sophisticated city girl, and her mother and aunt is very marked. Their painful and unnecessary solicitude for her is described in p. 139 as 'blood cruelty'. In spite of their fears, however, Dehin is no cheap slut.

pp. 37–40 Monica is contrasted with her husband Ayo. She is natural in her reactions while Ayo is pretentious and over-conscious of protocol. Their incompatibility is hinted at here. She and Kola have a lot more in common. Usaye is something of a bond between them. By p. 50 Kola is beginning to feel 'an insidious beginning of a great yearning'.

p. 50 *Simi* The language with which she is described suggests not only her great attractiveness but also the fatal nature of this attraction. We are reminded of cannibals (p. 50), snakes and bees (pp. 53, 54) 'the beast that lay in wait to swallow him' (p. 54), and the thornbush (p. 56).

pp. 59–60 The interrupted portrayal of this encounter has been commented on in the Introduction.

p. 63 Sagoe's nightmare or prolonged day-dream is the means of satirising the corrupt judge. The wardrobe, a symbol of cheapness and lack of good taste – 'cheap wood overlaid with varnish' – makes a good symbolic home for Sir Derin. It is interesting too that Sir Derin is naked (p. 68), as it were bared of the facade which he had kept up in life. Now, in death 'the truth has lately begun to matter'. The nightmare leads back to Sagoe's first encounter with the newspaper world (p. 68). A highly satirical passage.

p. 70 *The voidante philosophy* This is Soyinka the lighthearted essayist – in the mood of 'Salutations of the Gut' (*Reflections*, ed. Ademola, F., A.U.P., Lagos, 1962). The 'philosophy' is defined on p. 72.

p. 71 *'She farted like a beast'* Here and elsewhere Soyinka adopts a Chaucerian directness in matters flatulent.

p. 73 Winsala's entry – a dramatic near-fantasy. From now on the satirical touches come thick and fast. Sir Derin, the chief, the Managing Director, are all vehicles for the satire on falseness and corruption.

p. 91 Note how the real image of the waiter dressed in green – 'greenbottle' – fades into that of flies ('greenbottle' is formed by analogy with 'bluebottle' which is a type of fly) '. . . swarm of greenbottles on fruit . . . buzz . . .'

p. 91 Winsala's thoughts are given in a series of proverbs to suggest his glibness.

p. 96 Sekoni's dreams had ended in frustration. Sagoe's attempt to publicise the story meets the same fate; obstructed by the corrupt establishment. On p. 98 the situation is neatly summarised: 'Because the good Knight must be saved, they roast the sheik'.

p. 98 Sekoni's quarrel with his father for marrying a Christian girl (they were Moslems), his illness, his father's remorse, his pilgrimage are all portrayed in the compact, oblique way of the novel. All Sekoni's frustrated energy at last finds expression in sculpture.

p. 99 'Their run of forty times' – One of the activities of the Mecca pilgrimage is the circling of the Kaaba, which contains the Black Stone, seven times. Forty here is an exaggeration.

p. 102 Kola is painting a Pantheon of Yoruba deities, using his friends as his models. Egbo is Ogun, the explorer, warrior, creator god. Golder is Erinle, an animal spirit, Lazarus is Esumare, the rainbow, Usaye is Obaluwaiye's hand-maid. See the glossary for complete list of figures in the Pantheon.

p. 102 *Esau and Jacob* Obvious reference to the biblical story of the usurpation of Esau's birthright. A number of Soyinka's allusions are to the Bible. Dehin is referred to appropriately as Jael (p. 67) for sending a pain through Sagoe's head. The Biblical Jael had driven a tent nail through Sisera's head. See *Judges* chapter 4, verse 21.

p. 106 Sagoe's remark about Dehin's grandmother leads back to his first encounter with her... 'The grandmother *had* taken a long look etc.' This old lady is a grand matriarchal figure uninhibited by prudish attitudes to sex and marriage.

p.111 *Ikoyi* the old colonial residential area of Lagos now occupied by the African successors of the old administrators. Soyinka tilts at what is pictured here as the deadness of their lives.

p. 113 This section (Section 8) is primarily concerned with the chase and rescue of the young thief, Noah, but it is also a vehicle for satire. In it is portrayed the more general chase of the petty thieves by the bigger thieves in authority; it is the story of the mass, strong only in numbers bearing down on the individual. There is much implied social criticism here.

pp. 119–20 *'Perfunctory doles ....'* This is the sort of passage that could be called difficult. Soyinka portrays Egbo's thoughts with the same headlong tumble with which the mind can run through its business, recalling images formed in childhood: the Osun grove, the bridge etc.

p. 123 *'Egbo stirred in his sleep....'* Without notice we are taken back to the episode with Simi, p. 60. This kind of sudden switchback occurs frequently in the novel.

p. 126 Egbo's strange whim to pass the night under the bridge is no doubt connected with the associations of a bridge in his childhood at Oshogbo.

p. 128 Is Egbo growing out of Simi? It is interesting that the thought first occurs to him after his meeting with the self-assured undergraduate girl.

p. 128 This encounter develops rapidly; and although we are supposed to see in it the independence of the two people and the fact that they instantly find themselves totally in tune, it is one episode in the novel which seems forced and rather stagey.

p. 136 *'And then it's . . . .'* A typical side swipe at the rapid touchy assertions of nationalism which sometimes pass for the real thing.

p. 139 *'A buzz of wit. . . .'* With the Professor's party Soyinka's satirical genius comes into its own. Into this deadly sedate house 'the house of death', devoid of any real initiative, and enslaved to what other people say is right, enters the iconoclast Sagoe. His outrageous thoughts are fortunately not uttered ('humming inside him' p. 141); but soon the oppressive atmosphere of artificiality (the plastic fruit and foliage are symbolic) get him down, and he starts throwing the artificial fruit out of the window. By the time he bends down and kisses the plastic rose decorating Mrs. Oguazor's navel the scene has become a hilarious farce, reminiscent of the adventures of another young hero, similarly placed – Lucky Jim in Kingsley Amis' novel of that name.

p. 155 The parallel between Sekoni's death and Soyinka's poem 'Death at Dawn' has been mentioned in the Introduction.

pp. 155–6 A reflection of the differences between the interpreters is their differing reactions to Sekoni's death.

p. 160 Lasunwon is the least developed of the group. He is more of a foil to the others.

p. 162 *'Its good business. . .religion'* Soyinka has a more extended study of a businessman-prophet in Brother Jero, the leading character in his play *The Trials of Brother Jero*. Lazarus' portrait is not of an obvious charlatan. There are suggestions of complexity which are not fully explored.

p. 164 A good example of Soyinka's disregard for conventional prose structure is the description of Kola's grief – 'Kola risen . . . in his hands.'

p. 164 Lazarus and his church steal the centre, and almost edge the interpreters out.

p. 177 Kola's facile blasphemy is countered by Lazarus' quiet assertion of faith.

p. 188 Golder is something of a bonus in this novel. Interesting though his character is, he seems to fit rather loosely into the structure. He is linked at the end with Noah's death.

p. 202 Faseyi is almost overdone. His type does exist but his portraiture lacks the characteristic subtlety of the rest of the novel.

p. 203 *'So the pollen is blowing. . . .'* Kola's deepening feelings for Monica referred to here.

pp. 203–4 Glance at the tussles of exuberant students with authority.

p. 209 To describe Mrs. Faseyi as a stallion sounds odd, but it suggests her magnificent figure and personality. There is something male about her.

p. 212 Mrs. Faseyi is as advanced in her views as the young interpreters.

p. 213 To expose Ayo's pretentiousness he is isolated in feeling not only from his wife but also from his mother.

p. 215 The trials of a homosexual in an alien society.

p. 216 *'Cockroach gut. . .'* As a description of the literal minded swot this is a good image.

p. 217 *Giovanni's Room* A novel by James Baldwin which has been described as one of the most sensitive portrayals of a homosexual relationship in fiction.

p.220 The novel has resumed its tense narrative texture; it almost simultaneously depicts the past and the present. Sekoni's sculpture goes back years for its inspiration. All this background suddenly merges with the adventure of Kola and Egbo's search for the church.

pp. 223–4 Noah seems to be subjected to a kind of ordeal fire which he fails. The details are not very clear.

p. 235 Egbo's affinity with the mysterious undergraduate girl has been noted. Here he says of her, 'this is the new woman of my generation'. Gradually her image seems to eclipse even the reality of Simi.

p. 236 Noah reacts in fear where the thugs would have reacted with violence at Golder's homosexual advances, and falls to his death.

p. 236 Egbo's reaction to his discovery of Golder's nature is one of physical disgust.

p. 246 Egbo is lost in a reverie of childhood.

p. 248 Dr. Lumoye's raucous levity contrasts (even in her absence) with the unnamed girl's dignity and assurance, and it is clear who has the more valid moral code. His callously improper suggestions to the girl expose the hollowness of his conventional morality. Professor Oguazor's 'moral' stand is no less callous and phoney.

GLOSSARY

The Gods in Kola's Pantheon
Esu, spirit of disorder.
Sango, God of lightning.
Orisa-nla, the principal deity.
Esumare, the rainbow.
Erinle, an animal spirit.
Obaluwaiye, the respectful name for
Sopona, god of smallpox.
Ogun, the explorer, warrior, creative god.

Abetiaja: A Yoruba cloth cap with flaps over the ears (literally, that which covers a dog's ears).
adire: dyed cloth.
agba n't'ara: respect to an elderly body.
agbada: a voluminous Yoruba garment.
agbo: a potion of bark and roots.
agidigbo: a kind of Yoruba music.
aladura: a Christian sect whose services are characterised by rhythm and trance.
alakori: a term of abuse.
alhaji: one who has done the 'hadji', i.e. pilgrimage to Mecca
amala: a soft doughy concoction made from yam flour.
apala: a kind of Yoruba music.

ayaba osa, omo Yemoja: Queen of the sea, daughter of Yemoja (a water deity).

dansiki: a brief smock worn by men.

e figbati fun yeye: give the bastard a slap.

egbe: magic for vanishing.

ekan: elephant grass.

elegungun: ancestral masquerade.

ewedu: a slimy vegetable soup.

gaga: eye-glasses.

Gambari: local slang for a Hausaman (pejorative).

gidigbo: a rough form of wrestling.

ibeji: twins, or, more commonly, wood figurines carved in the form of twins, usually with exaggeratedly long heads.

ibosi: shame.

igbale: grave of exclusive cults.

ikori: a hunter's cap ending in a sort of pouch.

ilu oyinbo: the white man's country.

iyun: coral beads (highly valued).

koboko: leather whip.

kola: kola nut (a bribe).

maraccas: a kind of castanets.

Ogboju Ode: a famous work of Yoruba literature, by D. O. Fagunwa.

ogboni: a conclave of elders, a kind of executive council to the throne.

ologomungomu: a spectral figure.

omo alufa: vicar's son.

omo ole: a term of abuse.

omo tani: whose son does he think he is?

oriki: a chant of family names, titles, antecendents etc.

oyekoko moniran }
oyeroba } : meaningless gibberish.

oyinbo: white man.

'se wa s'omo fun wa': literally, 'will you act as a dutiful son should?', i.e. look after the elders.

tanwiyi: mosquito larva.